Making Scorecards Actionable

Balancing Strategy and Control

Nils-Göran Olve, Carl-Johan Petri, Jan Roy and Sofie Roy

WILEY

658.4012
MAKING

Copyright © 2003   John Wiley & Sons Ltd, The Atrium, Southern Gate, Chichester,
                       West Sussex PO19 8SQ, England

               Telephone (+44) 1243 779777

Email (for orders and customer service enquiries): cs-books@wiley.co.uk
Visit our Home Page on www.wileyeurope.com or www.wiley.com

This publication is designed to provide accurate and authoritative information in regard to the subject
matter covered. It is sold on the understanding that the Publisher is not engaged in rendering
professional services. If professional advice or other expert assistance is required, the services of a
competent professional should be sought.

Other Wiley Editorial Offices

John Wiley & Sons Inc., 111 River Street, Hoboken, NJ 07030, USA

Jossey-Bass, 989 Market Street, San Francisco, CA 94103-1741, USA

Wiley-VCH Verlag GmbH, Boschstr. 12, D-69469 Weinheim, Germany

John Wiley & Sons Australia Ltd, 33 Park Road, Milton, Queensland 4064, Australia

John Wiley & Sons (Asia) Pte Ltd, 2 Clementi Loop #02-01, Jin Xing Distripark, Singapore 129809

John Wiley & Sons Canada Ltd, 22 Worcester Road, Etobicoke, Ontario, Canada M9W 1L1

Wiley also publishes its books in a variety of electronic formats. Some content that appears in print may
not be available in electronic books.

British Library Cataloguing in Publication Data

A catalogue record for this book is available from the British Library

ISBN 0-470-84871-5

Typeset in 12/14 Garamond 3 by Footnote Graphics Limited, Warminster, Wiltshire
Printed and bound in Great Britain by Biddles Ltd, Guildford and King's Lynn
This book is printed on acid-free paper responsibly manufactured from sustainable forestry
in which at least two trees are planted for each one used for paper production.

Contents

Preface

Following the seminal work of Robert Kaplan and David Norton who first presented the concept 'balanced scorecard' in a *Harvard Business Review* article in 1992, we presented the experience gained through scorecard work in Sweden and England in a book published by John Wiley in 1999, *Performance Drivers – a Practical Guide to Using the Balanced Scorecard.*[1] It was quickly translated into a number of languages, proving the interest in scorecards in countries as far apart as Japan and Brazil. We refer readers to that volume for a full description of the rationale behind scorecards, and how to introduce them.

In this book we look much more closely at the experiences organizations have had in using scorecards: the *challenges* they have encountered, and the *key design issues* in making scorecards actionable. In doing this, we build on a number of cases from business and government. During the past 10 years we have also learnt from the scorecard experiences of many others: clients, participants in conferences, case descriptions in books, students doing research for their examination papers, etc. It seemed to us that the time was ripe for a stocktaking of what we had learnt, and that the outcome of this could interest others as well.

As in *Performance Drivers* there is an over-representation of Swedish cases, reflecting the fact that most of our own experience comes from our own country. Very few cases, incidentally, come from companies where we have been active as consultants, so they also reflect rather different approaches to introducing and using scorecards. Most of these companies are internationally active corporations.

There seems to be a greater 'market penetration' for scorecards as a tool for strategic control in the Scandinavian countries than anywhere else, possibly apart from the United States. Readers of our previous book have commented on how scorecards are used differently in different countries, detecting a Scandinavian flavour in our recommendations that may differ from the US use of scorecards. We are not sure about this, but it provides another reason why cases from this part of the world attract global interest. After all, most books and articles on management come from the USA or at least Anglo-Saxon environments.

We are indebted to Professor Takeo Yoshikawa in Yokohama who provided the Japanese material, to our TCG Cepro colleague Michael Collins who contributed to our chapter on IT, and to all the people who were kind enough to let us share their experiences: those we interviewed for the named cases and list in the Acknowledgements; their employers who accepted that we publish material on these organizations; many other people whose experiences we collected in informal ways over the past years; and our colleagues in The Concours Group, in particular its Stockholm office TCG Cepro.

In writing this book we had people like you in mind: people who already have been exposed to the idea of balanced scorecards, and may even have taken part in scorecard projects in your own organizations. We attempt to put your experiences into the larger framework provided by the experiences of many others. We also add many of our own hopes and concerns.

These remain the same as in *Performance Drivers*. In the preface for that volume, the objective for scorecards was expressed in the following way:

> to provide a more thorough and meaningful picture of a business, suitable for the discussions in which a growing number of company employees should participate:
>
> - *A total, comprehensive picture*: How do our operations fit into the overall picture? Can I understand why we do things the way we do, and does it make sense?
> - *A long-term view*: More and more of our time at work is spent on preparing for the future. The cultivation of competencies and relationships is an investment with effects that are often hard to see. How can we convince ourselves that what we are doing is right, and that others at the company are doing what they can to prepare for our common future?

- *Experience*: How do we make use of what we learn? Today many company employees deal directly with customers, make discoveries in the process of their work, and cultivate relationships with other companies and official agencies. How can we benefit from the knowledge which we thereby gain?
- *Flexibility*: The long-term focus and the ambition to learn from experience has to be combined with flexible reactions to a fast-changing environment.

These remain important and valid ambitions. We hope that our new book will provide further insights into how these intentions can be realized. If you have any experiences or suggestions that you want to share with us – or get up to date information about our future experiences – please check out www.makingscorecardsactionable.com

Nils-Göran Olve
Carl-Johan Petri
Jan Roy
Sofie Roy
Stockholm, January 2003

Acknowledgements

The following persons were interviewed for this book. Professor Takeo Yoshikawa of Yokohama National Univerity collected material on JIT for us. Material on Ricoh and Xerox is repeated from Olve and Sjöstrand (2002). Where no other credit is given, information on other companies comes from our professional contacts with them.

AMF Pension

Anders Ohrbeck, Chief Controller

British Airways at Heathrow

Peter Read, Director of Heathrow
Andy Garner, General Manager Business Development

Ericsson Enterprise

Sten Olsson, Manager, Management Systems
Kerstin Lilje-brinck

Helsingborg

P-O. Gunnarsson, Chief Executive
Bengt Vänerlöf, BSC Project Manager
Lars Johansson, Development Council
Jörgen Olsson, Chief Social Care Board
Annethe Lind, Controller Social Care Board

Hewlett-Packard (HP)

Sten Holm, HP Services Controller Northern Europe

Jönköping

Göran Henriks
Vera Moqvist
Eva-Lotte Köllerström
Kristina Bertov

Lund Heart and Lung Centre

Claes Arén, Director
Anna-Karin Bryder, Senior Development Officer
Ann Gyllenberg, Senior Development Officer
Karin Ottosson
Dr Hans Ölin

Nordea

Erik Öhman, Director of Group Planning and Control
Sven Edvinsson, Director of Group Planning

Oriflame

Robin Chibba
Joakim Tuvner

Scandinavian Airline System (SAS)

Matiss Paegle, BSC Project Leader

Skandia

Interviews have been made with 25 persons in Skandia, at various levels
and in different units in the organization. The names can however not be
disclosed because they have been promised anonymity for this book and
for one of the author's doctoral thesis (Roy, S., forthcoming 2003).

Volvo Cars Corporation

Jonna Sandell, Director Business Planning Process

Steve Walkin
Gerwyn Williams, Gerwyn Williams Consulting

The information in the case studies is included with permission from the following companies/organizations, who are the copyright owners:

- AMF Pension
- British Airways
- City of Helsingborg
- HP Services
- JAL
- Jönköping
- Lund Heart and Lung Centre
- Nordea
- Oriflame
- Ricoh
- SAS
- Scandia
- Volvo
- Xerox

The authors gratefully acknowledge these permissions.

Scorecards 10 Years On – Fading Fad or Maturing Management?

1

SCORECARDS AS EMERGING BEST PRACTICE IN MANAGEMENT CONTROL?

The concept of the balanced scorecard (BSC) was first presented in the early 1990s. By 2000 some surveys indicated that a majority of firms in the United States, the United Kingdom and Scandinavia used scorecards – or at least intended to do so soon. Others, like Bain's management tools survey,[2] indicated a slight drop in usage to 36%, but with a high average satisfaction with the tool. The number of software packages for scorecards on the market is growing and now exceeds 100. In only 10 years, the idea of the BSC has certainly made its mark.

At the same time there are reports of high failure rates. We have seen firms abandon their scorecard efforts. Others are struggling against the perception of the BSC as 'just another three-letter fad' propagated by consultants such as TQM, BPR, and ABC.[3] But were these failures? There are probably fewer BPR or ABC projects started now than 10 or 15 years ago. Still, important parts of their philosophy have been integrated into standard practices in modern management.

There is also another danger. Many such projects were not for 'real'. Managers used the terms because it was the current thing to do, but did not give the concepts a chance by applying them as intended. The same may be happening to the BSC: the ideas are rejected because they are not applied properly.

There are indications that the literature about scorecards has 'peaked' (Figure 1.1). Even after 10 years of the BSC we are aware of very few companies with more than a few years of successful and ongoing scorecard use. Some may see Figure 1.1 as a 'hype curve', indicating inflated expectations among those who take an interest in methods of management. To have lasting effects, the hype has to be followed by action. Organizations introducing scorecards need to work patiently for several years before they can claim to have reformed their control systems. With diminishing hype, the BSC will need to start producing tangible effects – at a time when it is still in need of continued support and experimentation.

Yet during our research for this book we found that several important corporations are only now launching major BSC initiatives. We met enthusiastic managers convinced that they will avoid the pitfalls encountered by companies who have discontinued their projects. They usually claim that others have laid too much emphasis on performance measurement, and too little on strategic control. Maybe after a period of trial-and-error the BSC is now emerging as a natural and necessary part of management?

So it seems time to make up our minds about the BSC. What can we learn from the past 10 years of the BSC? What should organizations using scorecards take note of in order to make their projects successful? These are the questions that prompted the present book. We build on the experiences reported in our previous book *Performance Drivers* (1999). But here we

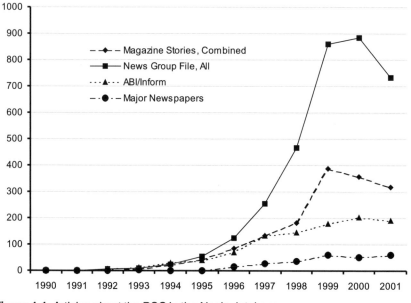

Figure 1.1 Articles about the BSC in the Nexis database.

take a much more careful look at the experiences people have had in introducing and using scorecards. We do this through cases from business and government. A few of them are told in some detail, because we believe that success with scorecards hinges on how they enter into the everyday life of organizations. Others are used as building blocks for a discussion of challenges and issues facing firms using the BSC. But first this chapter and the next provide a brief introduction to the range of different varieties of BSCs, and how they are used.

WHAT A SCORECARD IS, AND WHY

A BSC is a format for describing the activities of an organization through a number of measures for each of (usually) four perspectives. A simplified BSC may resemble Figure 1.2. Some business activity is described from four different perspectives, using a small number of measures for each. The description may refer to the business's current performance, or to its goals for the next period.

Some would say that this is just another performance report, combining financial and non-financial metrics. But there is more to the scorecard than immediately meets the eye:

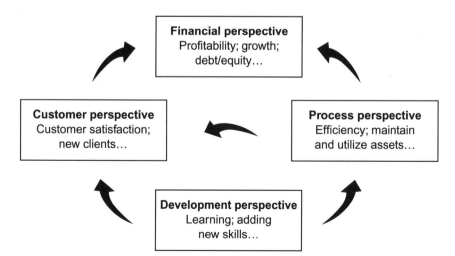

Figure 1.2 A basic BSC, with examples of typical contents for each of the four perspectives.

- The scorecard is balanced: the four perspectives aim for a complete description of what you need to know about the business. First, there is a *time dimension* going from bottom to top. Current profitability, etc. may largely be a consequence of what was done last quarter or last year; if new skills are added now it should have consequences for next year's efficiency and finance.

- The scorecard is balanced in another way also: it shows *both internal and external* aspects of the business. It is obvious that a 'well-oiled machinery' of internal processes is important in any business, and may not always correlate with external perceptions. On the other hand, customers' views and the contacts that have been established in the market-place are obviously important too. The scorecard shows both.

- Finally, the scorecard is *linked* through cause-and-effect assumptions. Among its most important uses is to reflect on how strong these linkages are, what time delays they involve, and how certain we can be about them in the face of external competition and change. In Figure 1.2, links are indicated just between perspectives; it is, of course, advisable to discuss links also between individual measures.

In Figure 1.2 we use four perspectives, as originally proposed by Robert S. Kaplan and David P. Norton in their initial article, published in 1992 in the *Harvard Business Review* (Kaplan and Norton, 1992). In practice, the names and identities of these perspectives have come to vary. The 'development' perspective was Innovation and Learning in Kaplan and Norton's first article, and became Learning and Growth in their later writings. The 'process' perspective is sometimes called Internal Business Processes. We tend mainly to use 'development' and 'process' for their brevity, but readers will find that the organizations we have studied have introduced their own names for these.

Organizations whose long-term goals are not financial may prefer to reorder the perspectives, and regard the financial perspective not as an objective but as a means to providing customer services. Or they can change it into the fulfilment of the organization's goal. We will discuss this in Chapter 2.

Since its first appearance, the concept of the BSC has been widely adopted as a new approach to management control both in business and government. A scorecard is an easy-to-understand generic format for describing the ambitions and achievements of an organization. It has proved useful for:

- Communicating strategic intentions, enabling managers and employees to realize intended strategies.[4]
- Discussing activities that are motivated by strategic aims rather than current necessities, such as the development of competencies, customer relationships, and IT, and how these will pay off in the future.
- Monitoring and rewarding such activities.

These aims are equally important in business firms pursuing long-term profitability and in non-profit organizations such as government agencies. Some of the most enthusiastic advocates of scorecards are to be found in public administration. Behind them is one important common theme: essential qualities of modern organizations – their resources as well as their performance – are poorly reflected in traditional accounting and control. Managers need tools to communicate about intangible or immaterial assets: to agree on targets for, and to monitor, their organization's performance in dimensions other than the traditional monetary ones.

GETTING A GRIP ON INTANGIBLES

In *Performance Drivers*, we argued that the interest in scorecards reflects the increasing dependence of both business and government on their intangible assets, *and* the need to engage employees in the pursuit of strategies where the long-term development of such assets is a key to business success. This need will be most apparent in organizations where many employees have customer contacts, and where long-term success is highly dependent on the interaction with customers and other external contacts. Such organizations need to spend time and effort learning about their environment, improving databases and systems, and creating positive attitudes towards the organization among all stakeholders. Scorecards will guide and focus these activities.

The idea of a BSC for business emerged from consultations with companies to identify a planning and performance control process suitable for the 1990s. Increased dependence on immaterial resources was a major reason why a quest for control tools using metrics other than traditional, financial ones seemed necessary. The time was ripe for a concept integrating several ideas that had gained importance during the 1970s and 1980s, and would develop in parallel with the BSC:

- Customer satisfaction indices, and the general idea that value as perceived by customers was important to monitor.
- 'Network' ideas of customer and supplier relationships as assets that a company should maintain and develop over time, important for future earnings and consequently an important part of the value of a business. Terms such as customer base, partnerships, alliances, virtual and imaginary organizations, emerged at about the same time.
- Process orientation and quality as critical for business success were promoted through acronyms such as TQM and BPR.
- Human resource accounting provided the roots for other types of 'intellectual capital' reporting, with ambitions to provide both internal and external parties with an improved understanding of the most important assets of a company.

These ideas could be integrated into the customer and process perspectives. For the development (learning and growth) perspective, there were comparatively fewer suggestions.

Using non-financial measures, of course, had a history going much further back. Local information systems (in a production unit or a sales department) attracted the attention of accounting research in the 1980s, but had, of course, always existed. Large corporations have used non-financial numbers in a systematic way for at least 50 years. And, as Kaplan and Norton have pointed out, there will always be hundred of numbers which are used in a company that should not be included in scorecards. The scorecard idea was essentially to articulate strategy through a particular format, integrating a highly restrictive selection of metrics.

Brand recognition, competences, processes, etc. are all part of an organization's intangible assets. The benefits of scorecards will be greatest in organizations where these are especially important, and particularly when many organization members are involved in maintaining and utilizing them. Assets such as customer relations, procedures, brand names, databases, etc. used to show up only as costs in planning documents and reports. Gradually, new metrics have been introduced such as customer satisfaction, cycle times, and brand recognition. A well-designed scorecard provides a unifying perspective for these, showing the intended relation between them and future revenues.

During the 1990s, interest in intangibles grew. Research in the European Union and the United States focused on how companies could manage and report immaterial assets, and the title of a Brookings Institute report (2001) summarizes the hopes attached to these efforts: *Unseen Wealth*. Through most of the decade, stock markets did see wealth in intangible assets. In the United States, the ratio between share prices and book values for large companies on average rose from a little more than 2 in 1990 to a high of more than 7 at the end of the decade.[5] It then declined, but not to its previous low. Obviously, this development was partly about asset-less 'new economy' firms. But also 'bricks and mortar' companies are increasingly focusing on their 'intellectual capital', rather than the material assets that are visible in their balance sheets. With the current emphasis on shareholder value, few will find it sufficient to base internal controls only on Return on Investment (RoI) or similar concepts which reflect traditional accounting concepts.

The link we see between intangibles and scorecard use may also explain why the idea seems to have attracted interest especially in industries and countries where 'knowledge-based' companies are common. But also other types of firms can benefit. A recent report[6] describes scorecard use in a carpet company in Mongolia!

USES OF SCORECARDS

Scorecards are tools for communication. They can be used in many different dialogues about almost any kind of activity. All organizations strive to please their customers, clients, or recipients in general; we all have our internal processes and routines; we all reap rewards from what we did earlier, at the same time as we need to prepare for the future; and we all have to think about causation over time. Introducing BSCs, however, also means *designing a customized management control system*. Scorecards are used to align business activities to the vision and strategies of a firm, monitoring performance in the dimensions used in the scorecards, and taking action appropriate for realizing the intended strategy.

Compared with other ways of describing what an organization does or should do, BSCs have two distinguishing features. One is the almost

simplistic format of the scorecard itself, where a restricted number of measures are used for each of four perspectives on a business activity: its *financial*
performance; its *customer interface*; its *internal processes*; and its *learning and
development*.

The other is the insistence that perspectives and measures should be
'linked'. A good scorecard documents a strategic logic: cause-and-effect
relationships between current activities and long-term success. Scorecards
aim to *change behaviour* through *communication* in order to *realize the intended
strategy*. The particular efforts an organization makes in order to learn, or
improve its processes, or make its customers happier, must be based on its
conviction that these efforts constitute the best path to future success. The
links in a good scorecard will visualize a 'business logic': how doing the
right things now is expected to produce long-term rewards. In this way,
scorecards translate strategy into terms that are meaningful for organization members in their everyday activities.

A difficulty in judging the penetration of scorecards is to decide what we
mean by 'using' BSCs. There are studies where half the respondents claim
that their companies use scorecards or soon will. We believe that companies where management control is really based on scorecards are much
fewer. The fact that most respondents believe that they (should) use scorecards is interesting by itself, as are the difficulties also reported. In fact,
there are very many different variants to be found among the applications
we have learnt about:

- A number of firms use scorecards as a format for discussing strategies
  only, and have not really introduced them as a tool for ongoing
  management control.
- Some companies structure their plans and reports into four or five
  perspectives derived from the BSC. However, they use these only for
  sorting existing measures to provide an overview. The resulting 'scorecard' does not really derive from any coherent strategic discussion.
  While this shows that the scorecard format is generally accepted and
  attractive, we do not expect companies who just use it for sorting pre-
  existing measures to realize its potential benefits.
- In some cases, scorecards were introduced as a substitute for budgets,
  while in other cases budgets and scorecards coexist. A fairly common
  ambition currently seems to be to combine scorecards with rolling

forecasts of cash flow. This is because budgets are perceived to have a dual role: providing performance targets, and foreseeing cash needs. The former role is taken over by scorecards, while the latter is handled through rolling forecasts.

- The scope of scorecard use within companies varies widely: just one scorecard (for the entire firm, or for some part of it); scorecards at one or two levels of the hierarchy; scorecards throughout the organization, sometimes including personal scorecards for individual members. So does the way different scorecards are linked. In some corporations, similar metrics are prescribed for everyone; in others, design is up to each scorecard 'owner'.

- This is closely linked to how measures[7] are meant to relate. Some companies (and, incidentally, most software vendors) expect numbers to be aggregated throughout the organization, while in others it is the logic rather than the numbers that matters. Some examples: certain measures obviously are easy to combine (like adding profits). But is it meaningful to calculate an average of market shares or employee scores? Has a division necessarily met its targets if the sum of its subunits fulfils expectations, but this hides large discrepancies among them?

- Some companies have used scorecards for projects. 'Learning and development' may then be for the project itself, if its life span is long, or for the rest of the corporation.

- Scorecards for corporate functions such as IT or human resources (HR) have been suggested and tried. This introduces the need to distinguish between a scorecard for, say, an IT *department* and for IT as a *business resource* for the entire firm.

- Scorecards for government and other non-profit organizations are gaining in popularity.

These applications show that the BSC is an attractive format for discussing human activities whenever there is a need to communicate ideas about causes and effects and priorities, or to check what has been achieved so far. There is no single best way of using scorecards. This makes it urgent, before starting a scorecard project, to consider what part or aspect of an organization and its activities is in need of such discussions, and who is to take part in them. This should determine the scope of the project, in terms of how much and which parts of the organization should be included, who should be involved, and at what stages: as a planning tool; for monitoring activities; and for reviewing achievements.

SCORECARDS AND INFORMATION DISCLOSURE TO THE PUBLIC

In this book we are concerned with the use of scorecards in running an organization. However, it seems appropriate to comment briefly here on scorecards as tools also for external communication.

Reporting performance in scorecard terms to the outside public, for instance, in annual reports, has been very rare. However, current suggestions for richer reporting using terms such as intellectual capital often show the influence of BSC thinking.[8] Recent events are having a huge impact on public trust in any information disclosed by corporations. It is hard to guess how this will influence the debate about adding more non-financial information to the facts that corporations are publishing, or are required to publish.

On the one hand, when even long-established accounting numbers are difficult to trust, who will believe a company's non-financial reports about its customers, its processes, and its development efforts? Can they be audited? Is not any claim about such assets too contingent on other external and internal conditions that are impossible to verify?

On the other hand, misleading or fraudulent use of accounting numbers may partly happen because modern business cannot be described in as simple terms as earlier. Translating emerging new business deals, partnerships, and competencies in monetary terms involves assumptions that are better left to the market. According to this way of thinking, scorecard-like information as a *complement* to external accounts is needed now more than ever.

In our interviews for this book we came across a related, but different issue. A few of the corporations we talked to saw insider-trading rules as a limitation on their *internal* disclosure of scorecard information. Public corporations have to obey strict rules about how information with a potential impact on share prices is disseminated. Top-level managers who have access to such information are registered as insiders to prevent them from buying and selling stock based on it. The companies we talked to would have liked to let many more employees have access to scorecard information such as trends in different customer segments, quality measures, etc. They told us that they could not do this, and had to restrict access to measures for just the local unit where employees work. 'Otherwise we would have to register several hundred employees as insiders!'

We found this interesting, because it seems an obvious but little-discussed consequence of the greater openness that many corporations now aim for. It also shows that this type of information really is strategically sensitive. Of course, it should be if a scorecard really 'tells the story of our strategy', as is the intention. But it may also indicate that in the longer run it will be necessary to disclose more such information to the general public – because it has to be handled daily by too many employees to be kept secret. Scorecards will be a natural format for this.

FAD OR EMERGING STANDARD?

The previous sections showed that the *aims and scope* of scorecard projects have varied. Early projects focused on performance management.[9] The BSC was soon promoted as a strategic control tool, to be used throughout a corporation and based on its over-arching strategic aims. This was prob-ably attempted in only a minority of cases. Multi-business corporations find it hard to articulate a corporate strategy, and financial measures are usually more acceptable and even sufficient at this level, especially in more differentiated groups. Much scorecard work therefore started at division or business unit level, or even lower down in organizations, where non-financial metrics and concrete assumptions about cause-and-effect relation-ships were found to be more attractive than traditional controls. Some companies even argued that scorecards should be built bottom-up rather than mandated from the top. One such company, Skandia, is described in Chapter 3. As we will see, after some years they partly changed their philosophy.

But there are also large differences in the *realization* of the intended aims. We have seen scorecard projects that never went beyond an initial score-card, although this was the aspiration. Management engaged enthusiastic-ally in articulating their strategy, but the resulting scorecard was never turned into control.

At the same time, other corporations pushed systematic measurement and reporting as the essential part of their scorecard projects, almost to the exclusion of strategic discussions or top-management involvement.

A consequence was that scorecards in some corporations were a set of overhead slides in the CEO's presentations, in others elaborate performance measurement routines without much contact with strategy. In some, the scorecard project became synonymous with a new software package for reporting numbers that already existed in data warehouses. As we will argue in later chapters, to get widespread and connected use of scorecards without lapsing into meaningless rituals may be the real challenge in scorecard projects. Popular books and articles, including our own, are partly to blame for the failures. Too little attention has been given to the problems of 'living with scorecards', an imbalance we intend to redress in this book.

Scorecards also tend to look very different in different organizations. Kaplan and Norton in their later writings (e.g. Kaplan and Norton, 2001) stress the use of the *strategy map*, a tool which we find highly useful and will discuss extensively in later chapters. This should be regarded as a different way of *representing* the scorecard, and we include it when we talk of the BSC. On the other hand, many companies have redesigned the original, four-perspective scorecard. We have given some examples already in *Performance Drivers*: Volvo using one short-term and one long-term scorecard, or Xerox reformulating their previous measurement framework into a sort of scorecard. In Scandinavia, a standard change has been to introduce a fifth perspective for employees or HR. This sometimes leads to a reformulation of the entire scorecard in terms of stakeholder groups.

Although such 'scorecards' are interesting reactions to the same needs that led to the BSC, we believe that they may have harmed the basic concept. The BSC is a flexible tool, but its usefulness cannot be judged from the reactions people have from using 'scorecards' that are very different from the original intention, or from failing to use them properly. One of our case companies told us that their scorecard project had encountered difficulties mainly in one division. This had run a local scorecard project a couple of years previously, which the present project leader believed was not handled properly. In a similar way, we were told by a group having operations both in Sweden and in one of the Baltic states that it was easier to introduce scorecards in the latter. They had less preconceived opinions and a greater expectation of change.

Reports that 55% of firms are now using the BSC need therefore to be viewed with a healthy dose of scepticism. What kind of scorecards do they have in mind, and how are they used?

What these findings do indicate is a lack of satisfaction with traditional controls. This is also the unifying theme in the cases we report in this volume. Our intention in this book is to take a critical look at why companies introduce scorecards, how they do it, and what challenges and important design issues they encounter. The selection of companies is largely based on access, with an eye to a mixture of large and small, private and public, local (Swedish) and international. These are introduced in Chapter 4. We find one story, Skandia, so interesting that we devote an entire chapter, Chapter 3, to it. It provides food for thought on many of the issues that we discuss later, and allows us to give an 'inside' perspective that adds new depth to the descriptions of Skandia's project in earlier books.[10]

Following these chapters, we proceed by using our cases and other experiences for a thematic exposition which we have organized into 'challenges' and 'issues'. These are introduced at the beginning of these sections. Challenges are the difficulties many organizations face as they implement and use scorecards. Issues refer to the most important design choices when an organization introduces the BSC and starts relying on it as an important tool for realizing strategies.

So is our conclusion that the BSC is a 'fad', or 'emerging best practice'? We think it all depends on how it is done. The scorecard idea is flexible. It needs to be adapted to one's own situation, and a number of design issues need to be addressed. That is why we have written this book. By digesting the experiences from our case organizations and our own practice working with scorecards in many organizations, we believe that readers who are managing scorecard projects, leading firms where such projects are attempted, starting new projects – or salvaging old ones – should get an awareness of the pitfalls and critical choices to be made. This should make it possible for them to make their own use of scorecards successful.

Scorecards in Use   2

As we said at the end of Chapter 1, scorecard designs vary. In this chapter we introduce various designs, in some cases previewing how our case companies visualize theirs. We also provide a brief summary of how to introduce and use scorecards. Although probably too short for newcomers,[11] this will serve as a refresher course for those who already have some scorecard experience. The summary also indicates which issues we believe are the most important. Through this we lay the foundation for the rest of the book, and its outline is presented at the end of this chapter.

SNAPSHOTS OF SCORECARDS

A scorecard is a description of a business logic, using metrics in several perspectives in a systematic way. The simplest one we have seen remains Halifax's Theory Z, which we reported on in *Performance Drivers*: 'If we have the right staff (development perspective) doing the right things (process perspective), then the customers will be delighted (customer perspective), and we will keep and get more business (financial perspective).' In the basic BSC we showed in Figure 1.2, this (reverse) Z pattern is just one among several possible paths through the figure. For another company, development may be about improving the customer base; for yet another, improving internal efficiency with unchanged service performance. These three possibilities are depicted in Figure 2.1. The important thing is that the scorecard tells the story of the intended business logic.

Every organization should pursue a unique strategy, based on its interpretation of the external and internal situation. This may, of course, combine a few such paths through the scorecard. To clarify this, it is often easier

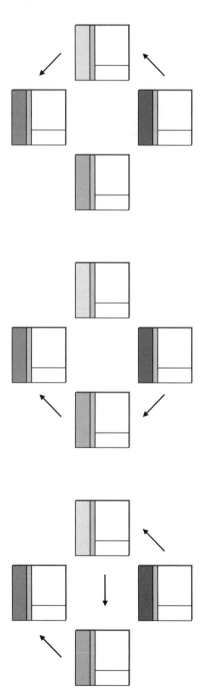

Figure 2.1 Business logics as paths through the scorecard.

to draw the scorecard as a strategy map (Kaplan and Norton, 2001). For instance, Figure 2.2 shows the four perspectives from bottom to top, and some important strategic goals are identified within each perspective. These goals are linked in a few causal chains through the strategy map. Kaplan and Norton use the term 'strategic themes' for such patterns. To the left in Figure 2.2 is a strategic theme aiming to improve the customer base; in the middle, improving customer value; and to the right, improving internal efficiency. It will be seen that some of the themes interact. We have also indicated through a feedback loop that improved financial health is a precondition for being able to afford continued development work. Over time, the process depicted in a strategy map should play out as a self-reinforcing 'virtuous circle': succeeding in our ambitions should breed further success.

Figure 2.2 is obviously just a textbook example. Still, we sometimes use maps almost as simple as this to trigger discussions in a group of executives, asking, for instance, which theme is the most important one. It challenges them to clarify their views about dependencies, time lags, potential, etc.

Graphs like these have proved helpful in articulating strategies. To test the quality of strategy maps, we find it useful to ask whether they make it possible for their users rapidly to understand the logic, ambitions, and/or achievements of the organization – in short, to gauge its health. As we explained in Chapter 1, users may exist at all different levels of the firm. If possible, we prefer to start with the entire firm. The test then is whether the board believes that the map – or scorecard – gives a fair and comprehensive view of the organization.

Drawing such scorecards as strategy maps often makes it easier to discuss the intended business logic. A scorecard for a department in a publicly funded university might, for instance, look like Figure 2.3. Such graphs should be developed together with the people who are going to use the scorecards, in this case the management team and – if possible – representatives of the employees. In Figure 2.3, we recognize that the aims of a university are not primarily financial by changing the financial perspective to a 'trustees' perspective'.

To arrive at scorecards which can be used in an organization, they have, of course, to be developed into agreed targets and action plans. The sequence recommended in the literature is through critical success factors (CSFs), metrics, targets for these, and action plans to achieve the targets.

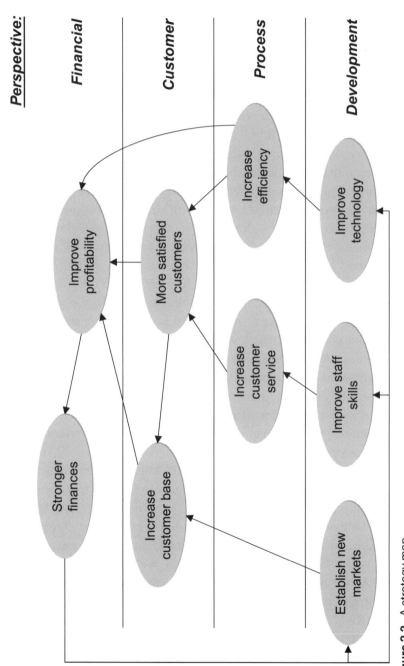

Figure 2.2 A strategy map.

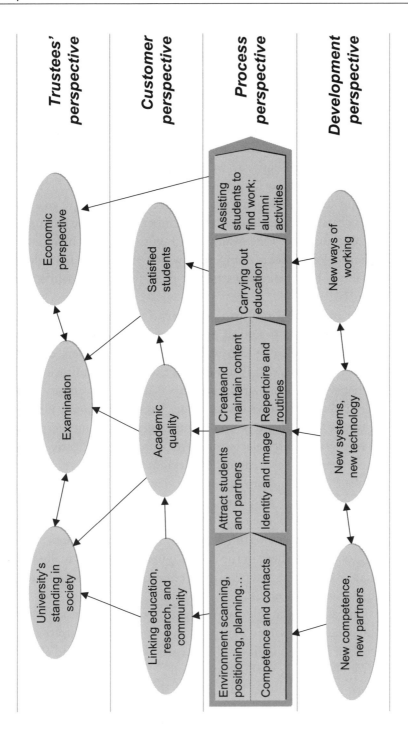

Figure 2.3 Strategy map for a graduate school within a university – initial draft.

An example from Ericsson Enterprise is given in Figure 2.4. (This, like other cases in this book, is introduced later.)

It can be seen from Figure 2.4 how Ericsson Enterprise have carefully identified 16 key (or critical) success factors (KSFs or CSFs), and associated one key performance indicator (KPI or metric) to each. For each KSF and its KPI, they have assigned one person in the leadership team whom they have labelled 'driver'. This person is responsible for monitoring its development. In later chapters, we discuss the development of CSFs, targets, and action plans such as those in Figure 2.4. Some find it easier to discuss metrics and targets, or even actions, before all strategic goals are in place. Others carefully identify a small number of strategic themes, and trace CSFs, etc. for each. One example is Figure 2.5, which comes from Nordea, another of the case companies which is discussed much more extensively later. They call their strategic goals focus areas, while actions are called initiatives.

(The reader may find it confusing that terms such as strategic goals are used differently between organizations. By retaining our case companies' vocabulary in this book, we also want to encourage readers to make a conscious choice of terms that is suitable for their own organizations.)

Yet another way of visualizing scorecards is used in the county government of Jönköping, which we discuss more later in the book. They use a cobweb diagram to condense in one graph targets and achieved performance. The 16 metrics were selected to cover different perspectives, but in this graph the perspectives are not shown (Figure 2.6).

Graphs like these should provide an overview of the organization's most important value-creating resources and processes. In Chapter 1 we mentioned the growing importance of intangibles. To put values on these individually is rarely meaningful, but by showing patterns and intended business logics, such as those in the above figures, scorecards make it possible for users to discuss and hopefully agree on the status, aspirations, and likely future of an organization.[12]

Discussions about strategies and targets are needed throughout the firm. For business units within a corporation, scorecards and strategy maps will reflect their business logics and strategies. But they should also show synergies from belonging to the corporation.

For service and staff units, they should show the rationale as to why services are not outsourced but kept in-house. In our experience, such

Ericsson Enterprise 2002   **ERICSSON ≡**

Condensed example

Vision: We make the Mobile Enterprise a reality for the business user
Mission: To be the market leader in Mobile Enterprise, providing personalized seamless access to applications, data and voice services anywhere, anytime, with any media

	Financial results	Customer/Channel partner	Employees	Internal Efficiency	Innovation
Strategic goals/ Wanted position	❖ Operating margin xx% ❖ We have ---- strategic acquisitions.	❖ Our channels and customers perceive our value proposition and competence in Mobile Enterprise as the best in the industry	❖ Enterprise employees understand and are committed to following our defined strategic direction. ❖ We are recognized as -----	❖ We have a tight efficient org. that pulls in the same direction with a leadership that leverage on competence in an optimal way. ❖ We get things done ----.	❖ We have established a leading position in Mobile Enterprise (market share > xx%, yy% in Europe). ❖ We are the channel of choice for all Ericsson offerings to indirect sales Channels.
Key success factors (KSF)	❖ **PBX Business (1)** Increased profitability in -----, (*Driver: xx Co-drivers: xx, xx, xx*) ❖ **Product Costs (2)** ❖ **Credit Management (3)**	❖ **Customer Orientation (4)** All employees understand their contribution to fulfilling customer needs in their daily work. (*Driver: xx Co-drivers: xx, xx, xx*) ❖ **Customer Recognition (5)** ❖ **Value Proposition (6)**	❖ **Communication (7)** Through effective communication of a common vision, managers on all levels are able to lead in a clear strategic direction. (*Driver: xx Co-drivers: xx, xx, xx, xx*) ❖ **Leadership Quality/ Strategic Direction (8)** ❖ **Employee Contribution (9)** ❖ **Performance Culture (10)**	❖ **Process Deployment (11)** We have clearly ---------- (*Driver: xx Co-drivers: xx, process owners*) ❖ **Performance Developm.(12)**	❖ **R&D Financing (13)** ❖ **Ericsson Recognition (14)** ❖ **Mobility & IP (15)** ❖ **Ericsson products (16)** Get agreements with other Ericsson units to bring their products/solutions to market through our channels. (*Driver: xx Co-drivers: xx, xx*)
Key performance indicators (KPI)	❖ Net Sales: x MSEK ❖ Operating income: x MSEK ❖ Cash flow: x MSEK ❖ Capital turnover: x ❖ Product related cost -----	❖ Partner Satisfaction: x % ❖ Customer Satisfaction: x % ❖ Top20 customers/partners -- ❖ Awareness of customer -----	Attitude survey (Dialog): -Human capital index: x -Empowerment index : x	❖ TTC precision: x % (vs requested) ❖ TTM precision: x%(T+Q) ❖ Motivation: x% (Dialog quest: x+x) ❖ Organizational efficiency--- :	❖ Sales of products/solutions from other Ericsson units: x% ❖ Operators/channel partners signed up to develop Mobile Enterprise business----- ❖ No. of Mobile Enterprise ---
Strategic actions	**KSF 1:** ❖ Provide a clear Road-Map (GW) **KSF 2:** ❖ Improved phase-out process (life cycle mgmt) **KSF 3:** ❖ ---	**KSF 4:** ❖ Raise customer/partner awareness amongst all employees (KS) **KSF 5:** ❖ ---- **KSF 6:** ❖ ----	**KSF 7:** ❖ Establish and maintain Enterprise Key Drivers as a key communications channel (KS) **KSF 8:** ❖ ---- **KSF 9:** ❖ ---- **KSF 10:** ❖ ----	**KSF 11:** ❖ Deploy new business processes (OW) **KSF 12:** ❖ ----	**KSF 13:** ❖ ---- **KSF 14:** ❖ ---- **KSF 15:** ❖ Deliver proof-points as defined at TG2 on time with right content and quality (SS) **KSF 16:** ❖ ----

Uppgjord (även faktaansvarig om annan) - Prepared (also au. ject respons. le if other)	Dokumentansv/Godk.- Doc respons/Approved	Datum - Date	Rev	Nr - No.
BEES (N.N)	LME/COO	2001-12-21	A	BEES-01:910

Dokumentnamn - Document name: BSC GRID 2002   Blad - Sheet 1 (1)

Figure 2.4 From strategies to actions – Ericsson Enterprise's "grid" (Source: internal material). Reproduced by permission of Ericsson Enterprise AB.

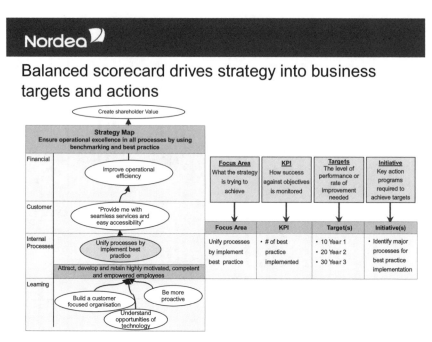

Figure 2.5 Relationship between strategy, targets and action at Nordea. Reproduced by permission of Nordea plc.

internal functions often lack strategic aims. Discussions about their role in the organization focus on their operational, generic tasks. The contribution of an HR or finance department to the success of a firm might be described in much more explicit terms in its scorecard. What qualities make it worthwhile to have these functions in-house, and how do we recognize high-quality performance? Figure 2.7 derives from our work with a company where it was agreed that the administrative department's customers, i.e. the other employees of the company, would consider the quality of support as essential in their choice of place to work, providing 'a good reason to work in this company'.[13]

On some occasions, we have found it useful to develop separate scorecards for, e.g.

1. IT's contribution to corporate success, and
2. the IT department as an internal service (IS) provider – see Figure 2.8.

The scorecard for the IT department (Figure 2.8(b)) would treat this unit more or less as a separate business, with the difference that its owners

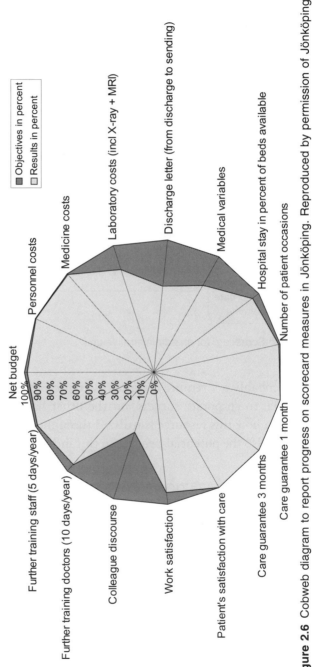

Figure 2.6 Cobweb diagram to report progress on scorecard measures in Jönköping county council. Reproduced by permission of Jönköping county council.

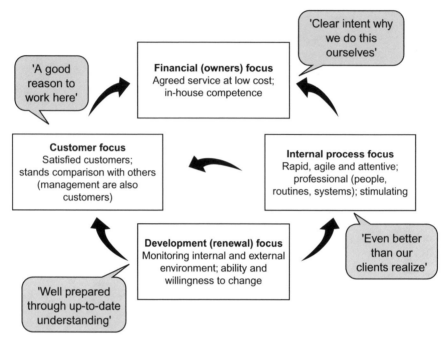

Figure 2.7 Scorecard for an administrative unit.

would probably not require it primarily to produce a profit. The contribution of IT to corporate success, on the other hand (Figure 2.8(a)), will depend on how this resource is utilized throughout the organization, and, of course, also the potential benefits in this industry.

HOW DO ORGANIZATIONS INTRODUCE SCORECARDS?

Aims for scorecard projects

BSCs provide a valuable tool for enabling employees to understand the organization's situation. They also provide information for management as the organization starts to develop and document on a continuous basis those measures for control which most quickly will guide it towards achieving its goals and its vision.

The outcome will be that daily operations are founded on a shared view of where the company is headed in the long run. With the scorecard segmented by area of activity, control of operations will be perceived locally

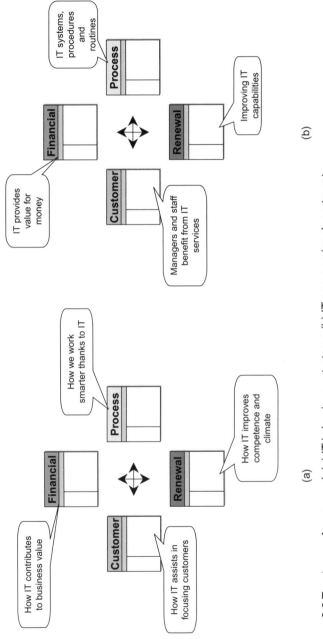

Figure 2.8 Two types of scorecard: (a) IT in business strategy; (b) IT as a service department.

as more relevant than with previous models. Employees will be more understanding and better motivated, and thus more open to change and forceful in implementing company decisions.

The organization also becomes better at learning, more perceptive and continually develops its competence.

All of this, however, requires that the introduction and continued use of scorecards is performed well. Since the idea of scorecards is so simple, the need for resource commitment and top management focus are often underestimated. A scorecard project can easily be perceived as just some kind of more elaborate performance measurement project. It may then even cause antagonism among employees by being seen as a new way to inspect their work. Or – more common in our experience – it is initially received well, but when employees get the (sometimes correct) impression that managers are not themselves really engaged in using scorecards to discuss business and performance in new ways, the enthusiasm evaporates.

So how can the process be designed to avoid these dangers? We comment on this using the following structure:

- *For what business activities should there be scorecards?* Among the first decisions is, of course, where to start. We also discuss the usefulness of scorecards for non-profit activities: staff units, government agencies, etc.
- *Developing the initial scorecards.* It is obviously of vital importance to launch the project in a good way.
- *Introducing and using scorecards – a process view.* Continuing on the previous point, we show the desired connection from strategy through control and learning back to strategy. It is in using scorecards on an ongoing basis that the real gains are to be had. It is also at this stage that support for the project may diminish, since top managers believe that the scorecards are safely introduced. 'Living with scorecards' easily gets too little attention, as it probably has in the literature also.

For what business activities should there be scorecards?

Some organizations start their scorecard projects with the higher echelons, others with a pilot project somewhere down in the organization. Some never reach below their higher echelons, others develop scorecards even for individual employees. A decision is clearly needed about which activities should be covered by scorecards.

Also, the dialogues where scorecards will be used need to be determined. A department scorecard could be used entirely for internal purposes (motivating employees, etc). It would normally also be used to agree with, and report on, performance to higher levels of management. It might also be published on a corporate intranet as part of a description of the department.

The unit chosen for the initial scorecard needs to be fairly complete and self-contained, or have a clear task and vision assigned by its principals. Otherwise, the attempt to develop a scorecard will only result in a host of questions about its vision and logic. Even this may be useful – some scorecard projects result in a 'proposal' from a subsidiary to corporate management about the role it wants. There are also practical matters involved: how large a part of the total organization will it be feasible and cost-efficient to include?

Extending scorecard work down to individual employees may be useful when these have more independent tasks; otherwise, teams would be the normal level at which to stop. How useful this will be also depends on a number of factors: the improvements aimed for in the project; links to development talks; effects on remuneration, etc.

Usefulness for support ('non-profit') functions within corporations

Scorecards are very useful for discussing internal support functions – cf. Figures 2.7 and 2.8. These functions provide the infrastructure in most organizations, and scorecards help in:

- Deciding that such extensive and expensive functions are needed, by articulating the links to expected benefits and their impact on profits.
- Prioritizing the demands of various users of such services.
- Encouraging the employees in support functions by showing how their efforts contribute to business success for the entire organization.

In our experience, the most common use of scorecards in this way has been for IT and HR functions and departments. As in any scorecard, all four perspectives should be used. Even an R&D unit has its finances, customers, processes, and internal development needs. That its 'business' is development does not mean that it should use only the development perspective! In this way, corporate management will get a full description of the IT, HR or R&D 'businesses' which form part of the corporation. This will be especially useful in comparing it with the alternative of outsourced activities. IT outsourcing sometimes turns out to be only a short-term success, because the decision was based only on current service deliveries, not the process and development assets which disappeared with outsourcing. This could be avoided with a scorecard that provides a more complete picture of the IT department.

As we have already shown in Figure 2.8, it will sometimes be useful to discuss IT as a department and as a function separately.

Use in government and other non-profit organizations

Profit-seeking organizations use scorecards to clarify links between current activities and long-term profits. In non-profit organizations there rarely is any such long-term, single goal. Instead, scorecards have an important role in enabling discussions about trade-offs between diverse interests, and the general level of ambition within a specific policy area. This is similar to the support functions we discussed in the previous section.

Scorecards have been introduced in central and local government organizations in several countries. It seems that the more successful cases so far are found at lower levels in such organizations, where scorecards provide ordinary employees with an opportunity to clarify roles and expectations, and to present their view of 'business logic' to their superiors. For instance, in some parts of Sweden the police departments use scorecards for town and patrol levels of their organization, deciding priorities between different kinds of actions and police duties. On the other hand, on a national level, the Swedish police have not so far introduced scorecards. Explicating the links between resource use, criminality, and public safety may be too complicated – indeed, a matter for research. However, strategies for the police will always reflect some 'strategic bets' about these connections, and – similar to our previous section about service departments in companies – scorecards could help to:

- Decide that extensive and expensive activities are needed by articulating expected benefits and, ultimately, their impact on social well-being.
- Prioritize the demands and needs of various groups of citizens.

- Boost the morale of employees by showing how their efforts contribute to society.

The four perspectives in the scorecard will need to be reinterpreted somewhat in the case of government or other non-profit organizations. We have found it useful to retain the four perspectives, reinterpreting each in the following way (also cf. Figure 2.3):

- *Financial perspective.* An owner's or principal's perspective, showing the ultimate contribution to the needs addressed by the organization (e.g. fight crime or poverty; or take custody of national art treasures).
- *Customer perspective.* An 'external' perspective, describing how successful the organization is in reaching and interacting with all its contacts in society. In addition to serving customers, such as a company, many organizations interact with less willing clients; e.g. criminals who are the targets of police actions. Their experiences should be part of the scorecard, but not an objective by itself.
- *Process perspective.* No major changes, since the internal processes of all organizations should be efficient and well managed. Just as in any scorecard, the principals of a non-profit organization should take an interest in how its 'capital' of processes is maintained and utilized. Improvements may not yet have been fully recognized by the organization's clients, just as in a business firm.
- *Development perspective.* Likewise, non-profit organizations will need to import and implement new technology and new skills as in any business.

Non-government, not-for-profit organizations include charities and voluntary organizations. Some of these have found it useful to agree on a 'business logic' that can be presented to employees, voluntary workers and donors alike, motivating them to support their activities.

Developing the initial scorecards

The initial development process consists of several steps that we will present below.[14] The final product will be a description of the business logic of the organization. This description may come in different shapes, as our examples earlier in this chapter show. It is usually presented in documents and slides, and often displayed on an organization's intranet or on wall charts. There is a danger that once these documents have been produced, they will be seen as proof of a successful project that has reached its final destination. But this is when the real work starts, that of using the scorecard as a strategic management tool throughout the whole organization. We will emphasize this aspect later in this chapter.

Preparing the project

As with any other project, careful preparations make up the groundwork for a successful BSC project. The company has to decide the scope and level of ambition of the project. We need to answer questions such as:

- *What is our level of ambition?* Initially, a project could concentrate on just a corporate scorecard, or as a pilot focus on some subsidiary. It could be restricted to a strategic map for general guidance, or aim for implementation as a full-blown control process.
- *What is our time schedule?* It may not be necessary to plan several years ahead, but there should be a shared view of what should be achieved during the next 12 months.
- *Who will be responsible for what?* Various competences will be needed, and it is essential for success to include important people and groups within the organization. Will they have the time and the will to engage in this?
- *Should we use consultants or not?* They can provide experience, a fresh perspective and work capacity to the project. On the other hand, it is important that the project is not perceived as something consultants do for us – the whole responsibility has to rest with the internal project team.

The first step then is to collect material on the characteristics and requirements of the industry and the company's current position and role. This starts by defining the industry, describing its development and the role of the company in the midst of this context. We recommend that the project team (or its consultants) do this through individual interviews with top management and with the most influential opinion leaders in the company. Significant customers, suppliers, and public institutions should also be included. In this way we build a platform for elaborating our vision and our future strategies.

Running the first seminar

In preparing for the first seminar it has proved useful to document the initial interviews, particularly any dissenting views on essential issues. In preparation for the seminar it is also important to find out what the people concerned believe will happen in the future. This procedure involves a combination of research and interviews with stakeholders and people at different levels in the company. At the seminar, the global picture provided by the participants is presented in summary form.

During the first seminar we need above all to confirm or, in some cases, establish the company's vision. Usually, a company will have had such discussions many times before.

Since the BSC model is based on a shared comprehensive vision, it is essential to ascertain at an early stage whether there really is a jointly held vision. The simple format of the scorecard triggers a concrete and realistic discussion, whereas existing strategies often consist of beautiful and non-committal words.

The next step during the seminar is to choose and establish the different perspectives on which to build the scorecard. For each of these perspectives we then have to break the vision down and formulate overall strategic aims, and identify critical factors for success. This step is about articulating, refining, and agreeing on a business strategy. There is an element of invention involved which is not easily described. Given the right participants and enough time, and a discussion leader who knows how to challenge the group, usually it is an intense and fascinating process.

Confirming the top-level scorecard

When the vision, strategic aims, perspectives, and critical success factors have been established it is time to develop relevant key measures. We need to evaluate the feasibility of taking a measurement for each of them, while at the same time checking the structure for logical consistency.

The great challenge is to find clear cause-and-effect relationships and to create a balance among measures in different perspectives. Short-term improvements should not conflict with long-term goals. Measures in different perspectives must not encourage suboptimization, but rather fit and support the comprehensive vision and the overall strategy.

The top-level scorecard is then put together for presentation and approval. This can be done through consultations, a second seminar, or at an ordinary meeting by the executive team.

Implementation is facilitated if everyone in the organization is briefed on the work and the thinking that have gone into the scorecard. Participants should receive advice about the continuing process of breaking down the scorecard: explanatory text, possible approaches, and suggestions for group work.

Roll-out

The next step is to derive lower-level scorecards from the top-level one. All employees should see clearly how the company's vision and overall goals affect day-to-day operations. This means that we need scorecards down to a level where they become sufficiently tangible and understandable to have an impact on daily actions.

The targets for every measure have to be aligned both horizontally and vertically (see, for example, Figures 2.4 and 2.5 earlier in the chapter), in order to be consistent with the comprehensive vision and overall strategy. Finally, to complete the scorecard, we must also specify the steps to be taken to achieve the goals and the vision which have been established. This action plan should include both the people responsible and a schedule for interim and final reporting.

Introducing and using scorecards – a process view

In many early BSC texts and projects, there was an understandable emphasis on the construction of an initial set of scorecards. 'Living with scorecards' therefore received too little attention. Figure 2.9 shows that the ambition should be to create management control systems for a learning organization. Data captured through information systems should be fed back to improve strategies through learning. This may also lead to a revision of the scorecards themselves.

- *Strategy development.* Developing the scorecards usually makes people see their company and its business model in a new way. This often leads to new ideas about the company's vision and to a reconsideration of its

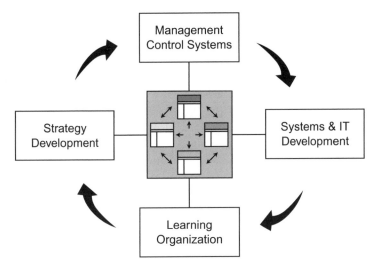

Figure 2.9 The BSC process (from *Performance Drivers*, p.147).

strategy. For this reason, the first steps in our scorecard process are about developing or confirming a strategy, as we saw in the previous section.

- *Management control systems.* Scorecards document how strategies are translated into measures and goals and provide comprehensive, balanced statements of the duties of managers and employees. In principle, the process should be repeated throughout the organization so that all employees are given a sense of participation and can understand their part in the overall strategic scheme. An important part of the process, therefore, is to link together measures in different perspectives and in scorecards for different business units.
- *Systems and IT development.* For the scorecards to be actionable through-out the company, the procedure for handling measurements must be user-friendly and not overly complicated. Data must be recorded, verified, and made available. Normally, the scorecard will draw on a combination of data already in use at the company, and of new measurements, some of which may be quite informal in nature. Some-times data will be imported from outside sources, such as market surveys or competitor benchmarking. Creating interest and high attention throughout the organization is often an essential part of a scorecard project.

- *Learning organization.* The primary function of the scorecard is to control company operations. By extension, there is also a more cumulative effect. As we gain experience in how a new customer database is being used, or how sales are developing in new customer segments, our assumptions about causal relationships will be confirmed or disproved. In this way, the use of the BSC can also facilitate learning. At both individual and company levels we will develop a better understanding of the relationship between what we do and how well the company succeeds.

As we said before, often organizations do not seem to be aware of the danger that the BSC process will be interrupted once a first set of scorecards has been prepared. To have the process continue, all these steps have to be well managed.

CHALLENGES AND CRITICAL ISSUES IN USING SCORECARDS

In Chapters 1 and 2 we have given a first introduction to the topics we will investigate in this book. In the next two chapters we turn to our case studies for narratives about what happened when a number of organizations introduced scorecards. Chapter 3, the longest, is devoted to Skandia, a Swedish insurance and long-term savings company. Chapter 4 gives shorter introductions to a number of cases that will recur in later chapters. We will also reflect on their varying approaches.

These cases are then analysed in two ways. Chapter 5 identifies a number of *challenges* we find that these companies faced. These are closely linked to our discussion earlier: how do you establish the appropriate scope of your project; how do you provide impetus for it, and keep it going?

The second type of analysis concerns the various *design issues* we believe scorecard projects have to address. We have selected six such issues that will be discussed in Chapters 6–11. They are shown in Figure 2.10, together with the path we follow through them. The issues occur both in introducing and using scorecards:

- *Strategy maps* – or, more generally, expressing strategies in scorecards, linking objectives and measures. How can this be done? We have already discussed strategy maps at the beginning of this chapter. Not

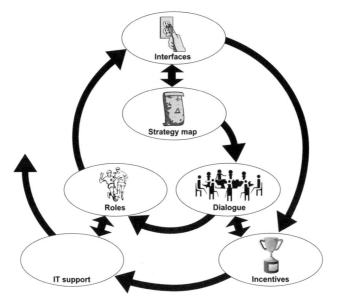

Figure 2.10 Issues to be discussed in Chapters 6–11.

all our case organizations make use of them, but those (such as Ericsson – cf. Figure 2.4) who do not will also have to deal with this issue.

- *Dialogues* – when and where are scorecards (or strategy maps, etc.) to be used? For scorecards to be meaningful, constant discussion of their underlying logic is essential. When employees perceive BSC as just performance measurement, all the negative effects of traditional supervision may occur. But it has often been welcomed when similar metrics are perceived as part of a living dialogue about what is worth doing, and how performance relates to organizational progress. This, of course, requires management to be able to engage in such dialogues – to have enough knowledge about their business and a viewpoint about its possible futures. The exact mixture of traditional budgets, scorecards, and forecasts will be a consequence of several things: the corporation's tradition and strategies; its competitive situation; industry conditions; and the level within the organization. Business units pursuing differentiation from the competition through long-term activities will have the greatest need for scorecards.
- *Roles* – what responsibilities have to be assigned for scorecards to function and have effect? These should cover a variety of aspects of 'living

with scorecards'. Obviously, every manager whose unit is part of the new control system is accountable for proper attention to its scorecard. The 'technology' of scorecards (definitions, formats, timetable, information provision) needs to be the responsibility of someone, often in the controller's department. During the first year or two, this may also include promoting and training for scorecard use, and then the responsibility is given to a special task-force near top management. If software is introduced, someone usually in the IT department will be accountable for its functioning. As data is collected about the various metrics, someone should periodically assess this in order to learn about cause-and-effect relationships. Did the patterns play out as expected, or should the links in strategic maps be reconsidered?

- *Interfaces* – there will usually be several or many scorecards in an organization. How should these relate? Sometimes there is an expectation that scorecard measures should be uniform throughout an organization, and aggregated in the same way that financial numbers are. In practice, conditions in different units often make it natural to use widely different measures.

- *Incentives* – what rewards are needed for scorecards to work? For some time directly after introducing scorecards, the attention paid to 'new' measures itself encourages performance improvements – especially for employees who were themselves involved in setting targets. For a more lasting impact, non-financial measures must be made 'competitive' with the financial and traditionally more visible ones. We have not observed any project where changes in formal compensation were part of the original design. Many arrived at this issue slowly and reluctantly, probably because large financial incentives were rare in Scandinavian companies until recently. Traditional values do not encourage them, and a highly unionized workforce has stressed other priorities in its wage negotiations.

- *IT support* – how should data be handled? Is an IT-based system necessary, and how can one choose between alternative solutions? A scorecard project will find it easier to 'take roots' if measurements are easily available and accessible. Our preference is for starting in a quick and simple way, even if this requires some manual work. In the longer run, most organizations benefit from having scorecard information readily available over an intranet.

In positioning these issues along a spiral in Figure 2.10, we want to indicate two things:

1. we believe the issues should be addressed in this order, and
2. some issues are closely related.

One such relation is between strategy maps and interfaces. Both concern links between objectives: in one scorecard, or between different scorecards. A second relationship is between dialogues and incentives. Motivation will depend on the way scorecards are used in dialogues between members of the organization. When incentives are linked to scorecards, it just introduces a more formalized component into such dialogues. The final relationship is between roles and IT. It is in fulfilling their different roles in using scorecards that people may need IT, while IT also introduces new tasks that have to be assigned as roles to somebody.

Summarizing the plan of this book then, we have:

- Chapters 1 and 2 – Introducing scorecards and setting the agenda for the book ('the concept')
- Chapters 3 and 4 – Narratives of scorecards ('applying the concept')
- Chapter 5 – Challenges in introducing and using scorecards ('what may go wrong?')
- Chapters 6–11 – Six important issues that organizations faced in introducing and using scorecards ('what needs to be done right?')
- Chapter 12 – Concluding thoughts ('prospects')

Most of the chapters are designed to be read separately, if the reader so wishes; but we then advise that Chapters 3 and 4 are consulted for background information on our cases if the organizations concerned are not already well known to the reader.

Skandia's Experience from Navigating into the Future   3

In this chapter you will get to know Skandia, a Swedish insurance and long-term savings company, and their work with the Navigator – their equivalent to the BSC. The chapter begins with an illustration about how the work started, and continues with a description of how the work with the Navigator has developed over time and how the employees in one of the companies in the Skandia Group have used the tool. This description is based on interviews over several years, and participation in meetings during autumn and winter 2000.[15]

The descriptions below serve as an illustration of the challenges and issues that an organization can face when working with multi-dimensional management tools. The stories also embrace how the organization has managed to deal with these challenges, and what has come out of the work.

THE FIRST GENERATION OF NAVIGATORS AT SKANDIA

The Swedish insurance and long-term savings company Skandia has often been considered a pioneer in working with the visualization of their intellectual capital. This work started at the end of the 1980s when Skandia Assurance and Financial Services, Skandia AFS, was established. The organization was built on an, at the time, unique way of organizing. The CEO, Jan Carendi, had an idea about working with 'specialists in cooperation', which suggested that Skandia AFS should function as a bridge between wholesale distributors and brokers. The distributors were regarded as specialists in selling long-term savings products to their established customer base. Skandia AFS therefore saw their chance to provide them with the administration and packaging of long-terms savings products. By doing this, both parties could focus on what they were best at and what they enjoyed most. The specialists' knowledge could thereby be developed and customer service continuously improved.

Carendi started thinking about all the knowledge that the 'specialists in cooperation' had and continuously developed during their work. The specialists' knowledge was seen as, and still is, the organization's most important asset but, unlike other more tangible resources, it was not visualized in the financial reports. Rather the opposite – the investments that were made in the employees' development and learning only turned up as red numbers in the profit and loss account. This created a number of problems for Carendi. During the first few years he found it difficult to get financial support from the rest of the organization because he did not show any profits. In addition, the company's financial value did not at all correspond with the company's potential future value.

It was these thoughts that triggered the search for new tools to visualize and manage the organization's intangible assets. In 1991 Carendi appointed the world's first director of intellectual capital, Leif Edvinsson, to work on the task. Edvinsson and his team started developing a set of tools and a language that were meant to help in communicating the ideas around intellectual capital. Their ambition was, according to Edvinsson, that the tools would lead primarily to a shift of management's focus, to an improvement in the cooperation between the different units in the company, and thereby also an increase in the pace of innovation. This would, in turn, increase the leverage in the organization.

The major tool that came out of the process was the Navigator. The Navigator is structured as a building (see Figure 3.1 below) consisting of five different building blocks – renewal and development, process, human, customer, and financial focus. The purpose of this building is to show that the organization's future is dependent upon the existence of a balance between the different parts of the organization. If there is not a balance between the building's different blocks, or focus areas, then the house will collapse. The story goes:

If the company does not have a solid foundation, it will not stand long. If it has not got any walls, it will be no company, and if it does not have a roof rain and snow will destroy the walls and the foundation.

The house was inspired by Kaplan and Norton's idea behind the BSC and its different perspectives. To customize the model to Skandia's unique situation, a few adjustments were made. One adjustment was the addition of a human perspective, or human focus as Skandia prefer to label it. In Skandia there were several arguments for adding this focus to the model. One was that a separate human focus was needed in order to emphasize that the human resources were seen as the most important resources in the organization. The focus was therefore also placed at the heart of the model. Another

Skandia's Navigator

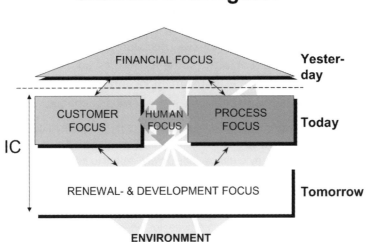

Figure 3.1 The Skandia Navigator. Reproduced by permission of Skandia AFS.

argument regarding the human focus was that management at Skandia argued that there is a multiplier function built into the human focus that enhances the other focus areas' value. By visualizing the human focus, the effect of this multiplication becomes more explicit.

Communicating the Navigator

Using the ideas underlying the Navigator that they developed, Edvinsson and his team started to missionize the concept mainly externally but also internally in Skandia. They produced supplements to the annual reports, CD-ROMs, and booklets that presented and communicated the concept. In the widely spread supplements, measures and tools that supported the new way of thinking were presented. By doing this Skandia wanted to spread their ideas and get others to adopt and even develop them. They argued that the more people that began thinking about and working with these things, the better. Skandia would thereby get support for their new ideas, and could thereby also get increased leverage internally as well as externally.

Edvinsson tried to initiate a change of thinking among the employees in the organization by changing the external image of the organization. By telling others what was going on at Skandia, Edvinsson hoped that the different organizational units would start using the Navigator as intended.

He, and Carendi, thereby wanted to give the employees time to understand the new ideas and learn the new language that they brought about. To start change projects this way, i.e. by creating external pressure, is not unusual in organizations but it is also a high-risk procedure owing to the fact that the organization sooner or later has to expose its 'results' no matter what their status. Beginning with the establishment of internal processes to make things happen thus seems to be a safer way of creating change.

All around the world scholars and practitioners began to pay attention to how Skandia managed its intellectual capital. This triggered action among external actors, and many organizations slowly started to adopt and develop the thoughts. A problem was, however, that internally in Skandia there was less awareness of the work that Edvinsson and his team were doing. Their work therefore remained for a long time on a conceptual level. Few of the employees knew what the Navigator was, let alone what it was for. The old budgeting and reporting systems remained in use and people did not take time to learn and use this additional tool that had become available to them. In addition, Carendi did not want to push the organization too hard. He stated:

> To get people to work with the Navigator the efforts must come from them – we cannot force this process upon them. This does however take a lot of time, and we need to be patient. We need to implement the concept slowly so that people get to know the language. By continuously talking about the concepts both internally and externally, the understanding will also grow and sooner or later the employees will see the need for this type of tool themselves. Those are the kind of triggers we need.

The main challenge that the organization faced was that there were too many different reporting, management, and information systems for the employees to pay any attention to the Navigator as well. Not all employees took the time to understand what the Navigator was for or how it could come to support their daily and long-term work. As many organizations have experienced when trying to implement the BSC and similar tools, the employees initially see it as a fad that will soon fade away. They do not think it is worth spending a lot of time learning a new system that management probably will substitute with another system in a year or so.

However, in 1998 something happened at Skandia that changed this initial attitude. The Navigator had now existed in the organization for more than five years but had still not had any visible effect on the internal work. At this point, lots of organizational changes took place, and in connection with this a new board was appointed. With them came new directions for the work with the Navigator.

The five years that had passed since the introduction of the Navigator to the organization had not led to any changes within the organization. Yearly reports had been released to visualize the development of ideas around the intellectual capital. Within the organization the situation looked somewhat different – most of the employees had still not worked with the tool. Many had not even heard about it. However, when the new board started their work they felt that considering all the successful investments that had been made to spread the ideas externally, it would be a waste not to take the opportunity also to get the tool implemented internally. The board believed that the tool would have positive effects in the organization and therefore decided that from May 1998 it was to be compulsory to use the Navigator.

To support this decision the old budgeting and reporting systems were changed. By leaving these old systems, management thought the employees would become more engaged in working with the new tool. No competing planning and evaluation tools would take time from their usual work and the Navigator work would thereby be given more attention. The use of the Navigator was to become a corporate-wide tool for managing and comparing different companies in the Skandia group.

Hence, from 1998 the Navigator was to become everyone's concern. It was not to be a surveillance tool, but a tool that could support all employees in their long- and short-term activities. Navigators were to be developed on all levels of the organization: individuals, units, companies, and the board were to have their own Navigators, enabling employees at all levels of the organization to get both holistic and detailed information about the organization.

The ambition to have scorecards on all organizational levels, including the individual level, is rather unusual. At Skandia, however, the ambition was to spread the tool organization-wide. To do this, everyone was encouraged to construct their own Skandia Navigator. This would make the employees get used to that way of thinking and get to learn the new language.

But there was rather a long way to go before Navigators were established on all organizational levels. To make this vision come true, several initiatives were taken. One was to appoint a new group that was to provide instructions on how and why to use the Navigator. In line with this task, the implementation group also got to develop a web-based system. This system was to embrace the Navigator and its accompanying tools, and serve as a knowledge sharing, development and management system. To have a web-based IT support system was seen as crucial to get the work with Navigator rolling. It would enable communication and management organization-wide.

A third initiative was to run workshops for everyone in the organization to ensure that they all knew how and why to use the tool. This time, management was to make sure that all employees accepted and used the Navigator.

DEVELOPING THE SECOND GENERATION OF NAVIGATORS

What we have seen so far is how the first thoughts about the Navigator developed. We have seen some of the challenges that the organization faced when trying to get the employees to accept and use the tool, and how old management systems stole the Navigator's attention. Next follows a description of how the implementation of the Navigator continued, how various supporting functions – IT-based as well as roles – were developed and what challenges the organization met during this work.

> The board's decision to make the work with the Navigator compulsory was an effort to get the employees to actually work with the tool – to make them get over the resistance to learning and working with a new system. The board wanted to emphasize that the work with the Navigator was not an over-blowing fad. The Navigator was there to stay. The initiatives that were taken were seen as the first step towards developing a second generation of Navigators – supported by IT, and by other types of help functions that would make the work easier.

The immense efforts to communicate the ideas behind the Navigator were made in order to get everyone involved in the work. In other organizations it is more common that the BSC is a tool for management, leaving them a much smaller group to convince and teach. In Skandia, the number of people to convince made the task much more complex. It was not only that a lot of employees had to be taught, but they all also had different backgrounds, different functions and different experience with this type of tool. However, if Skandia were to succeed in convincing its employees, then they also expected a much larger pay off.

> Together with the implementation group, management did everything they could to provide the organization with all the help functions they would need. As mentioned above, the major investment was the development of the web-based Dolphin Navigator System (Dolphin). This system was thought to enable organization-wide communication of the work with the Navigator and thus also new possibilities to live up to the ambition of developing a well-functioning, knowledge-management system.

The development of this computerized system, which would support the work with, and follow up of, the Navigator, had started already in the middle of the 1990s. The group that later became responsible for developing Dolphin had started developing a first version of the system in 1996. It was at that time a rather simple MIS system used by 100 people, spread out in the global organization. The problem with that system was that all updates had to be sent around the world using floppy disks. Considering that the system was updated at least monthly, the number of disks in travel was numerous. At the time, however, this early version of Dolphin was seen as a good start of an organization-wide management system.

In 1998, a formal decision was made by the corporate board to develop Dolphin to support all Skandia's work with the Navigator. The reason for developing this tool internally was that management found that they had already created a foundation for this work, and by continuing to build on this foundation they would get a tailor-made tool for their own version of the BSC. However, despite functioning as an IT infrastructure for the Navigator, the ambition was also that Dolphin would become an intranet-based solution for knowledge creation, knowledge sharing, and knowledge management. The Navigator was to be the central tool enabling visualization of the organization's intellectual capital. Implementing this system and making it accessible to all employees would be a way of both visualizing and triggering change. If the employees saw that changes took place out in the organization, then they would also use the tool to initiate change.

Different models within the system would support this change process. The Process Model in Figure 3.2 became the most important one.

The Process Model had been developed early in the 1990s to support the work with the Navigator. The model can be seen as an extension of the Navigator that visualizes the process through which the connection between the long-term strategies and the short-term operations is clarified. This was meant to create a language that would communicate methods for managing and following up ongoing activities. According to Edvinsson, Skandia needed '*an intellectual capital grammar and a number of measurement tools specifically developed to enable monitoring and evaluation of the movements of these intangibles*'.

The Process Model was developed to fill these purposes. By working with it, the employees should be able to translate their vision into daily operations and to follow up the outcome. This translation is done through a cause-and-effect relationship that connects the organizational vision and objectives to the daily activities that are followed up with different indicators. These linkages should be identified through a number of steps beginning with the formulation of a vision and objectives. To reach these goals, success factors

IC Management Tool:

The Process Model
Translating vision & strategy into action

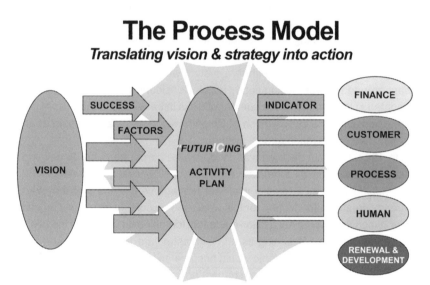

Figure 3.2 Skandia's Process Model. Reproduced by permission of Skandia AFS.

that are seen as crucial to reach the objectives have to be developed. These should be supported by a number of activities that are monitored through indicators in the Navigator.

As can be seen in Figure 3.2, the layout of the Navigator is similar to Kaplan and Norton's BSC. There are, however, some differences between the models.[16] First, the BSC model is hierarchical, starting from the top with the vision, moving down to goals, success factors, measures, and activity plans. The Process Model, on the other hand, is laid out vertically visualizing a process. The process begins with vision, moves forward to success factors, activities, etc.

Another difference is that goals are not explicitly stated in the Navigator. Instead, the vision and objective represent the overall aim of the organization. Furthermore, the activity plan is based on the success factors, and not on the results shown in the indicators as in the BSC. For Skandia, this is a way of being more proactive in their work. The employees should know what action to take based on the vision and success factors identified. This is Skandia's way of *FuturICing*[17] – their way of always taking action that is tightly connected to the vision rather than taking action based on

what their indicators show. Hence, instead, they follow up the activities
with indicators. The indicators are divided into the five focus areas that
become visualized in the Navigator.

> Dolphin, the web-based solution, can be used to link the vision, success
> factors, activities, and indicators, creating a chain of cause-and-effect link-
> ages. A built-in function, named Process Model Relations, allows the users to
> connect the vision to the success factors, and then to activities and indicators.
> However, connections cannot be made vertically in the model. That is, indi-
> cators cannot be connected to each other to visualize the linkages between
> the different focuses. A development of this function is in the pipeline with the
> next version of Dolphin. Being a one-dimensional tool, strategy maps (cf.
> Figures 2.2 and 2.3), can thus not be developed in Dolphin.
>
> Working with the Process Model and thereby linking the vision to the
> strategic objective, then continuing to link this to success factors, to activities
> and then finally to indicators has thus been an effort to create a language that
> tells the story of the strategy. This is central to the work with the Navigator. By
> looking at a unit's Navigator one should be able to tell what is being done in
> the organization to reach the vision. In this story, the indicators play an
> important role. They tell whether or not the unit or organization is on track
> towards the vision. In Dolphin, indicators are identified through work with the
> Process Model and are visualized in the Navigator. The Navigator thereby
> comes to function as a reporting tool. An alternative way of using the tool
> could have been to use the indicators to identify what action needs to be taken
> in order to reach the vision – not just to find out whether or not we are on track
> towards it.
>
> The indicators that are reported into the Navigator through the Process
> Model in the Dolphin system have a special colour code that functions as an
> early warning system. The units or employees set targets for each indicator.
> Then, when they manually[18] report the actual result for each month (or each
> quarter) into Dolphin the colour of the numbers displayed in the Navigator
> indicates whether they are on or off target (Figure 3.3). Red indicators (e.g.
> Total Sales) mean that the activities are off target; green indicators (e.g.
> Telephone and Employee) that they are on target; and black indicators
> (e.g. Customer Service and Breakage) that they are close to target. There are
> also diagrams in Dolphin where the changes over time are displayed in
> relation to the target. These functions, the colour coding and the diagrams,
> give the employees a quick overview of how the organization is doing, and
> thus enable them to take action accordingly. They also enable management
> to see how well the different employees and units are doing, and thereby give
> them a better overview.

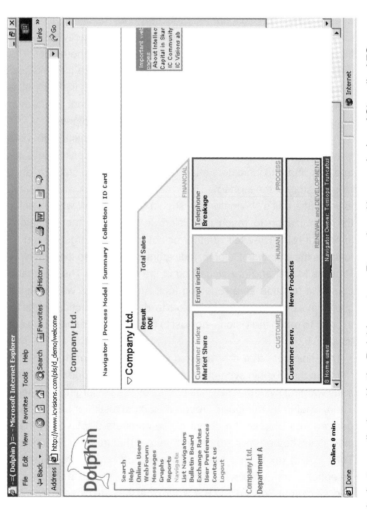

Figure 3.3 The Navigator as displayed in the Dolphin system. Reproduced by permission of Skandia AFS.

However, the system was not made completely transparent. Access is limited by built-in user levels. Management have full access to all Navigators allowing them to compare the individual employees' and units' measures. They can also require that the unit add indicators to their Navigators so that they can easily benchmark a number of units. Employees, on the other hand, have access to their own unit's Navigator but not to the other employees' Navigators. This limitation has been made to reduce the information overflow in the organization. By using Dolphin the employees are expected to get to know Skandia's objective, the objective of their own unit and to understand it in such a way that s/he will be able to influence how to get there. This was not thought to be achieved through information overflow but instead through sufficient information to enable innovation and learning.

How was Dolphin introduced and used?

Skandia had developed Dolphin to restart the work with the Navigator. The group responsible for the development of the tool, IC Visions, therefore felt a strong need to get the tool implemented and working. Because of the large investments that had been made in the Navigator and Dolphin, both management and other employees had high expectations of its functions. This put great demands on the introduction and implementation of the tools. To deal with this, IC Visions decided to take a number of initiatives. One was to develop a users' guide and a built-in help function in Dolphin.[19] These functions were to be available to all users in an effort to make Dolphin a natural part of their work.

To enable the implementation, another initiative was taken. Workshops were arranged where technical information about the system was given, as well as information about the Navigator and its purposes. In some units, three-day computerized business games, built on the Navigator concept, were arranged so that the ideas behind the tools really would sink in. Management and the group responsible for the implementation of the tool emphasized the importance of both understanding the system and the concept to make the work successful. The workshops and the business games were seen as important parts in creating this understanding. It seems as though the communication of the ideas had some success. The business game workshops gave some real 'aha'-experiences. In one of the Skandia companies the participants in the game commented:

> You understood that it [the company] doesn't work if you only invested in the financial focus. All the other focuses fell[20] and you lost your leading market position. You understood that the short-term thinking was not sufficient to keep the company performing well in the long run (Support Unit).

You got to understand the causalities in the company better. That things actually affect each other. That was a bit of an 'aha'-experience. (Unit manager).

I understood that the different focus areas are connected to each other and that they affect each other. I also got a better understanding for the importance of a goal and a vision to be able to get everyone to work in a specific direction. And to follow these up on a regular basis (Employee, Skandia Connection).

The business game had thus led to an understanding of how the organization hung together. And how this could be visualized through the Navigator. The workshop also led to the actors beginning to understand what the Navigator was good for, i.e. how it could be used. Many employees' original impressions of the Navigator had been that it was a reporting system with some additional dimensions. This slowly changed into an understanding that the tool also could be used for management and strategic work. And that this work was going to be everyone's concern.

In addition to these positive effects, there was also a more technical introduction to the Skandia Navigator and the Dolphin system. Important during this introduction was that initially one day was set aside to work with the Skandia Navigator concept. Once the participants understood the idea behind the Skandia Navigator, they moved on to a one-day introduction to the Dolphin system. During these introductions the employees were shown how the system worked, given personal usernames and passwords, and got to develop their own Skandia Navigator with support from the Navigator ambassadors that were appointed in each company. Three other types of courses were also held in the organization. One was an introduction to Dolphin: why and how it should be used. Another was a more advanced Dolphin course that was held for interested employees. During this course the employees got to learn more functions in the system, and how the system could be connected to the employees' everyday work. Finally, there was a Skandia Navigator course introducing the concept and its underlying ideas.

In April 2002 a third-level Dolphin course was also being developed, which started in Autumn 2002. This course's target group was the ambassadors who now needed to deepen their knowledge about the Navigator and its underlying ideas. The ambassadors were selected by the implementation group on the basis of their interest in the Navigator and its implementation. They were mainly controllers and actuaries that had close contact with the organization's management and control. Hence, despite the fact that Skandia's aim had been that the Navigator was not going to become an 'auditing tool', it was now the controllers and the actuaries that became drivers of the implementation process. Perhaps the acceptance among the employees and the implementation would have been different if others had been chosen as ambassadors.

The ambassador role is often seen as important in the implementation of BSCs. The ambassadors were what is often referred to as the 'necessary fiery spirits' that push the implementation of new models or new ways of working. In Skandia it was often the controllers or actuaries that were fiery spirits in the process and therefore were chosen as ambassadors. The implementation group decided to take advantage of their enthusiasm to trigger other employees to use the tools. The ambassadors' task was to ensure that the employees in each organization knew what the Navigator was, what it was for, and how it applied to each individual's work. In some companies the ambassadors also gave the employees homework where they, by using Dolphin, got to answer a number of questions. This was a way of almost 'forcing' the employees to learn the system and thereby get over the boundaries of using it.

The ambassadors' role was thus seen as crucial for the implementation of the Navigator. They made sure that everyone in the organization had their own Navigator and that the different organizational units reported through the Navigator. That the other employees listened to them may have been a result of the fact that most of the ambassadors were regarded as having important functions in the organization. Most of them had positions that were close to management and their influence in the organization was thus seen as considerable.

Facing technicalities

In the implementation of Dolphin and the Navigator the organization did, however, face some slight problems. There was a tendency among the employees not to see the difference between the system and the concept. One of the employees stated:

> *Dolphin is the same thing as the Navigator to me.... That's probably useful to know. When I talk about the Navigator, I think of Dolphin. I think many of us do.* (Group Manager)

The employees thus had difficulties understanding that the Navigator was a management system and that Dolphin was its technical support system. They instead saw them as one thing, which resulted in a situation where the employees used the Navigator as a reporting system and not as a tool for planning and managing their unit as intended. There was thus a rather large gap between how management had intended that the Navigator should be used, and how it actually was used. The Navigator was used as a diary of what had already happened rather than as a tool for aligning the efforts in the organization. For example, when someone had performed an activity – e.g.

gone through training – he would add this activity into Dolphin when the training was completed. The alternative would have been, through the work with the Process Model, to identify the need for training, set a target for it and then fill in the outcome of the training. The comments below illustrate this. An employee describes the Navigator in an interview conducted in mid-1999.

> *It is a follow-up system. At least that is how it works today. I don't know if that is positive or not.... I would like to see more effects of it, to see how the different parts affect each other* (Employee, Business Support).

The Navigator was thus seen as a profit-and-loss account with some additional dimensions. There did not, however, seem to be any awareness that this was not the way the employees were expected to work with it. Another employee stated something similar, indicating some embarrassment about the lack of use of the tool:

> *To be honest, I haven't gotten started with it properly. I haven't actively worked with it. But I see it as a diary on what I have done. It is a way of showing to your boss what you have done. It is also a way of seeing what the others are doing, and thereby get a better understanding for their situation* (Employee, Support).

Some employees also had their personal Navigators, but they mainly used them to report to their manager what they had been doing and how this corresponded to the goals they had set. However, many of the employees had not taken time to work with the tool as intended, and this began to worry management.

Support from management

Full support from management is often pointed out as important in working with tools such as the BSC. This was no different in Skandia. Management gave its full support to the process and allocated the time needed to get the work rolling. It had realized at an early stage that the new ideas would require plenty of time to sink in and become accepted. This involved learning a whole new language, which usually takes time. To stimulate this learning, management had produced a number of brochures and articles that communicated the new language. In addition to this, Skandia established a 'Future Centre' in a small harbour town outside Stockholm that was meant to become the organization's knowledge centre. This was to be the place where employees met, shared experiences and knowledge, and learned the new way of thinking that had been developed in the organization.

However, in mid-1999, after five years of implementation but still very little use among the employees, management became somewhat frustrated. It was time that all its investments paid off. New regulations about the compulsory use of the Navigator were therefore sent out along with various tools that were to make the use easier. The Dolphin system was one effort, and workshops another. Still, after one more year the tool had not become as widely used as management wanted. It was mainly used as a quarterly reporting tool and not as the management tool that it was designed to be. Management now sent out new encouragements to the heads of all the Skandia companies, promoting its use and its usefulness for both individual and unit development.

The heads of all Skandia companies now *had* to make sure that the Navigator was used on a more general and frequent basis. No reporting was to take place through any other system than Dolphin and the Navigator. This was to make the Navigator a natural part of everyone's work.

As an outcome of these requirements, new efforts were made in the organization. Next, we illustrate this by describing one unit, Skandia Connection (not its real name), one of the companies in the Skandia Group. This was one of several companies where lots of time was set aside to 'really get the Navigator working'.

NAVIGATOR MEETINGS

So far you have read about how the Navigator and its supporting tools were developed. You have seen some of the challenges the organization faced during the implementation of the tool, and also how they developed supporting functions to make the work easier. Next, you will be able to follow in some detail how the employees at Skandia Connection worked with the Navigator. You will get to know some of the challenges that the company faced and how they dealt with them, but also how they developed the model to suit their unique situation. The efforts made in different parts of Skandia have varied a lot. This describes one of the more ambitious instances of the company's work with the Navigator.

In this section we thus move from having described the whole of the Skandia Group's work with the Navigator (Wholesale, Administration, and Investment in Figure 3.4), to describing a company situated in the administrative part of Skandia. We then continue in the last part of this chapter to describe the whole of the Skandia Group's work.

Skandia Connection restarted their work with the Navigator in the second half of 2000. Up until then the different Navigators in the organization had

Independent Retailers   **Independent Fund Managers**

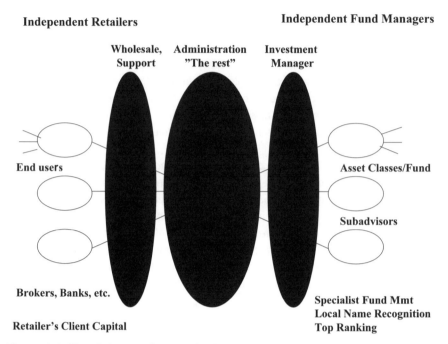

Figure 3.4 Skandia's way of presenting its organization. Retailers and Fund Managers form part of Skandia's 'imaginary organization', i.e. these are other companies that Skandia considers as partners with whom they collaborate on a more or less permanent basis.[21] Skandia consists of Wholesale, Administration, and Investment. Reproduced by permission of Skandia AFS.

been developed by either the unit or the company manager, together with the company's fiery spirit – the business controller. Together they had identified a vision, success factors, and indicators for each unit, and reported these to the board on a regular basis. The problem when the manager and the business controller created Navigators for the various units was that the employees in the units could not relate to their own Navigators. They did not feel that their Navigator represented the work that was done in their unit, and thus did not work according to the activity plans set. During an interview one employee said:

> *The group Navigator doesn't have any function. I can't relate to it. It has been developed by our group manager and I don't even understand what's in it* (Employee, Skandia Connection).

This comment was supported by another employee's concern. The Navigator did not make sense. It did not have a function, and was therefore not being used as management intended.

The current Navigator doesn't make sense. We haven't been involved in the process and therefore the variables in it don't have any practical implications for us. We must be involved in the process to be able to act accordingly (Employee, Skandia Connection).

The challenge that the company faced was thus that the employees did not feel that their Navigators filled any function. To them the Navigator was a reporting tool that the manager used, and that they were expected to work with but still did not.

In September 2000, Skandia Connection's manager decided to change this situation and put aside plenty of time to restart the Navigator work. He was determined to make the tool understood and used by everyone. The pressure on him was high because his goal was that all units should have developed their own Navigator before the board meeting in December. He should be able to report what was going on in his organization by showing the board the various Navigators. But to do this, he did not want the units to 'just put something together'. He believed that the work with the Navigator would pay off sooner or later, and therefore took the opportunity to do the work properly this time. To get this support, and pressure, from management was a prerequisite to get the work started. The employees themselves would not initiate the work.

What they had learnt from their previous work with the Navigators was that it was pointless to develop the Navigator for someone else. Having someone else developing the Navigator led to it not having any effect on the employees' work. To get away from this problem, the manager decided that everyone in the organization should be involved in the process. If everyone was to be part of the process, then the time was right to get mobilized.

One unit in Skandia Connection that really took the work seriously was the General Support unit. They initially set aside six full days to work with the Navigator in order to make sure that everyone understood the process and the outcomes of it. The group managers said:

It's really important that everyone agrees on what we're putting into the Navigator, otherwise we won't work accordingly (Unit manager).

The manager of the group thus found that to get the Navigator to work as intended everyone needed to understand, and be part of, the process. Developing a shared understanding thus became the aim of the work with the Navigator. To be able to reach this aim, the employees sat down and started discussing what they should do. They started by looking at Dolphin and the indicators that were in the system at the time. They decided that they needed to start from scratch, and recreate their Navigator. Their current Navigator did not make sense to them, and they thought that starting from the vision in the

Process Model and developing the Navigator step-by-step from there would change this.

At the beginning of this work some confusion arose because the group did not really agree with the structure of the Process Model in Dolphin (Figure 3.2). Someone therefore suggested that they should leave the system for a moment and instead use the blackboard to get started. This triggered a discussion where someone else argued:

> Yes, I agree, but at the same time we have got this set framework in the Dolphin system that we are expected to use. How do we deal with that? (Employee, General Support).

The group saw Dolphin as being somewhat constraining at times during the work with the Navigator. Their discussion continued:

> The system is very stale at times. It is wrong if the system restricts our thinking and our ability to move forward in the process. It is supposed to be an instrument, a tool that helps us get on with the work (Employee, General Support).

The employees found a solution to their problem. The system was sometimes not flexible enough to support their work, and the employees did therefore not see the point in continuously using a tool that did not meet the desired functionalities at all times. They argued that it would be better to use Dolphin more restrictively, i.e. to use it at times when they found its functions helpful.

> I think we should skip working directly in Dolphin. It only gets us stuck in technicalities. Let's do the job on paper instead if we find that easier. Thereafter we can use the system as a presentation tool, and a place where we keep documents, etc. (Employee, General Support).

At the end of the discussion, people agreed to the last suggestion and started working with this in mind. What was characteristic of the group's way of working was that they went through the different parts of the Process Model very carefully to ensure that everyone agreed upon what was put into the tool. For example, they did not only discuss what their shared vision should be, but also what a vision was and even if they really needed a vision. Questions such as, 'If there is an overall vision for the organization do we really need our own vision, or is it sufficient just to develop goals within the different focus areas?' were discussed. These discussions were part of their ambition to bring up all relevant questions so that they could create consensus in the group. This would also create good prerequisites to get the Navigator working.

Cause-and-effect diagrams
During their careful definitions of the different parts of the Process Model the employees also tried to develop the Navigator and the Process Model by

connecting the different parts to each other. They discussed things such as, '*If we want to have the most satisfied customers in the business, what is required of us?*' By using the Navigator's focus areas, one of the participants created slides where the different parts of the Navigator were connected (Figure 3.5). The goal in customer focus was, for example, connected to the success factors in the internal process focus and human focus.

The employees continued with their work by going through all their goals and success factors and cause-and-effect diagrams. Each part of the model, each goal and success factor, was carefully defined and documented so that they would know what they meant next time they looked at the models. This careful definition of the different parts of the tool seemed to be important to the group. It was a way of increasing the possibilities of coming to consensus about what was put into the model, and thus what the employees had agreed upon.

When the support group had finished their first version of the diagrams, they put all the diagrams together on one slide. Their vision, goals, and success factors were connected. By doing this they noticed how some parts of the model seemed more important than others and how some things that they previously had thought were really important did not appear to be relevant any more. For example, a couple of the success factors in the

Figure 3.5 Cause-and-effect diagram in the customer focus. Reproduced by permission of Skandia AFS.

financial focus were deleted because they were not found important enough for the employees to pay attention to. What the group was still missing, however, were indicators that would enable them to follow up their actions. This was the group's next task.

Finding the right indicators

Identifying the 'right' measures is often seen as the largest challenge that organizations face in their BSC work. It is difficult to find good representative measures of processes that are often qualitative and difficult to capture. Identifying measures is often done in two different ways. One way is to develop measures from scratch, i.e. finding suitable measures that have not been used in the organization previously. This is often a time-consuming and difficult process. Owing to this, organizations often choose to use already existing measures, i.e. measures that have already been developed and that are found in various systems and reports. This was the primary way in which the group at Skandia chose to work.

In the Skandia Group there were some financial indicators that management wanted each unit to report through the Navigator.[22] These were derived from the existing financial systems in the organization. However, much of the work done in Skandia is intellectual and qualitative work and the various companies and units therefore needed to add measures that represented this work. In the support group at Skandia Connection they started with indicators that they found relatively easy, such as accessibility, which was seen as an important part of satisfying the customers. The group defined accessibility as the percentage of a certain period of time that they spent answering the customers' questions, and the number of customer phone calls that they answered per month. At the time, the goals were set to 90% and 3000 calls. Aiming at answering 3000 calls within a certain time was seen as a way of continuously improving customer service and a good way of reducing the sales managers' workload.[23] The support group thought that by being able to answer a lot of phone calls the customers would see them as a competent group, and they would thereby continue to turn to support with their questions.

A problem that the group identified when they started working with the Navigator was that the distributors often asked sales managers the type of questions that they were supposed to ask the support unit. This increased the sales managers' job, reduced the telephone supports' workload, and thereby also their training opportunities. If they did not have a sufficient customer base, then management could not justify investing time and money into training. As a result of the work with the Navigator, the support unit saw their chance to change this. Increasing the customers' interaction was therefore seen as a way of learning new things and building customer relations, and was hence regarded as important.

To enable this the group needed to rethink how their situation could be changed. They concluded that one way of doing this could be to increase the number of phone calls they answered per month. They argued that by having many customers calling in and by being able to answer many of the calls, their image as being a capable group of employees would improve. The group concluded that they were to aim at answering 4000 calls per month instead of 3000. This, they thought, was a good ambition and prognosis on how they could improve their activities. The indicator targets were thus set to indicate the group's ambition. The targets were hence not a prognosis for their coming workload. However, to be able to reach their aims they also needed to take action.

Below is the discussion about how the group planned to take action to be able to reach their presented goals. What the discussion illustrates is how the employees, during their work with the Navigator, identified a few challenges in their current way of working that they needed to deal with. Through such discussions they tried to find solutions to these problems and follow these up by identifying suitable indicators.

> *We need to market our competence to the customers. Maybe one way of doing this is to visit the customers and present us to them. They always only meet with the sales managers.24 No wonder they [the sales managers] get a better survey result. It's easier to give someone whom you have met a high mark, than people you have just spoken to* (Employee, Telephone Support).

The suggestion to have a more offensive approach seemed to be a good one. The other employees agreed and tried to find ways of doing this. There were, however, those who found this way of working problematic:

> *I agree, but at the same time there is a risk that if we market ourselves separately from the sales managers we may communicate that there is a conflict between the groups or that we represent different organiza-tions. We need to appear as one organization that cooperates to help the customers* (Group manager).

The discussion continued with some suggestions of solutions to the problem.

> *Why don't we join the sales managers when they go away to visit the customers? That way we get to introduce ourselves both to the*

*customers, and at the same time the brokers get to understand what
kind of competence we possess* (Employee, Telephone Support).

Two months later everyone from the telephone support group had joined a
sales manager on one of their field excursions. Each employee had contacted
a sales manager and informed him or her about the situation. The sales
managers appreciated the initiative and they therefore arranged for the
support group to join the sales managers on a suitable occasion. Then this
event was going to be followed up on a regular basis, so that all customers at
some point would meet someone from the support group. The problem of
being invisible to the customers thus seemed solved. But then another
problem arose.

During the efforts to define measures the group discovered that many of
the indicators that they needed could be taken from the current customer and
employee surveys that Skandia Connection did on a regular basis. Most of
the 'softer' indicators used in the Navigators were taken from the customer
and employee surveys. The problem was that the group did not know what
questions were asked in the customer survey, implying that they needed to
check what the measures actually indicated. They therefore decided to go
through the surveys and possibly change questions that they felt did not fill
the desired function.

*We need to go through the surveys and try to affect the questions
asked so that they really reflect what we want to find out. Today, many
of the questions are identical for both us and for the sales managers.
Our roles and relations to the customers are too different to be
captured in the same type of questions* (Employee).

During a two-hour meeting the group sat down and discussed how they could
reformulate the survey questions. For each question they went through they
discussed interpretation possibilities, possible misunderstandings, and what
they would get out of the result. They found it important that the customers
understood that their competence was not supposed to be the same as the
sales managers. They were different.

The work with the Navigator had thus led to the group looking upon their
own role in relation to the rest of the company in a new way. They had
identified some challenges that they needed to deal with in order to avoid the
uncomfortable comparison between themselves and the sales managers.
Changing the survey questions was one solution. The group also found that
they needed to do something more to change their image in relation to the rest
of the company, and to the customers. They therefore decided to change their
name. They found that the name General Support breathed less competence
than they wanted. They did not only want to be the customers' *support*. They

wanted to be able to help the customer *develop* their business. Therefore they felt that Business Support was a name that better reflected the image that they wanted to communicate, not only to the customers but also to the rest of Skandia. Having a different image was important to the group, not only to stand out from the 'others' at Skandia but also to create an internal image in the group. They, as a group, would be seen as more competent and this would strengthen their image in relation to the rest of the units within Skandia Connection.

Hence, by working with the Navigator the group became motivated to change their identity and their relationship to others within the Skandia Group. They felt as though their intense work with the tool had paid off. The comments below indicate how the employees felt about the work with the Navigator at the time.

> *I think we have gotten a clear and shared image of where we are heading as a group* (Employee, Business Support).

> *I've got a feeling that we are finally speaking the same language when we are talking about vision, goals, and indicators. And we know where we put our priorities* (Group Manager, Business Support).

Most employees in the group agreed that the work with the Navigator had developed a shared image and a shared language in the unit. Through the collective process they had developed a new way of communicating – a new way of talking about things. Some other employees commented:

> *We have gotten a shared platform to stand on in our work, and it has become clear to everyone. I have also increased my understanding of the usefulness of my individual Navigator* (Employee, Business Support).

One important reason why the group had been able to develop a shared image was thought to be that they had been able to allocate a lot of time to work with the Navigator:

> *It was really good that we got so much time to work with the process and that everyone joined the discussions. I think that it is important to enable us to get a shared image and then be able to continue with our daily work* (Employee, Business Support).

> *It has been great to get time to discuss everything. Everyone has really had a chance to speak out* (Group Manager, Business Support).

The process had also given the employees an opportunity to get to know each other:

Finally I'm beginning to understand what everyone in this unit does (Employee, Business Support).

The business support group then summarized the work they had done in a revised Process Model (Figure 3.6).

It is interesting to note that this model was not structured as the official model that was used in the organization (Figure 3.2). The group had added goals to the model. By doing this they wanted to emphasize the importance of explicitly stating what they were aiming for. Having goals, and not only an overall vision, was also a way of making the vision more tangible.

Another difference was that the group had swapped places for activities and indicators. This was done to emphasize that they wanted to measure how well they were meeting their goals and then be able to take action accordingly, instead of measuring whether or not they had completed their activities. They argued that this made their activity plan into a strategic agenda rather than a daily list of activities as in the original Navigator. What they should do on a daily basis would become clear just by looking at their Navigator.

Figure 3.6 Business Support's Process Model. Reproduced by permission of Skandia AFS.

As we have seen through the comments above, the employees found that the work with the Navigator provided them with a shared image about the organization and what they as a group were aiming for. However, during the discussions they had also come to think of another problem. As a group they now thought they had a common image of the organization, but how could they communicate this to newly recruited employees?

> *Finally I understand why I should use the Navigator. Before someone else has just put numbers into the focus areas and we have seen how they change, but never understood why. I'm glad to be able to be in the discussion from the beginning* (Employee, Telephone Support).

> *I agree with [previous employee]. It is really important to follow the process from the beginning. Otherwise, everyone sits there with his or her own definitions and doesn't understand what the others are saying. How do we integrate newcomers in this process? We can't go through this every time someone is recruited* (Employee, Telephone Support).

The comments indicate the importance of being engaged in, and part of, the development process, which also had been the group manager's aim with the Navigator work. The employees felt that they needed to be part of the initial process to understand it and to engage in its continuity. In a changing organization where new employees are continuously being recruited, as in Skandia, it is especially important to make the employees understand and work towards the same goals, and understand why they do so. But, as indicated by the discussion above, it is also very difficult.

> At the time the employees did not find a satisfying solution to the problem of introducing the Navigator to newcomers but they were aware of the problem and knew that they had to deal with it. One suggestion that came up was to introduce newcomers, and others interested, to the group's Navigator by showing them the cause-and-effect diagrams (see Figure 3.7). The employees themselves found that this way of presenting the Navigator made its structure much clearer. The cause-and-effect diagrams became a way of telling the story of their strategy, and how they intended to follow it up.

Strategy maps such as Figures 2.2 and 2.3 are usually presented as useful in developing a scorecard (see, for example *Performance Drivers*, and Chapter 6). It is interesting to note here that the Business Support group used the maps to visualize and tell the story of the scorecard, after first developing its parts separately.

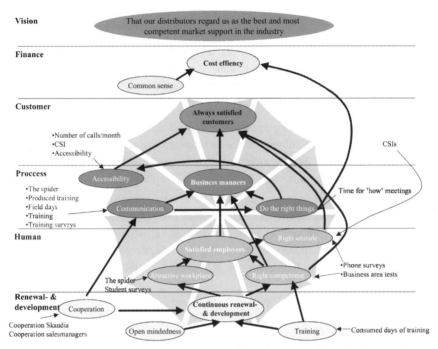

Figure 3.7 Business Support's cause-and-effect diagram of the Navigator. Reproduced by permission of Skandia AFS.

Connection to bonus

Having a Navigator for the Business Support group was, however, not seen as enough to get the group to work accordingly. Therefore, the next step in the group's Navigator work was to connect some of the measures in the Navigator to the group's bonus system. This was also something that the corporate board had encouraged for some time. In a letter that the CEO sent out to the heads of all Skandia units in mid-1999 he stated:

A personal Navigator constitutes an excellent tool for the personal Appraisal and Development Dialogues. The objective of a personal Navigator is that an employee may gain greater understanding of Skandia operations, and will be able to see how his/her daily work contributes to the achievement of Skandia's goals.

Connecting performance measures to the bonus system was not new to the Business Support group. Before the use of the Navigator the group had had goals for accessibility, and if the group reached its goals, then the employees got a certain bonus. From now on the bonus was also to be connected to other goals in the Navigators.

To determine what measures were to be connected to the bonus system, the group discussed the possible effects of this. They concluded that the measures that they currently had in their Navigator encouraged different behaviour for different employees. For example, 'Direct Answer' was one of the indicators in the Navigator that the group manager wanted to connect to the group's bonus. Direct Answer referred to the group's ability to answer a customer's question directly, i.e. on the first call without having to check the answer with someone and then return the customer's call. This measure would signal that the employees were competent enough to be able to answer the questions directly. Hence it would emphasize that it was encouraged to increase the learning in the unit. However, for some of the employees the measure would encourage them to put the customer on hold and then find out the answer, leading to very long and fewer calls. This would also be contradictory to the goal that they should answer 90% of the calls within 25 seconds.

Below are examples of questions that came up during the discussion that was held in the support group in late 2000. It turned out that the connection between the Navigator and the bonus system was not a simple task. The employees discussed the possible connection between the Navigator and the bonus system and how they, as individuals, would respond to different connections:

> If Direct Answer is being connected to the bonus system I'm sure that we'll have much longer calls than we do now. Then we'll not be able to relate bonus to accessibility or number of calls answered per month (Employee, Telephone Support).

> I would not act that way – I would probably try to encourage my customers to write me e-mails so that I can answer questions that way as well (Employee, Telephone Support).

> OK, it seems as though you will respond differently to the different measures. Maybe it is better if we have one or two measures connected to the group's bonus, and the rest connected to the individual bonuses. That seems fairer (Group manager, Telephone Support).

The connection between indicators and bonus was thus not easy. The employees were different and were aware that a certain connection would lead to suboptimations in the group. The only satisfying solution, was therefore, that the bonus was done on an individual level rather than on a group level, i.e. depending on each individual's behaviour, s/he got a customized bonus connection. This was thought to lead to the group's goals being fulfilled but the employees had their own ways of getting there.

Summarizing the Navigator work at Skandia Connection

After the bonus discussion was held at the end of 2000 the group had completed six full days of work with their shared Navigator. Business Support's next step was to present their Navigator to the rest of Skandia Connection. This was to be done at the yearly conference held to discuss strategic questions in Skandia Connection. Before we look into what happened at that conference, some of the comments from Skandia Connection's summary of their work with the Navigator are illustrated. The comments are examples of what some of the employees claimed that they had learned during the workshops and some of the issues that they still found problematic with the Navigator:

> *It is great that we have set off so much time to discuss and come to consensus on what we, as a group, see as important for the company's success. I feel that we have gained a shared understanding about what we are currently doing and what we should be doing. It is just a matter of going out there and doing it* (Employee).

> *I agree. I finally understand the purpose of the Navigator and its construction. And we have a shared language to use to talk about these things. It's great!* (Employee).

This snapshot of the discussion emphasizes the benefits from gaining a shared image and vision. The group found that the time they had invested in the work with the Navigator had paid off. They had reached the shared understanding that they had been aiming for.

Thus far the Navigator had only been used as a tool for visualizing and clarifying the goals in the organization. The step to follow-up activities that would lead the group towards its goal had still not been taken. In the Business Support group, however, the employees seemed to be satisfied with the results they had reached thus far and felt that, finally, the Navigator had proven to be a useful tool.

> *And finally I have got a positive image of the Navigator and its purpose. Previously I have only seen it as a burden* (Employee).

Even though there were many positive voices heard, the employees still suggested some improvements. Some found the Navigator too static, others that the cause-and-effect linkages were not explicitly visualized. Also, Dolphin, the IT support system that was meant to help the employees in the process, was regarded as difficult and even perceived as a restriction. The discussion below indicates some of these challenges.

I still see a problem with the Navigator though. It is too static. Now we've got it all written down on paper. But when we sit down at our desks it is so easy to forget about what we have said and go back to the good old habits. And even if we really work according to the Navigator, there is so much happening in the organization all the time that the Navigator becomes outdated straight away. We need to find a way of keeping it updated. We cannot meet for three days every time changes take place in the organization (Employee).

No, especially not with all the structural changes taking place all the time (Employee).

This is something we need to think about (Unit manager).

I also find that the Navigator lacks the kind of causalities that we saw during the simulation game. If you forgot to invest in one focus it had obvious effects on the other parts of the Navigator. Is there any way that we can make our efforts more visible? (Employee).

There is a project going on in the implementation group where they are focusing on how to build cause-and-effect linkages into the Dolphin system. But that will take a while yet (Financial Controller).

Then I think we need to do something ourselves in the meantime. We need to see, to visualize, how the different parts of the Navigator are connected (Employee).

Yes, and I think we should do this outside the Dolphin system. It is too restricting (Employee).

From the dialogue above we can conclude that there were still several challenges that the group faced in order to get the Navigator to run smoothly. Some efforts were made at management level in Skandia to make the work with the tool easier. IC Visions, the company in the Skandia Group that developed Dolphin, were making efforts to develop cause-and-effect linkages in the system, so that the model 'really' told the story of the strategy.

Another ambition with the system was to develop a simulation model in Dolphin so that the users could test what their decisions led to. The system could then be used to test questions such as 'What effect does it have if I invest four days of training instead of working with customers?' The effects of doing these sorts of tests are still to be discovered.

As a part of the continuous improvements of the many functions in Dolphin, IC Visions also put time into developing the tool so that bonus modules could be integrated with each Navigator. Connecting the Navigator and the incentive models is believed to be an important part when changing the employees' behaviour so that they act as desired. At Skandia they thus saw the connection to a bonus system as an important instrument to get the employees to use the Navigator – and to do the right things. This is, however, not always the case. As we will see in Chapter 10, other processes can also function as triggers to increase the employees' commitment and interest in scorecards.

DIFFERENT AMBITIONS IN VARIOUS UNITS

Let us return to the yearly conference that was held at Skandia Connection. Because Skandia Connection is an organization where half of the staff are spread out in different parts of Sweden, they arrange a yearly conference where everyone gets together for a week. It is the manager of Skandia Connection who initiates and sets the agenda for these conferences. The main aim is always for the employees to get to know each other better, but there is also an additional aim for each conference. At the yearly conference in January 2001, which was held at a skiing resort in Sweden, the aim was to work with strategic planning. Below is a story about how all the units presented their Navigators at the conference, and how the overall Navigator for Skandia Connection was to be updated on the basis of these presentations.

One reason for updating the company's strategy was that Skandia Connection had just become a limited company with new requirements on profitability. Previously, the company's finances had been part of the Skandia Group's finances, which meant that all companies within the Skandia Group did not necessarily have to make a profit to exist.[25] To deal with this new situation, management decided that the new situation required an update of the strategy.

The strategy work began by letting all the different groups present their respective Navigators. Many of the units were rather confident about the Navigators that they had spent the last few months creating. But there was an obvious difference between the different units' understanding of what the Navigator was and how it was supposed to be used. Some units, such as Business Support, had spent days on developing their shared Navigator. Others had constructed it during a two-hour meeting. Therefore, some of the groups presented their strategy work by using the Navigator framework, whereas others had made their own versions of the model. In some of the groups the Navigator had been developed by the group manager just before the trip, and in others all employees had worked together in the process. Then when they all got together and tried to merge all their different models into one shared Navigator for Skandia Connection, chaos was unavoidable. There was a clear conflict between the locally adjusted Navigators and the possibility of coordinating these.

These differences in how the Navigators had been developed especially became evident when the employees were split into smaller groups to discuss Skandia Connection's new vision. The mix of employees was made so that people that usually did not work together got the opportunity to do so. All groups also got a copy of the company's existing Navigator to use as a starting point. It was inspired by Business Support's cause-and-effect diagram, meaning that it was a new language and a new way of presenting to most employees.

One of the groups started the discussion, beginning by looking at the structure of the current Navigator. 'Do we really need a new vision, or is the current one good enough?' The group started going through the Navigator asking, 'What do we want to change and what do we feel is aligned with our work?' They revised the vision somewhat. They felt that the current vision did not live up to the manager's definition that the vision should give direction, be something to strive for, breathe ambition, offensive, and be easily understood. It needed to be more challenging. They discussed back and forth, and came to an agreement on a vision that was filled with words that breathed ambition. They needed and wanted to be at the forefront at all times.

They quickly moved on to discuss the success factors. The employees from Business Support tried to work according to the BSC model, and therefore started by identifying goals that supported the vision, but the others wanted to move on and work according to the Process Model. The confusion was complete. There was disagreement on what role the focus areas had – should they be included from the start, or just in the identification of measurements? Most of the employees in the group argued that the focus areas did not really fill a function until they were put into the Navigator 'house'. Hence, they decided to skip the focus areas until the measures were identified, and instead discussed success factors. They concluded that the current ones represented what they needed to do to reach the vision. These were only qualitative success factors, and no financial success factors were therefore discussed.

The group was suddenly running out of time and they needed to move on to identify suitable measures. Together they tried to find measures that were aligned with success factors, but found this really difficult. The group decided that the best thing to do was to look at the employee and customer surveys, and try to take measures out of these. For those success factors that were still not connected to a measure, the group found that it might not be necessary to do this either – as long as the employees knew what their tasks were, they thought it was OK.

This is an example of how an organization uses already existing measures in their scorecard. The risk of doing this is, as we have seen above, that they thereby also miss important measures that can enable the desired changes.

> The work at the skiing resort was somewhat chaotic. The employees that got together to develop a shared Navigator obviously had different levels of engagement and motivation to work with the tool. It became obvious that the way that the Navigator had been communicated within the different units was determinate for how the employees worked with it. In the company there seemed to be too many different images and versions of the Navigator existing that consensus about how to work with it could not be reached. To change this, a new decision was made. It was time to turn the work with the Navigator into a routine.

TURNING THE WORK WITH THE NAVIGATOR INTO A ROUTINE

At the corporate level in Skandia, different efforts were continuously being made to get the Navigator integrated with the daily work. An additional example of this is the integration of the Navigator into the quarterly reports. This is an activity of which everyone in the Skandia Group has to be a part.

> When the Navigator was first introduced in the Skandia Group, the work with the yearly budget was the most important management tool in the organization. After 1998, when the work with the Navigator became compulsory, this was, however, changed. Making budgets became optional and a continuous planning process handled through the Navigator was instead to be implemented. This process was to be started every year in August/ September and be carried out in all companies within the Skandia Group.
>
> The process starts with a discussion about changes in the existing Process Models. Discussions are held about changes that have to be made to adjust to the current, and expected future state of the business environment. On the basis of these discussions, the goals, success factors, and indicators are updated in the Process Model in Dolphin. Some compulsory indicators will have been identified and must be measured. For example, the number of premiums, assets under management, and market share are three measures that corporate management wants each company to report. The goals for the next year have to be stated, as well as a capital plan for the next three years. The information put into the Skandia Navigator should be discussed internally in each company, but is also supervised and supported by Skandia's financial

support unit, Business Control and Support. In this group there is one newly recruited employee who is responsible for communicating the ideas behind the Skandia Navigator and supporting the whole organization with its implementation and use of the tool. As part of this role some representatives from the Business Control and Support unit travel around to the different companies in the Skandia Group and discuss the company's plan and the Skandia Navigator/Process Model into which it is put. Then, in December each year, the plans are to be presented to the Skandia Group Executive Management Board. This is done in a joint meeting where all the CEOs from the companies in Skandia participate and present their future strategies. This meeting is seen both as a presentation and as a knowledge-sharing meeting.

To make the business planning more dynamic and useful, the strategic objectives, success factors, key indicators, and activity plans should be updated and managed on a continuous basis. According to the Business Control and Support unit they should at a minimum be updated on a quarterly basis. This should be done through quarterly book closing[*] and business review meetings[†] that are meant to secure the long-term planning within Skandia. At these meetings controllers and managers from the different companies in the Skandia Group participate.

In addition to the continuous business planning reports, the top-down control and the bottom-up communication in some of the companies within Skandia are also done through monthly reports, that is, the employees communicate what happens in their units in monthly reports and management take part of these reports and thereby get an update of what is happening in different parts of the organization. These monthly reports have existed for several years.

The reports are constructed by the different units in the company and describe what has happened during the last month in each part of the organization. The reports are initially created on a unit level in the organization. In the report, an employee from each unit summarizes what has happened in the unit and how well this is aligned with the unit's targets in its Navigator. It is thereby both performed activities and how well these meet the goals that are reported. After this summary has been written, the unit reports are sent to the company manager who, in turn, summarizes the different units' reports and sends the final report to top management. The monthly reports are thus aggregations of the individual Navigators up through the units and companies to the corporate level.

---

[*] Even though the focus is on the financial perspective during this meeting, all perspectives within the Navigator are discussed.

[†] During this meeting the whole organization's strategy is discussed, embracing all the Navigator perspectives.

In some companies, the monthly reports have changed somewhat in the last few years. As a consequence of the work with the Skandia Navigator, the monthly reports are now structured on the basis of the Skandia Navigator's focus areas. The reports have to address how well the unit has met its goals, success factors, and indicators. Questions such as, 'What efforts have been made in the organization to work towards the goals?' and 'How do the units develop their success factors?' should be answered. The employees must also specify their indicator goals, and how well they meet these. If the Business Support unit has answered 3500 calls, and the goal is 4000, then the employees in the unit need to analyse this gap and discuss possible ways of bridging it. Comments are thus to be made for each indicator, why and how goals have/have not been met. On the basis of these reports, management can create action plans by looking into things such as what they need to do to meet the goals.

As part of the communication improvements in the company, Dolphin is also updated on a regular basis. This enables management at all levels of the organization to see what happens in the organization and take action accordingly. Updates should therefore be made at all levels in the organization. At Skandia Connection the employees update their individual Navigators and unit management check, analyse, and comment on the changes. These updates take place at least every six months. This continuous work with the Navigator enables a dialogue between management and the employees to take place, and thereby also creates an awareness at all levels of the organization about what is going on and how divergences from the plans can be dealt with.

An example of action taken, based on the monthly reports, was an initiative to improve the information in the organization. Reported through the monthly reports, via an indicator in the Navigator, management found that the employees were dissatisfied with the information in the organization. Monday meetings were therefore arranged. Every Monday morning at 9.00 a.m. a meeting was held to inform the employees about what had happened during the last week and what was planned for the coming week. The meetings were also tape-recorded, and were then made available via telephone to the employees who were not able to attend the meeting. After these efforts had been made, the information indicator approached its goal.

Despite the monthly reports and the updates of Dolphin, there are also regular surveys conducted within the organization as well as externally. 'Insight' is the name of the corporate employee survey that the employees fill in on an electronic form on the intranet. This survey consists of two parts: one part where questions are general for all employees in Skandia, and another part where each unit within the organization can add their own questions that they wish to follow. These surveys are conducted every six months. The results of the surveys are discussed internally within each company and action should be taken if any of the indicators do not show the desired results.

There are also two types of customer survey: one survey that each company sends out to its customers, and one that an external survey company does of all insurance companies in Sweden. The company-specific surveys are sent out regularly to the customers to evaluate whether the company meets its customers' demands. The other survey, conducted by an external organization, enables benchmarking not only for Skandia's own organization but also across the whole industry. This survey is seen as important for Skandia – especially with their high ambitions. Skandia's current goal is, by 2005, to be the best in the industry in five different areas. This goal requires both continuous improvements and continuous follow up to ensure that they are on the right track. The work with the Navigator is expected to support this process.

SOME CONCLUDING COMMENTS

What can be concluded from the description of Skandia's work with the Navigator is that it has been a rather long and challenging road but one that seems to have had many positive outcomes. The early start of the work with the Navigator gave Skandia many opportunities to learn new ways of working with, and developing, the concept and its supporting tools. For example, the early introduction of Dolphin led to the organization initially facing some difficulties with its functions while also ensuring that the system thereby was continuously tested, improved and thus could become the well-functioning support tool that it was meant to be.

The Navigator itself has also been repeatedly tested and developed as new demands have emerged and new improvement possibilities have occurred. This has strengthened Skandia's employees' belief in the concept, its future pay-offs, and thereby their desire to work with it and learn from it.

Case Histories   4

Chapters 5–11 discuss challenges and issues in using scorecards thematically. We have interviewed a number of organizations about their scorecard use, and we also build on other experiences and ideas about emerging 'best practice'.

As a background, we first present some case stories. We find it interesting how different factors have led companies to introduce scorecards. The texts below are based on our discussion with the organization concerned, and so they differ in emphases and scope. We then return to most of these organizations in the following chapters, and in several cases we have kept the presentation here brief because later we add much more detail.

For ease of access, we have ordered our cases alphabetically.

AMF PENSION

Company background

AMF Pension is a Swedish pension insurance company, founded in 1973 by the employers' confederation and the central labour union to handle a system providing pension payments for its members – now 2.4 million of them, a major part of the Swedish population, which is less than 9 million. This system was non-discretionary and came on top of other forms of pension agreement. Until 1998, AMF Pension had a service monopoly, and its goal was low costs. In this year, a new agreement made it possible for employees to choose between available insurance providers that they wanted to entrust with part of their compensation, which had formerly gone automatically to AMF Pension. In the following years, a sequence of 'pension elections' were organized in Sweden. To prepare for these and for its new existence in a competitive market-place, AMF Pension rapidly started to build a marketing department and introduce some new products. Although few Swedish companies had so many customers, most people had not been aware of the existence of AMF Pension, nor had they had any reason to think of pensions as something requiring active consumer choice.

AMF Pension did well in the 'elections', getting 66% of the new business. Still, losing the remaining 34% required adding to the product range and approaching new customers. Its assets are now SKr198 billion, and it still has only 160 employees operating in a single office in Stockholm. These comprise its own fund managers.

Internally, people at AMF Pension talk about going from an 'unknown' monopoly in 1997, through being an 'election campaign company' gaining wide-spread recognition among Swedes from 1998 to 2000, to now being established as a 'pension company' – a major player in a highly competitive market.

Scorecards at AMF Pension

In AMF Pension, management developed scorecards for the entire company, for its departments and subdepartments. Everyone among its 160 employees was involved in this exercise. At this time, AMF Pension was preparing for the 'pension elections', and so it was logical that the scorecard work should be developed top-down. The targets set for the election were used as a starting point. The CEO and some other members of the management team were new to the firm, and the whole team spent many hours portraying a business logic for AMF Pension in terms of a 'virtuous circle' and strategy map. These built on the fundamental values of the company: 'simple, safe, and human'. They meant that AMF should stick to strategies emphasizing scale economies, openness, and 'no frills', but add closeness to 'normal people'. In the virtuous circle and the strategy map, this translated to cost savings enabling low premiums, attractive pension solutions for the majority of employees, and reinforced economies of scale. It also meant that certain developments should be resisted, for instance, using brokers and offering more specialized pension plans.

This top-down message was then translated into lower-level scorecards, department for department. Scorecards acted as a way of rallying the organization and providing guidance through its changes.

Having 'won the elections', the situation changed. The 'giant change in our way of thinking', as one of the executives called it, had to be followed up by now becoming an ongoing, established 'pension company'. Now targets were set not to win an immediate election but one that was three years away, and scorecards became the method for all parts of AMF Pension to find ways to support this vision. So the scorecard work the organization was engaged in during 2001 was much more build-up oriented.

AMF Pension faced a situation which is rather uncommon. It was to lose its monopoly at a predetermined date, and had to compete for the business it was to retain. It had to do this in a very visible way through 'elections'. This required that all 160 employees change their mind-set.

We know few examples where the task for scorecards to assist in agreeing on strategy, communicating strategic change, and monitoring new behaviours, has been so clear. The company decided from the start to have scorecards for all work groups, and that these would be developed through a series of seminars – more or less as described in Chapter 2. This happened concurrently with the preparations for the 'elections'.

Having succeeded in its ambitions, AMF Pension is now using scorecards to discuss its focus in the new market situation.

BRITISH AIRWAYS AT HEATHROW

Company background

British Airways Limited was formed out of the merger of a number of smaller UK air transport companies in 1935. Following a Government review, Imperial Airways and British Airways (BA) were nationalized in 1939 to form British Overseas Airways Corporation (BOAC) – the forerunner to the modern-day BA. The company's service network is one of the world's largest and through its membership of OneWorld, the most international of the global airline alliances, the network extends to some 570 destinations in 135 countries.

BA has invested £1 billion in service and comfort during the last decade, and won the prestigious Business Traveller's Award as 'Best Airline of the Year' for 11 years in succession, in addition to a number of other awards. Its fleet of aircraft is one of the largest in Western Europe, numbering 344. The airline has its head office outside London, in Waterside, near Heathrow. BA serves both Heathrow and Gatwick airports in London. About 60 000 people were employed in the BA group during 1999.

Heathrow is the world's busiest international airport. It is also the world's second busiest cargo port. Regarded as the hub of the aviation world, over 90 airlines have made Heathrow their base. Approximately 64 million passengers pass through Heathrow every year, heading for any of approximately

170 destinations. There are also some not-so-important facts to know: over 80 million items of baggage pass through the airport each year; every day over 26 000 cups of tea, 6500 pints of beer and 6500 sandwiches are sold to the public at Heathrow; The Heathrow Lost Property Office receives approximately 200 telephone enquiries per day; some of the most peculiar items of lost property found at Heathrow include a glass eye, a suitcase of dead fish, a false leg, and the whole front of a Ford Escort car.

In 1997 the operation at Heathrow was in great need of a change programme. The British Airways' performance was poor and a new manager was brought in from BA Cargo, where he had participated in a re-structuring effort using the BSC concept as a change instrument.

Scorecards at Heathrow

When the manager was first brought in to turn around BA's operation at Heathrow, he was only in charge of the baggage-handling unit (employing some 3000 persons). He immediately decided to use scorecards as an instrument in the change process.

Early on in the process, the new management team at Heathrow went for an off-site meeting where they discussed what had to be done to turn around the operation. The initial instruction to the group was not, as is suggested in the BSC literature, to challenge the unit's vision and strategic goals, but rather to pay attention to the details. Each unit had to describe how they thought the customers judged their performance, and then derive measures from this perception. The metrics in the scorecard were thus developed from the customer's viewpoint (for all four perspectives). The reason why the manager did not want to start the initiative with an open discussion on BA Heathrow's mission and purpose was the immediate need for improvements. The organization was in a crisis and every possible improvement was important.

The results from the off-site session made the scorecard very tangible. The metrics as such were understood, and they could easily be verified as important indicators from the customers' point of view. All metrics were also tailored to the specific situation. The new manager encouraged the unit managers to define their set of performance indicators independently. As long as they could explain why each metric was an important indicator to which to pay attention, it passed the relevance test. The only thing that was required of the unit managers, mandated by the new manager, was to use scorecards to describe the unit's operation.

Scorecards have been used since the turn-around project, and new operations have been added to the manager's scope of responsibility. As mentioned before, to start with, the manager was only responsible for the baggage handling at Heathrow, but soon also front-line customer service was included in his unit – doubling the size of it from 3000 to 6000 employees.

The reason why the new manager decided to work with scorecards was that his experiences from Cargo were positive. The concept as such was not too complicated to communicate, but it was still based on a robust theoretical platform.

The decision to use scorecards was the manager's own. There were no instructions within BA that BSCs should be used as the preferred management control system. According to the manager, there are few mandated concepts. Rather, each unit is allowed to decide what kind of management principles they prefer to use. As far as the manager knows, scorecards are not widely adopted in the BA organization. Just a few units use them on a regular basis.

Scorecards are now the management control system at BA Heathrow. Each unit in the organization plans its operation according to the dimensions in the scorecard, evaluates investments according to it and monitors performance along its dimensions. Also, the manager at Heathrow has decided to report the unit's performance to his boss in a scorecard – even though the superior manager has not asked for it.

The next step in the development of scorecards at BA Heathrow is to develop strategy maps that describe how the efforts in the organization are linked. Another step has been to promote scorecards at the level above in the organization. The Customer Service unit (some 25 000 employees) has run some off-site sessions to establish a notion of what will characterize BA's customer service. The working material thus far may easily be implemented in a scorecard, but that has not yet been done.

Scorecard projects are often initiated by enthusiasts, e.g. a manager who has picked up the idea from some colleague, from a conference, or a book. As the concept basically is so simple, this often leads to very different interpretations and practices. At Heathrow, the new manager brought with him experiences from his previous job. As baggage handling is a highly concrete activity with short cycles, it was probably natural to involve many employees and start out from concrete activity measures. It is interesting that the positive experience seems to have generated interest in other parts of BA and may lead to a spreading practice of the BSC. This also is something we hear happening in other organizations. Without consciously intending to run a pilot project, wise companies pick up successful experiences and let them spread. This does, however, mean that recommendations in the literature to use corporate strategies as the starting-point, cascading them down in the organization, cannot be used.

ERICSSON ENTERPRISE

Company background

Within Ericsson, the Swedish-based telecom corporation, Enterprise is the business unit responsible for its range of products and services for enterprises: 'We make the Mobile Enterprise a reality for the business user' through messaging systems and mobile solutions. Enterprise has 50 000 customers worldwide, and in 2001 had a turnover of SKr7 billion. Like other Ericsson units, it has been hit by the problems in the telecom industry. Over the past two years, Enterprise has changed from a direct sales to an indirect multi-sales-channel organization.

Ericsson Enterprise started using scorecards in January 1999. It has become highly accepted as a language for agreements and responsibilities. Before scorecards were introduced, there were only a few non-financial measures in use. The scorecards for units within Enterprise include both commonly defined measures and some selected by each unit, which together provide the targets.

The process leading to scorecards for 2002 was characterized by the project leader as

> ...our most successful ever. It was the first time the management team gave adequate time to this. They had three meetings of four hours each where they processed the scorecard on the wall until they had a shared view of the situation.

Scorecards at Ericsson

Enterprise is one of many Ericsson units using scorecards. Group-level management has encouraged the use of scorecards, but for many years there was no uniform format or group scorecard. A degree of similarity came from the fact that almost all use the 'Cockpit Communicator', a presentation software developed in Ericsson and later spun off as a separate firm (4GHI Solutions AB).[26]

In 2002, group management took a more proactive stance concerning scorecards. The new COO Per-Arne Sandström was quoted in the internal Ericsson newspaper.[27] He expressed a top-down view, where strategies are the starting-point for corporate goals. These in turn determine business unit goals, which must be followed up. 'Balanced scorecard is the name of the method used in Ericsson to describe targets and check how well different units succeed in reaching their goals. The model can be compared to a traffic light, where green means that work is going on as it should and targets will be reached. Yellow is a warning. Red means that things are going wrong and something radical has to be done to succeed.' He also explained that compensation programmes should act as a necessary push to provide that little extra effort.

Several Ericsson units have long experience in using scorecards, but it has taken them several years to arrive at the present stage. (An example is given in Figure 2.4.) Like Skandia, Ericsson group management has encouraged BSC use but not formally required it. Nor is there a corporate scorecard, although corporate goals provide the starting-point for group planning.

We saw that AMF Pension started out from the top – but this is a small company (although it handles large sums of money). A company like Ericsson Enterprise may have a role within the Ericsson group which is clear enough to start scorecard work at this level. We would have expected this to be more difficult at Heathrow's baggage handling, but it seems that its task of serving customers was also clear enough to provide enough guidance for its scorecard.

HELSINGBORG

Organization background

Helsingborg has a population of close to 118 000 inhabitants making it Sweden's ninth biggest community. About 85 000 people reside in the town itself. It is situated at the narrowest part of Øresund between Denmark and Sweden, and the distance across the water to Helsingør in Denmark is not more than 4 km. Its history as a centre for commerce and collecting tolls goes far back, but until the middle of the nineteenth century Helsingborg was just a small town. Thanks to the railways and a new harbour, a strong expansion then started, and now it is a major trading centre, the harbour is the second largest in the country, and the European highways E4 and E6 cross one another just outside the town.

Helsingborg started their work with the BSC in June 1999. The initiative was a result of the city government wanting to change its management philosophy towards becoming more market oriented. The community needed to become more competitive in relation to other communities. The vision was to become both the most attractive town in Sweden and to provide a comprehensive and good service throughout the life of each inhabitant. High quality in harmony with nature was the key concept. To reach this goal,

Helsingborg strived to provide a good platform for trade and industry while strengthening its environmental profile and its identity as an attractive cultural and tourist town. The BSC was to support this process.

Scorecards in Helsingborg

Up until 1999, budgets and balanced sheets had been the most important tools for managing. These were no longer considered to be sufficient. The city administration now wanted a more balanced and holistic view of their organization. Intangible values and trust needed to be visualized. These were the things that citizens wrote and read about in the local newspaper, but they were invisible in the plans and reports used to govern the city. As a result, administrators and politicians might overreact on newspaper stories questioning the city's priorities or service levels, partly because there was too little knowledge about actual facts and consumer attitudes. The city's chief executive felt a need to change this.

At the beginning of 1998 he took the initiative to introduce the BSC. In one of the city departments the controller had introduced scorecard-like methods for measuring quality and consumer reactions to city services. These ideas were now to be used for the entire city. The intention was to promote new ways of looking at, and managing, the organization from a more holistic perspective, where information about finances and the results achieved would be integrated. While there were doubts among some civil servants, especially accountants, this attracted positive interest from the politicians and led to a decision by the city council in June 1999 that scorecards were to be the shared platform for the management of Helsingborg's entire organization.

Progress was somewhat wobbly during the first years. There were changes in project leadership and the number of scorecard perspectives was reduced from six to four. But during this time, many civil servants took part in training programmes and gradually the concept became accepted. A turning point came with a large seminar involving 80 people, including all the most important politicians and civil servants, in June 2000. Its goal was to communicate the BSC language, show the results so far, and discuss how this could contribute to the improvement of the city management. The participants also got to try the tool in practice. Sceptics, including accountants, became convinced. During this seminar, the city's chief executive formulated 10 commandments that were to permeate all work with the BSC. These commandments were:

1. The BSC is to be our management tool.
2. The BSC is a tool for management and control.

3. Everyone needs to understand why to use the BSC – this is the individual's own motivator.
4. Plenty of time must be set aside to work with the scorecard – the usual budgeting time is to be cut in half.
5. Everyone must be involved in the process and talk to each other – dialogue is required.
6. The BSC is not a project – it must be an enduring process.
7. Fiery spirits and engines are necessary to drive the process.
8. It is an apparent responsibility for committees and administrative boards to ensure that everyone that wants to be involved gets involved.
9. Resources (time and money) must be set aside.
10. Political management groups must legitimize the work

With these commandments in mind the work with the balanced scorecard began.

Helsingborg provides a classic case for the BSC: a need to communicate strategy throughout a large organization; an awareness that traditional systems do not capture less tangible resources and effects which are becoming increasingly important; a need to convince sceptics that this is a serious effort, and will not lead to increased work compared with traditional budgeting.

But we note here also that some inspiration came from a previous local initiative to use scorecards, and that it took three years from the somewhat tentative start to a stage of relative maturity now.

HP SERVICES

Company background

Hewlett-Packard (HP) is the second largest IT company in the world, with a turnover of US$45.2 billion and 88 000 employees. In 2001, not a good year in the IT industry, it still made a profit of US$0.6 billion, and through a pending merger with Compaq it is now becoming even larger. HP's strategy is to focus its inventive capabilities across three key dimensions of the emerging technology landscape:

1 enabling intelligent, connecting devices and environments
2 enabling an always-on Internet infrastructure
3 enabling a new generation of applications delivered as e-services.

'By understanding the relationship among these three, we can help transform the experiences people have with technology and the role it plays in business and life.'

Scorecards at HP

BSCs are an important part of business control throughout HP. They form the top-most layer in its information hierarchy (Figure 4.1). The same information is available throughout the world to all HP employees who have the appropriate access rights. The contents of scorecards are adapted to the different types of business within HP, but, for instance, a customer service unit in Sweden will have the same contents in its scorecard as one in Australia.

In some ways, HP has the most mature use of the BSC among our cases. It is highly structured, and, compared with all our other cases, is more top-down. We tend to see this as a consequence of HP's US identity, but it probably also has been perceived as natural and necessary owing to HP's global reach. Being part of the IT/IS industry also makes it natural for HP to provide excellent information systems, including scorecard information, for its managers, and this by itself drives a development towards more unified scorecard solutions.

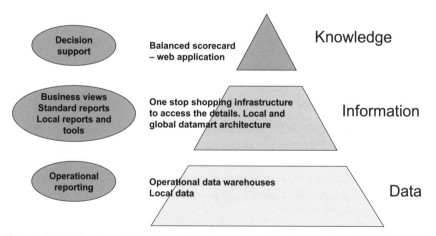

Figure 4.1 HP's view of its information hierarchy. The future direction is that web-enabled tools should make decision makers more self driven in their gathering of information. Reproduced by permission of HP Services

JAL INFORMATION TECHNOLOGY LTD

Company background

JAL Information Technology Co. Ltd (JIT) is a Japanese IT company whose service covers not only system consultation but also systems development, maintenance, and field services. JIT is a subsidiary of Japan Airlines (JAL) and was established in 1996 through a merger of two former JAL companies: one systems development company and one IT field service and network service company. Their major customer is JAL itself, and the second major customer group is JAL's subsidiary companies such as travel agencies and logistic service company. There are also some sales to general clients outside JAL.

JIT's sales figure in 2001 was ¥22 billion, on which it made a profit of ¥1.5 billion. The number of employees was 1225. Recently, IBM was entrusted with JAL's overall IT outsourcing, and JIT became a subsidiary of IBM in July 2002.

Scorecards at JIT

JIT started to investigate the possibility of introducing their BSC in the autumn of 2001 and developed it in April–May 2002. Scorecards began to be used in the entire firm from July 2002. JIT used the scorecard process to develop its corporate strategy as a strategy map, which then was broken down into scorecards for JIT's three strategic business units (Airline, Solution, Service), for each division in these, and the departments (such as Personnel) in JIT's headquarters. In the process, executives and heads of all units had extensive discussions about strategies and ways to achieve them. From a rather ambiguous situation, this resulted in a unification of the entire company's strategy, in particular, its needs in terms of human resources. Headquarter departments improved their understanding of target customers. This now forms the basis for a continued, closer cooperation in the organization to carry out the strategies. Scorecards are used monthly to discuss performance.

JIT's experience of scorecards as yet is brief, but it seems to have approached the BSC in a very systematic way. We also find it interesting that joining IBM provided the main reason for implementing scorecards.

JÖNKÖPING

Organization background

The county council of Jönköping is one of Sweden's 18 county councils. Its main task is to provide health and dental care for the 335 000 people living in the council. The organization has about 10 000 employees, and a turnover of SKr5 billion.

The work with the BSC started in 1996 when Göran Henriks, Chief of the Department of Learning and Innovation, and his colleague Mats Borjestig, Chief of the Department of Medicine in the eastern part of the county, went to a quality conference in Stockholm. In the organization they had worked with quality improvement for some time and wanted to integrate the quality work in their planning process as well. The problem that they had was that the budgets and plans set up were never fulfilled, and they looked for a possible solution to this problem. At the quality conference, one of the speakers introduced them to the BSC. Göran Henriks and Mats Borjestig saw this as a great opportunity to improve their work.

Because Henriks and Borjestig knew how difficult it could be to introduce new management models, they decided to test the BSC on different parts of the organization before an official decision to use it organization-wide was made. Borjestig's Department of Medicine became the first test group. They tried the tool for a year before three other groups were introduced to the tool. The test groups were then increased to nine in 1998 and finally to all 99 departments in 1999. Since then, all reports in the organization have been made in the BSC format.

Scorecards in Jönköping

The BSC has become an accepted and widely used tool since its introduction in the organization. The BSC has become the format that everyone at all levels of the organization uses to communicate their plans and their results. It is used more or less on all levels of the organization for long-term strategic work and short-term plans. It has thereby become a natural part of all planning and follow-up processes in the organization, and a way of moving away from the 'purely financial discussions' to more holistic assumptions about what is going on in the organization.

Instead of the yearly budgets that the organization used to do, the work with the BSC has led to planning reports three times a year, made in a BSC format. These reports are then followed up on a regular basis to ensure that the work is going according to the plans. The plans and the regular reports have also enabled benchmarking of the different units in the organization as well as aggregation of the measures. The changes taking place in the organization are thereby made visible to the employees, enabling them to take action when needed. The BSC has thereby become a way of giving direction to the organization.

Jönköping adds two more facets to our collection of experiences. First, that the BSC was here closely connected with quality management. Secondly, that it was tested at a smaller scale for two years and only then introduced throughout the county. In local (and central) government organizations such as Jönköping or Helsingborg, it is also necessary to find ways of bridging between the BSC and the requirements for budgets and other reports. These may be both formal, legal requirements and a matter of what politicians have been used to. There may, however, be similar pressures in business firms, from board members and corporate management who are wary of abandoning traditional control methods. To avoid excessive administration, it is, of course, always necessary to find ways of cutting out old practices, but not until the new methods function well.

LUND HEART AND LUNG CENTRE

Organization background

The Heart and Lung Centre (HLC) in Lund provides specialized care for patients with cardiac and pulmonary diseases. The centre has 650 employees that together generate a turnover of about SKr0.5 billion per year. The fundamental idea behind the organization is that during diagnosis, treatment, and nursing care the patient will find that the staff are working together, without organizational dividing lines, in order to try to cure or alleviate the patients' disease in the best possible way. The HLC forms part of the University Hospital in Lund, so it also trains doctors, nurses, other clinical staff and undertakes research.

The centre's vision is that, where there is a choice, the HLC will be the natural and obvious one for patients and those referring them, as well as for employees, students, researchers, and those financing research. To reach this vision, in 2000 the centre started working with the BSC. With the help of the BSC vision, strategic objectives and success factors for activities were established at different levels of the organization.

Scorecards in Lund HLC

The work with the BSC started after an extensive reorganization in April 2000. The new, rather complex, organization required new ways of managing and following up its activities. The BSC was introduced by the new director of the HLC. In his previous job in another part of Sweden, he had been highly involved in a variant of TQM. The official line in the University Hospital was that this should be introduced, but the new director had found this method too cumbersome. When he 'discovered' the BSC, he preferred to try it in connection with the reorganization that he initiated.

The BSC soon became widely accepted by the employees at the centre. They found that it was a good way of identifying what they as a group wanted to achieve and how they would achieve it. The BSC became part of the continuous improvement efforts that were made at the centre.

As discussed more in later chapters, Lund HLC is another case where one person brought about its adoption of the BSC. As in Jönköping, there was an expectation that another quality management method should be used, but the new director wanted to try BSC on the basis of his previous experiences. We are impressed by the way he went about changing to a matrix organization and developing scorecard targets throughout his organization. It provides an interesting example of how the BSC can be used in part of a non-profit, government-run organization to boost local identity and clarity of vision.

NORDEA

Company background

Nordea describes itself as 'the leading financial services group in the Nordic and Baltic Sea region and a world leader in Internet banking'. Its customer base is nearly 11 million customers, of which 3.1 million also are e-customers. In addition to the Internet, it is represented in 1370 locations. It is organized into three business areas: Retail Banking, Corporate and Institutional Banking, and Asset Management and Life.

Nordea was formed through a series of cross-border mergers involving four major Nordic financial institutions. This was consolidated in November 2001 with the creation of a new business and management structure, and the merger integration is expected to be completed by the end of 2003.

Scorecards at Nordea

Some parts of the companies that merged to form Nordea had used scorecards. Notably, the CEO, Thorleif Krarup, had previous experience himself and believed in the model. The first planning process in the newly merged corporation, not yet including Christiania Bank, was carried out in the autumn of 2000. An evaluation of this led to a 'new planning and performance management model' (PPMM). This was accepted by the group executive board in April 2001. Although budgets are still used, the PPMM constitutes the central management tool of Nordea for the fiscal year 2002, and for 2003 it will be extended to lower-level units not yet covered.

The PPMM consists of three parts which will be discussed more later in this book:

1. BSCs
2. Rolling financial forecasts (RFF)
3. Service level agreements (SLA).

RFFs are made quarterly and cover the following five quarters. As the name indicates, they are forecasts, not targets. In combination with the BSCs, they will gradually replace traditional budgets. SLAs are used for internal service providers, documenting what has been agreed between these and receivers of their services.

In the annual report for 2001, Nordea described the PPMM as follows:

A new planning and performance management model

In the strategy and business planning process for 2002, a new common planning and performance management model has been applied, introducing the Balanced Scorecard (BSC) to drive strategy into actions, rolling financial forecasts always to have an updated view on future financial performance and service level agreements better to govern cooperation between internal service providers and receivers. The overall purpose is to increase groupwide focus on shareholder value creation, ensure aligned and focused strategy implementation and support the development of a common Nordea corporate culture.

Making strategy operational

The purpose of the BSC framework is to make strategy operational. The idea is to select a number of areas in the strategy where changes are required. These are referred to as strategic focus areas.

For each of these focus areas a key performance indicator is defined, i.e. a concrete measure and an initiative to be completed which will contribute to achieving the target. The key performance indicators include cost/income ratio, market position, customer satisfaction and employee satisfaction. Business strategy, target and activities are thereby linked and strategy becomes operational.

The BSC has been developed for the Group as a whole and each business area has its own BSC. Where the Group's BSC has served as a guideline for the BSCs of the business areas, the scorecard of the business areas will provide the guidelines for the scorecards of each of their subordinate units. Each business area is responsible for the implementation in its own area. The BSC has been implemented in business areas and will be implemented in Group Staffs and Group Corporate Centre during the second half of 2002.

Rolling financial forecasts
In order to always have an updated view of future financial perform-ance, quarterly rolling financial forecasting has been introduced. There is no element of target-setting in this process. Instead, the latest available inputs regarding the major drivers of financial result are considered in order to provide the best possible estimate of future earnings.

Management's attention will then be on discrepancies between the financial forecast and the targets within the financial perspective in the respective BSCs in order to be future oriented and to decide on potential corrective actions, rather than explaining historical perform-ance.

Service level agreements
In order to provide a clear understanding of the services to be provided by internal service providers, such as IT, HR etc. to service receivers (mainly the business areas), service level agreements have been introduced consisting of four key components:

1. *Clear definitions of scope of services provided.*
2. *Defined measures in order to track quality, costs, content and timeliness of services delivered.*
3. *A governance structure establishing decision processes and clear responsibilities.*
4. *A structured process for building and maintaining the service level agreements.*

Nordea combines several traits that can be found also in others among our cases. Its BSC project is partly the result of a major strategic change, in this case realizing the intentions with the merger and creating a Nordic–Baltic bank. It has been introduced fairly rapidly, perhaps for the same reason. As we said earlier, Thorleif Krarup himself is a believer, after having worked with the BSC in his previous job. And the BSC is combined with other controls in what Nordea call their PPMM model.

ORIFLAME

Company background

Oriflame Cosmetics is an international corporation domiciled in Luxembourg that markets a complete range of high-quality skin care, fragrance, and cosmetic products through its own direct sales organization in over 50 countries around the world. In 41 of these markets, Oriflame has a local presence through wholly owned subsidiaries. Oriflame also owns ACO, a leading skin-care brand in Scandinavia, which is distributed exclusively through pharmacies.

The brothers Jonas and Robert af Jochnick founded Oriflame in Sweden in 1967. A rapid expansion took place culminating in an Initial Public Offering (IPO) on the London Stock Exchange in 1982. When an opportunity to expand into Eastern Europe arose after the fall of the Berlin wall, Oriflame was one of the first companies successfully to enter these markets. In the period from 1989 to 1997, a total of 26 new markets were opened. The growth in Eastern Europe was phenomenal and the financial exposure to the former Eastern Bloc countries increased. The expansion in Eastern Europe took place through the newly formed Oriflame Eastern Europe S.A. (ORESA) of which Oriflame International S.A. (OISA) held approximately 25%. In 1997, OISA and ORESA merged and later changed its name to Oriflame Cosmetics.

The share price fell after the macro economic instability in Russia and surrounding countries in 1998 and in October 1999 Oriflame completed a leveraged buyout, which delisted the company from the London Stock Exchange. This was done by the Jochnick family, together with the Swedish private equity firm Industri Kapital, with the objective further to develop the company in a private environment.

Over one million independent sales consultants market and sell the Oriflame products directly to the end-consumers as well as purchasing the products for their own needs through a direct sales concept. Oriflame is among the fastest growing cosmetics companies in the world, with a market-leading position in over 20 countries.

Oriflame has a long history of profitable growth. The compounded average growth rate of sales has been 17% per year since 1990. In 2001, Oriflame's net sales amounted to €447 million.

Scorecards at Oriflame

Early in 2000, the CFO initiated a project, sponsored by the CEO, to review the business and financial planning process in the company.

Considering, for example, the fact that Oriflame operates in a very volatile industry, the financial budgets which were currently in use were often misleading even before the end of the first quarter. The budgets were typically produced by the managers in each country, at a detailed level, and then negotiated with headquarters. The separate country budgets were then aggregated into regional budgets, which were summarized in a corporate budget (which was presented to the board). This process consumed a lot of time locally as well as centrally, and the information in the budget often became out of date early in the year. The cost of the budgeting process was hence considered higher than the value of the information in the budget.

To manage these difficulties, a pilot project was initiated which would evaluate alternative modes of business planning and evaluation. Early on in the project, the group zoomed in on the BSC and financial forecasts as an alternative to the traditional budgeting process. The group's task was then to analyse whether these two control mechanisms would be a feasible alternative to the traditional budget.

The project group's conclusion was that scorecards and financial forecasts would be a feasible alternative to budgets, and seven units were appointed to test these two methods to see how they would work in practice. The units (mainly sales companies in different countries around the world, but also some units at the corporate head office) received instructions on how to develop the scorecards during the autumn and winter of 2000–2001. The results were then presented at a joint conference in March 2001.

The scorecards presented focused on the logic behind the perspectives and metrics, i.e. the strategy maps describing each local company's business logic. The pilot units' presentations were much appreciated by the corporate management team and hence all units in the organization were instructed to develop their own scorecards during the summer of 2001. The emphasis in this continuous effort was also put on the strategy maps, rather than on the actual operating procedures.

The Oriflame case deviates from the others in some respects. It is a company with a very specific business model: direct selling in many countries; own manufacturing of products centralized to just two factories; a range of fast-moving products where logistical coordination is important; and centralized production of catalogues for all markets. In introducing the BSC, we would expect Oriflame to develop an official, top-level version of its business model, and then impose this on all countries.

Instead, it will be seen that management allowed seven different units to make their own interpretations of Oriflame's business logic as it applied to each of them. Following this, all units have now developed their scorecards, inspired by the pilot units' work and some corporate guidelines. Compared with our expectation of global uniform usage, Oriflame seems to regard scorecards as much more differentiated 'contracts' between unit managers and headquarters.

RICOH[28]

Company background

Ricoh Co. Ltd manufactures and sells copying machines and other information-processing products such as digital cameras. It was founded in 1936 and is headquartered in Tokyo, Japan. In 2000, its net sales were ¥755 billion (about US$6.5 billion) and its employees numbered more than 12 000.

Scorecards at Ricoh

Ricoh introduced scorecards for its 51 business units in October 1999. The intention was to create a management system emphasizing strategy implementation, since the lack of growth in the Japanese economy made it crucial to focus the organization on the medium-term strategies that had been determined. That Ricoh received the Japanese Quality Award in 1999 helped greatly in their introduction of scorecards.

According to Ricoh, introducing BSCs had the following consequences:

1. All business units achieved their strategies.
2. Relations between top management and business units were improved.
3. Ricoh's president came to a better understanding of the business logic of each business unit.
4. Top management understood the stage of development for each unit, and strategic imperatives for all businesses.

Ricoh follows the usual intention of the BSC: to increase strategic focus. We will come back to Ricoh in discussing leading and lagging measures.

SCANDINAVIAN AIRLINES SYSTEM

Company background

The Scandinavian Airlines System (SAS) Group offers air travel with a base in its home market in Northern Europe. The SAS Group also engages in airline-related businesses such as hospitality management. Through Star Alliance it cooperates with a dozen other international airlines. In 2001, the SAS Group had revenues of SKr51 433 million and made a loss after taxes of SKr1140 million. This followed a successful span of seven profitable years, and reflected extremely bad business conditions for airlines, especially following 11 September 2001. But there had also been other major changes in the SAS. The group was restructured in May 2001. Up till then, it had been a consortium co-owned by the three Scandinavian states, with no real group structure and large differences in business and planning concepts between its various subsidiaries. Now these – a few airlines, its hotel business, etc. – were organized into a new structure.

In addition, from January 2002 two more airlines (Braathens and Spanair) were acquired, reducing SAS's share of the group to 55%. This triggered one more reorganization in July 2002, and further adjustment of the new governance model that had been started in 2000.

Scorecards at the SAS Group

In 2002, the SAS Group introduced a new governance model. The intention was to clarify roles, but also internal demarcations so that costs and revenues would be clearer. The SAS management philosophy is as follows:

The SAS Group's steering philosophy is based on the belief that result responsibility promotes business professionalism and motivation. The SAS Group is developing towards a group consisting of independent and professional operations. Each business shall be competitive within its field of operation. The steering and governance of the SAS Group shall be characterized by the values of the SAS Group.

This reflects that further acquisitions and divestitures may happen. All companies should be customer focused, be competitive and have a strong sense of responsibility and pride. The 'glue' that keeps the group together is largely the common values ('*We that work at SAS care, can be trusted, are progressive and professional*') and the steering model that is shown in Figure 4.2.

It is recognized that this is a balancing act, where a less tight follow-up process and clearer SLAs promote independence, while at the same time a group perspective on issues such as IS/IT and HR, and the targets in the BSCs, shall promote the idea of *one* SAS. Scorecards will play an important role in the assessment of each company. They will be important tools for the boards. There are about 20 companies in the group, and more than half have board members from outside SAS.

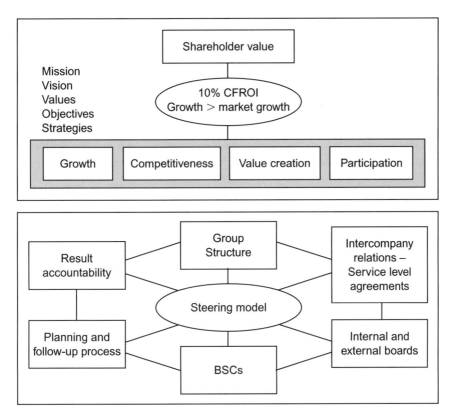

Figure 4.2 BSC's role in SAS's steering model. Reproduced by permission of Scandinavian Airlines System.

Like Nordea, SAS emphasizes the link from its long-term financial goal to what it calls its steering model, where the BSC is just one part. Also like Nordea, the use of SLAs is to be combined with scorecards. There seems to be a stronger emphasis here than in our other cases on using scorecards in the boards of the various companies within SAS.

VOLVO CARS

Company background

The Volvo Car Corporation (VCC) describes itself as 'makers of some of the safest automobiles in the world'. Seventy-five years old in 2002, the VCC has been part of the Ford Motor Company since 1999. Through 2500 dealers in

100 countries it sold in excess of 400 000 cars in 2001. Of these, 56% were sold in Europe and 33% in the United States.

Scorecards at Volvo Cars

The VCC introduced scorecards in the mid-1990s. The term is used for a variety of formats for planning and reporting, most with little direct resemblance to the BSCs in the management literature.[29] There are four areas that all parts of the organization should focus on and report how they contribute to:

1. profitable growth
2. customer satisfaction
3. next-generation cars
4. next-generation employees and leaders.

It will be seen that these are broadly similar to the finance, customer, and development perspectives in a 'normal' scorecard. But they highlight the importance of renewing products and people at the VCC.

In this book we focus on the VCC's use of scorecards in developing new products. VCC has a special unit, Project Management, with an overall responsibility for car projects, which reports directly to the CEO. This unit is very small, and projects are mainly staffed by employees belonging to other functional parts of the VCC. A special team (Business Process Management) is in charge of developing tools for project planning and control. Its challenge is to create metrics and procedures that will keep projects on track, and achieve long-term returns on VCC's investments in development. Project planning and control, however, also has to coexist with planning and control in the line organization, where almost everyone working in projects belongs. It should also be compatible with requirements from Ford.

The VCC characterizes its development work in this way: 'Because the Volvo Car Corporation designs cars completely digitally, the designers and engineers work more rapidly and intelligently than most of their competitors. Today, it's not only possible to design a car in a computer, Volvo's experts can also test drive it and perform crash tests - all before a single prototype is built.'

But development projects do not always concern an entirely new car model. An updated annual model also will be considered as a project, so there are always numerous projects going on, of different sizes.

Volvo was one of the pioneers in introducing 'scorecards', although the methods we described in *Performance Drivers* were rather different from those proposed at about the same time by Kaplan and Norton. We find it interesting that the VCC has continued to use scorecards since becoming part of Ford, and also to investigate how they are used in the part of the VCC which more than any other has to take a long-term view.

XEROX[30]

Company background

Xerox has been one of the fastest-growing American companies of the post-war era. The business of much of the company is based on the xerography principle, that is, of making copies on ordinary paper.

In the early years, Xerox had a monopoly position which enabled it to achieve a return on assets (ROA) of 25%–30%. At the end of the 1970s, however, its patent expired. The Japanese entered the market, and in 1979 they introduced their first xerography-based photocopier to the American market. Because of its market position, Xerox at first did not consider the Japanese products to be a major threat, but it soon found out that the Japanese products were being sold at a price equal to Xerox's production costs. Furthermore, the Japanese products were of superior quality. Consequently, the ROA curve dipped sharply, plummeting to a low of 4% in 1983.

In the 1960s, Xerox made the fortunate move of acquiring 50% of the Japanese company, Fuji Xerox, which in 1980 received Japan's highest citation for quality, the Deming Award. From 1979 to 1983, when Xerox was in the depths of its slump, management tried to launch the expression 'leadership for quality'. Xerox then 'benchmarked' itself against Fuji Xerox and was subsequently able to raise profitability to a level of 18%. Not only did the ROA improve, but the company's efforts were crowned with the Malcolm Baldrige Award (1989) and the European Foundation for Quality Management (EFQM) Award (1992). To achieve this success, groups consisting of participants from all over the world were appointed to develop strategic guidelines for Xerox.

Scorecards in Xerox

In 1990, Rank Xerox conducted a comprehensive review of its efforts to meet high standards of quality. This work resulted in a management model drawing on the ideas of Baldrige, Deming, Xerox's own work, the International Organization for Standardization (ISO), and the EFQM. The model helped top management to focus on a total of 42 specific measures. The model was further developed and named the Xerox Management Model (XMM). The XMM focused on 31 specific measures in six different categories. Since the model had the same format all over the world, it was possible to benchmark the different units, thus simplifying learning and development. The model also provided a framework when the unit was certified once a year. In addition, the measures and categories were reviewed and published every quarter in a Self-assessment Portfolio.[31]

The XMM process was pursued very systematically for some years. Although all 31 metrics were measured, it turned out that corporate management focused on only four or five. Looking back, there was a danger of over-complexity even with this small number. Many of the metrics required judgements, and senior people from Xerox subsidiaries were assigned to act as outside corporate assessors. They would visit other Xerox units and grade performance on each metric on a scale from one to seven. A major effort was then made to have corporate management discuss this information during two-day sessions. But the assessors were not as harshly realistic as they should have been. When things were presented as improvements, which top managers knew were not, they came to regard it as a waste of time. As control officially was through a matrix organization, it also turned out to be hugely difficult to devise metrics that portrayed the responsibilities in an under-standable way.

Then Xerox was hit by a new competitive situation in the late 1990s, and at the same time made some mistakes in reorganizing its sales force and customer administration. Focus became much more short-term (survival). Most of the XMM structure was dismantled. Measures were still used for more operational purposes such as print volumes and stock turnover rate – and, of course, finance. But corporate management focused on just a few metrics, essentially cash generation and the balance sheet.

In the new situation there has also been a realization that the scorecards used previously were too generic. Business needs to be conducted in differ-ent ways in different countries, and when the current difficulties have been conquered, it is likely that top management will focus on sources of differen-tiation, unique competencies, partnerships, etc. – making KSFs more varied across the organization. In the longer run, just having KPIs relating to cash flow will not be enough.

The mode of control which is now emerging will be less complex and more focused, with more stress on follow-through. Management processes need to be disciplined and structured. It is essential that people understand them and expect them to be acted upon.

The Xerox experience shows that an elaborate technique for scorecard measurements does not guarantee success. The problems hitting the company may partly explain why the XMM process was abandoned, but also it was applied in a way which was later regarded as bureaucratic and too complex. On the surface, Xerox seems to have applied it diligently and systematically. But apparently it did not lead to strong commitments or enough action.

An interesting observation is that Xerox was successful in using metrics over a very long period through benchmarking between countries and units, and creating challenges for managers. When top management needed to take a more differentiated approach, and created changes that required corporate management to act forcefully, XMM turned out to be of limited use.

What does this tell us about the use of scorecards – as we have seen, XMM originated as a quality control project? Such models carry the temptation to use large numbers of metrics, and try to create, monitor, and compare 'complete' descriptions of performance. As proponents of score-cards, we suspect that scorecards, and maybe strategy maps really describing sources of uniqueness in Xerox, might have worked better – and may do so in the future. But, of course, we cannot know this. At least the story cautions us not to confuse an impressive façade with good management control!

Challenges 5

THE TROUBLES WE'VE SEEN...

Most authors who write about BSCs believe in the concept to the extent that they forget to mention the challenges and troubles that some experience with it. As consultants and teachers we have heard of numerous implementations that did not yield the expected results, and as researchers we have assessed why and how organizations use the concept in practice. In addition to our own hands-on experiences, we also gained a deeper understanding of the concept in Scandinavian practice by organizing a theses competition among master students in the five Nordic countries on the theme of BSCs. Over three years, we read 100 Master theses and learnt how the concept was implemented in many organizations. It is clear that far from all succeed. A foreign colleague told us the following true story, which is not unusual:

> Approximately a year and half ago, 'NADIR', a US multinational, implemented a BSC for all of its major business segments, business units, functional areas (HR, IT, Procurement, Supply Chain, etc.).
>
> Each of these submitted their scorecard on a monthly basis. Somebody in the planning and strategy department would then compile all of the scorecards and place them in a very neat Binder which was about 8 cm or 10 cm thick by the time they received all of the various scorecards. This binder was then submitted to the CEO and CFO of 'NADIR', and the rumour was that they would go through each scorecard and make inquiries or judgements based on what they saw. In reality, the binder was extremely difficult to read, understand, and draw any conclusions from. The scorecards were very unbalanced, covered many different topics from one to another and typically showed all measures in the 'Green' (which means all good news) and nothing in the 'Red'. These results were interesting given their stock was falling to a low

level, the ROI by company was in single digits at best and the organization had not delivered on much of the integration savings that they had promised over the past two years.

Another interesting point of the scorecard was that it was developed by the CFO and therefore it was financially driven and, again, had no balance to it of any real value. A consultancy helped the Global CIO develop his own Functional Group Balance Scorecard. The scorecard was balanced; however, it was about the time when the CFO mandated a different point of view and approach. The CIO's scorecard was basically dissolved and the CFO's became their new template.

In the past year or so, 'NADIR' has initiated a major cost-reduction programme across all business segments, functional areas, and major process focuses including supply chain, sourcing, and others. This re-orientation has led to less attention on scorecards.

A sad story, isn't it? In this chapter we want to address some of the difficulties we believe exist. Readers who are themselves part of a BSC process may recognize some of them and put their own experiences into context. The troubles you have may be typical when implementing and operating scorecards – not anomalies, following from bad implementation of the concept. Identifying this will help some in overcoming the difficulties. And others may become better prepared for challenges they are likely to encounter.

In Chapters 6–11, we then elaborate on how we believe scorecards should be designed in order to be actionable. There is no one-to-one connection between the challenges discussed here and the issues presented in these chapters. Problems in implementing and operating scorecards such as 'NADIR' experienced arise because inappropriate choices have been made on a range of design issues. All of those we discuss in Chapters 6–11 need to be addressed, and conscious choices made on how they are to be handled.

CATEGORIES OF CHALLENGES

What went wrong in 'NADIR's' scorecard project? A simple list would probably include:

- *They did not convince the organization WHY they needed scorecards.* You need to present a reason why people should do as you want. Resistance to change is one of the most obvious challenges for any new idea to overcome. In the 'NADIR' case, people were understandably reluctant to mark their performance in red. When cost cutting became the agenda, it seems even top management themselves were no longer convinced *WHY* they would persevere with their scorecard project.

- *WHAT they attempted to do was wrong.* Scorecards can be used in so many ways that this is a dangerous thing to say. But 'NADIR' seems simply to have ordered all units to deliver reports on their performance, with no coherence or known link to strategy. That thick binder was meant for the CEO and CFO. They or their staff would inspect and interrogate units whose scorecards warranted it, in the same way as they used to do with financial numbers. Even if this had worked, we do not believe this is a good form of control in a modern organization.

- *HOW they did it was wrong.* Even if you want to use scorecards as a format for checking people's performance, there are different ways to introduce them. When discussing their scorecards with our consultant colleague, 'NADIR' people clearly had a vague idea about how they were to be used: 'rumour was...'. It does not seem the project was properly explained. Making it easier for people may include using appropriate software, dismantling other types of control, and linking the new procedures to established routines.

We will use *WHAT, WHY,* and *HOW* as keywords in discussing challenges. What you do, why and how, have different connotations when you start a new BSC project as well as later, when it is a matter of making BSC use a continuous habit throughout the organization. Because of this, we discuss separately these two time frames, giving us in all six categories of challenges. In Table 5.1 we have listed some of the challenges we have identified. We will begin with *WHY,* since the reasons for your BSC project should predate the decisions on *WHAT* to do and *HOW.*

For each cell in the table, we later in this chapter use our case companies to illustrate how they dealt with these challenges. As they were willing to talk to us about their BSC projects, we may expect that these are (mainly) successful. So we will add observations from some other, anonymous, cases to provide an overview of possible answers to *WHY, WHAT,* and *HOW.*

WHY is essentially about providing *motivation*, *WHAT* is choosing the right *application* for the BSC, and *HOW* is having sufficient *resources* for your BSC project:

Table 5.1 Challenges to be discussed in this chapter

	During initial development	During the continuous process
Why	Perceived as a temporary and unnecessary project, certainly less important than existing previous control methods	Lack of attention and interest as other duties out-compete BSC-related tasks (depends partly on rewards, of different kinds)
	Scorecards not linked to strategy	BSC turns into a ritual with little perceived importance or meaning, and the link to strategy is forgotten
	Suspicions and fear	
What	Inappropriate scope and ambitions for what parts of the organization the BSC should cover, and for what it will be used	Stagnation – intended 'roll-out' is discontinued, or no gradual exploring how scorecards can be applied in new ways
	No good mix between bottom-up and top-down	Not used for learning
	Measurements difficult (or too many)	
How	Lack of support from top	Relation to other planning and control unclear
	Wrong people taking part	Insufficient time allocated to BSC-related tasks
	Project not introduced so all concerned understand their part in it	BSC turns into a measurement ritual
		Lack of appropriate software
	Excessive workload	

- *Motivation.* A need for organizational changes, or the opportunity to have a greater influence on one's situation, often provide rational reasons for people to engage in BSC projects. There may also be more immediate rewards. On a more emotional plane, motivation may require addressing people's fears. In 'NADIR' people did not want to expose their poor performance. In other cases, top managers realize that discussing scorecards will mean *they* have to expose their lack of knowledge about subunits' activities. It is easy to tell people that costs should be lower and profits larger, as in traditional budgetary control. To engage in an intelligent dialogue about business logics and how sub-units should prepare for their future takes much more knowledge. When scorecard efforts die because of this, it is not a weakness of the BSC but of the organization as such.

- *Application.* We believe that 'NADIR' attempted to use scorecards in a poor way. In Chapter 2 we described a broad range of applications, where a number of choices had to be made about what the BSC should be in each particular organization. Faced with this range of possibilities, there is an obvious danger that organizations try to have them all. This is rarely a good idea – or it will at least require a huge change effort. Many find it hard to decide what *not* to do. A choice that will work involves a diagnosis of the situation on hand, where essentially everything we write about in this book comes into play.

- *Resources.* We mentioned lack of knowledge as a common reason why the BSC sometimes fails. Knowledge is, in fact, one of the most important resources in scorecard projects. Not primarily knowledge about the BSC as such, but rather the facts needed to start discussing what the organization should do. This is, of course, a weakness that has little to do with the BSC as such, and we have often seen projects lead to a resurgence of interest in data on customers, costs, competitors, etc. which seemed healthy. The need to bring forward such material is one reason why the second most important resource is sufficient time. Many people in the organization need to allocate sufficient time and effort, and this is not purely a matter of being motivated to do so. There are obvious constraints from other duties, and from other change projects competing for time and attention. Occasionally, more dedicated resources such as computer software may also be required.

Some of the design issues we introduced in Figure 2.10 and discuss in later chapters link directly to some challenge in Table 5.1. Most of them, however, connect with several. To take two examples: how dialogues are conducted, and how roles are assigned are not just *HOW* issues but also require clarity of task (*WHAT*) and purpose (*WHY*).

ONE MORE SAD STORY

To illustrate the challenges, we use one more negative case story. This is not a true story, but an amalgamation of some experiences we had or heard about. We wrote it for use in seminars, and quite often participants tell us this actually happened in their corporation, and ask us who has told us!

The Polish subsidiary

It is November 2000. One of your friends works as a controller in a Swedish corporation, which recently expanded their business to a couple of countries in Central Europe. In the autumn of 1999 the company established BSCs for the group as well as for its subsidiaries. In January 2000 the Polish company consisted of a Swedish management group and five Poles. According to its BSC for the year, the most important targets to be achieved were:

Financial perspective:
- Net income: Skr10 million
- Sales growth (value as well as volume): 50%

Customer perspective:
- Brand recognition: 50% of the target group will mention the company when asked to name three possible suppliers of this kind of product
- Eighty percent of customers are satisfied or very satisfied

Internal Process perspective:
- Ninety percent of the orders are delivered within a week
- A complete integration of administrative systems with those of the parent company over the Internet is implemented

Learning and Growth perspective:
- Ten regional agents/service providers have been appointed and trained
- Another five co-workers have been hired locally and started work, and also received training at the parent company
- Discussions with three potential suppliers have begun (on behalf of the Swedish manufacturing company).

These targets were also included in the Polish company's business plan, which also included a 'budget' for 1999. The latter is called a 'rolling forecast' and is arranged after cost categories. It was meant to be revised quarterly, but the past year's intense activities have left no time for this.

The group scorecard was set up through a series of discussions among corporate management. Following this the scorecards for the local sales companies were put together quickly and, to be honest, without any in-depth analysis or discussion. However, the companies were clearly expected to reach their stated targets.

Your friend now approaches you for advice on the following situation: The financial manager of the Polish company called her yesterday and told her that good economic developments in Poland will lead to a bigger profit than expected. This is partly due to the fact that the operating expenses are lower than estimated and partly to a higher margin on sales than expected. The small team of employees has done a terrific job.

Your friend had then started to talk about the BSC, and her feeling was that her Polish colleague had not given this any thought at all. But he promised to get back with an estimate of the current position. Today your friend received a 'very preliminary estimate' on her e-mail:

Financial perspective:
- Net income: SKr15 million
- Sales growth: value 40%, volume 25%

Customer perspective:
- Brand recognition – no estimate made
- Sixty percent of the customers are satisfied or very satisfied

Internal Process perspective:
- Time of delivery – no follow up, believed to be approximately 2 weeks
- Integration of administrative systems not finished due to problems on the Swedish side

Learning and Growth perspective:
- Five regional agents/service providers have been appointed and trained
- Another two employees were hired locally and are now being trained at the parent company, and they will start working next month
- Discussions with one possible supplier were started at the beginning of the year, but they were then put on hold due to excessive workload.

When moving to Poland in 1997, the CEO of the Polish company made a deal through which, during a five-year period, 30% of his remuneration is estimated to consist of bonus payments based on company profit.

Your friend is concerned about this and asks for your opinion. According to budget, the Polish company is doing very well. But the scorecard does not seem to be taken seriously. She feels that group management should continue to use this new tool for internal control, even though she knows that they have not given it much attention during the past 12 months.

This story is different from 'NADIR's'. Here, the intention was to apply scorecards for a reasonable purpose: to guide and monitor a new venture in Poland. (We are not told how scorecards were used in other parts of the corporation.) This is a situation where scorecards should be useful, since there is a need to invest in the new business and in marketing, so profits will be an inappropriate objective for the first few years.[32] The scorecard quoted in the story also seems a reasonable one. The metrics are not very sophisticated but commendably few and possible to measure. Even without strategic objectives and success factors, the metrics reflect an intended strategy. The task for the new company is to build up its operations and establish well-functioning and modestly profitable activities in Poland. Being recognized as a possible supplier by the targeted customers is an important ambition.

Compared with this, actual performance seems much more short-term in focus. Profits are up, but almost everything else is below expectations. Higher growth in sales than in volume, combined with higher profits than expected, seems to indicate that prices have been increased – maybe 'skimming' the market. This, combined with slow delivery and low customer satisfaction, is likely to prove disastrous for the company's more long-term ambitions. If these remain the same, the current year's performance should not be celebrated.

Seminar participants easily identify one reason for the course of events: the CEO's bonus model. This predates the scorecards and should have been renegotiated, since his task now should not be to maximize profits. They also quickly identify that there was not much participation in developing scorecard targets, and that scorecards have been dormant during the year.

So some of our 'challenges' in Table 5.1 seem to have been met, others not at all. There is a link to strategy; it is reasonable to apply scorecards to the Polish company; and measurements should be possible. But it surely was wrong that the subsidiary was not involved during the 'initial development'; when scorecards were developed at the headquarters, all concerned did not understand their parts; and at least for the CEO in Poland there were clearly other controls that mattered more.

In terms of the issues (Figure 2.10) we discuss in later chapters, there were bad design choices for at least the following three: dialogues, roles, and incentives. There was a lack of dialogue, no local roles concerning scorecards in Poland, and incentives to focus on short-term profit rather than the scorecard.

This had an effect on the business as such, but also on the ambition to use scorecards 'during the continuous process' (Table 5.1): lack of attention to them, and measures being made out of duty rather than interest. When a scorecard project has reached this stage there is an overarching challenge in reviving it, because by now many feel that the BSC has been tried and failed. What has failed is, of course, the way it was applied. Yet it is tempting for those in charge of the project to claim that scorecards exist – and they do. But they are not in any way effective. A restart is necessary, and to admit honestly that wrong choices were made.

From the story it should be clear that choices made early in implementing the BSC are crucial for its success. *WHAT* was handled was at least partly right, but *HOW* it was done did not address *WHY* it was motivated. We now look into how our case companies handled these challenges.

DURING INITIAL DEVELOPMENT

Why

So how did our case organizations provide motivation for their projects and make them perceived as important and linked to strategy? Did they manage to avoid suspicions and fear?

In Chapter 3 we saw how it took Skandia several years before its Navigator project had more widespread effects. Most of the events we described took place when many people probably thought that scorecards had been implemented, and scorecards did exist. But when employees finally had to start taking note of these, they were not accepted as a relevant description of their work. Up until then, as we stated in Chapter 3, employees probably regarded scorecards as a fad and did not think it worth spending time on something that might change soon anyway. Top management had to issue orders, and local units devote sufficient time, before scorecard work started in earnest.

Skandia is not alone in encouraging scorecards for some years before finally mandating their use:

Ericsson Enterprise
Group-level management has encouraged the use of scorecards, but for many years there was no uniform format or group scorecard. In 2002, group management took a more proactive stance concerning scorecards. As we stated in Chapter 4, the new COO was quoted in an internal Ericsson newspaper.[33] 'Balanced scorecard is the name of the method used in Ericsson to describe targets and check how well different units succeed in reaching their goals.' He also explained that compensation programmes should act as a necessary push to provide that little extra effort.

This comes at a time when Ericsson is undergoing extensive changes, as are all companies in the telecom industry. It is tempting to see a connection between this and the renewed corporate interest in scorecards, and it may provide the motivation which has been lacking earlier in most parts of Ericsson. It can be compared with our other case companies, several of which faced obvious changes that prepared people for new ways of working:

AMF Pension

With the changes in Sweden's pension systems, there was a strong awareness of change, and scorecards became one of the new CEO's tools for clarifying and communicating directions.

JIT

When JIT became an IBM subsidiary, they could no longer manage their company by using only a financial performance measurement such as profits, but had to apply other performance measurements such as quality, delivery on time, low-cost operation and customers' satisfaction. In the process of making the mid-term business plan, they have introduced strategic management into their business plan based on the concept of the BSC.

Nordea

As a newly created group, there were expectations within Nordea that common procedures should be introduced. Scorecards were introduced to get a balanced view of activities, but even more importantly to monitor Nordea's ability to generate results in the future.

In contrast to this, the budgets used previously were felt to be too rigid in the face of changes in the markets. Scorecard targets are revised only in exceptional cases, but a relevant view is maintained by combining them with forecasts that are revised quarterly.

People are attracted by the hope that scorecards will be more relevant, or simpler to work with, than previous methods.

Helsingborg

The traditional ways of managing the organization had long been considered misleading. They were purely financially focused and did not take any 'soft' variables into account. This became apparent every time the local press questioned city service, and the city government's responses could not match the issues raised since service measures did not exist, and targets for what was acceptable had not been set. The council therefore decided to implement a tool that provided a more balanced and holistic image of the organization. Among the benefits expected from the BSC were a holistic view, improved ability to react quickly, and improved communication and understanding between employees and citizens.

Jönköping

The old budgeting and planning process did not work as desired. Management constantly had to adjust the numbers in the budget to fit the changing circumstances and the fact that the organization rarely lived up to its plans. They felt they needed to make the planning processes more qualitative, and felt that the work with the BSC could be a possible way of doing this.

Furthermore, the organization did not find a suitable way of visualizing and strengthening management's thinking in the organization – a way of giving strategic directions in the ever-changing and political environment. Also, goal documents were not coherent. There were many goals but there was no internal ranking order or priority made between them, making it difficult to reach the goals.

Measurements were made for control purposes with the aid of statistics. Care services were evaluated on the basis of the consumption of resources and number of inputs instead of whether they created health. Management felt that they somehow needed to deal with this.

Nordea

There were problems with the 'ownership' of budgets. To achieve financial consolidation, they were largely based on assumptions sent out from headquarters. In contrast, scorecards reflect local ambitions and expectations.

Oriflame

The budgeting process was perceived as too costly – consuming a lot of time, but only producing modest value. Operating in a volatile market, most details in the budget became invalid even before the end of the first quarter.

Top management's attention to the project also served as an important catalyst. As we stated in Chapter 4, the CFO initiated the project and the CEO sponsored it.

Scandinavian Airlines System

Previous reports varied from none to 40 pages – using one, concise format actually reduces workload. Only two pages per company are allowed. Those who prepare reports realize they go directly to top management, and that – different from previous reports – the new reports will be understood.

So the most obvious way of providing motivation seems to be external changes, or lack of satisfaction with existing procedures. Without these, people may be hard to convince. This also means that sometimes the need to provide motivation for a BSC project is localized to some people only:

BA Heathrow

One challenge was to get everybody to accept the outcome according to the scorecard. In the beginning, some managers argued that the figures were incorrect, and that the performance in their unit was much better than the scorecard suggested. To show his devotion to the metrics in the scorecard, the manager told the unit managers that he would measure some of the important metrics manually himself if they did not implement measurement procedures themselves. Even so, some of the subunit managers claimed that the poor results depended on the quality of the metrics, not on the actual performance.

Lund HLC

The most difficult group to convince that the BSC was a good way of working was the doctors. They were more focused on research, clinical work, and development, and did not really want to set aside time to work with the scorecard as well.

Organizations usually introduce scorecards for some reason. The three most common ones are closely related: a changed business situation; a new CEO; and a perceived lack of relevance in existing management control. All are represented here. It is vital for success to be able to articulate the need for change, and 'market' the BSC internally. Even more so when there are pockets of resistance. Demonstrating the need for change may sometimes require very hands-on efforts, as at Heathrow.

What

How do organizations apply the BSC and choose an appropriate scope for their projects? What do they target in their early stages?

Some organizations aim for total coverage from early in their projects, and make a point of pronouncing this in public documents:

Helsingborg

All activity areas shall develop balanced scorecards, the contents of which shall be of a general nature and form the basis for comparisons within and between different units and activities over time, where possible.

The scorecards shall be accessible for citizens, employees and other interested parties within accepted ethical norms.

They shall be easy to understand and clear for different constituencies so that each and every one without specific pre-

> *knowledge shall understand their contents. The information in the scorecards shall in a simple explanatory way be possible to trace to their source, in order to achieve optimal credibility. (Official document)*

But much more down-to-earth guidance is of course also needed:

Helsingborg
A so-called 'balance handbook' summarizes how measuring is to be performed: by whom, how often, how measures are presented, etc.

It may be useful to let people try the methods before going 'live':

SAS
From August 2001 to January 2002, companies were encouraged to 'play' with the new model, e.g. to experiment and try different KPIs. It was not difficult to have the basic idea accepted. Now when the system is 'live', improvements are still needed in terms of the relevance of the KPIs and recognizing achievements. For instance, SAS has the ambition to implement capital-market-oriented KPIs as part of its scorecards

Where scorecards are to be combined with other control tools, it is important to clarify where they should be used:

Nordea
Of the three components in the new PPMM, the BSC will be the one that ultimately extends the furthest down in the organization. RFFs will be made by units one level below business areas but are not seen as meaningful below this level. SLAs will be rather few.

Some enthusiasts even regard it as important to make other organizations adopt the BSC:

Jönköping
The ambition of the initiators was that all county councils should be working with the BSC in 2000. To create prerequisites to reach this goal, one of them became involved in the Federation of Swedish County Councils where representatives from all county councils participated. To get others to work with the BSC, Jönköping had to get their work going quickly.

We discuss these issues more in later chapters. It is, of course, desirable to be as clear as possible in the early stages of a BSC project about how scorecards are intended to be used, for instance, how far down in the organization, and to what extent they will replace previous planning models. At the same time, managers usually want to see some effects before committing themselves irrevocably to the new way of controlling the organization. It is a difficult balancing act.

How

How do organizations make sure their projects have enough support from the top, access to needed knowledge, sufficient time, etc.? The most obvious need is to prove that the BSC will not lead to an increased workload, at least not permanently:

Oriflame
Scorecards and financial forecasts have not been added on top of the normal planning procedures. Rather, the corporate office now focuses on top-level financial figures, not all the thorough financial budgets, and instead has asked the country managers to devote their time to the strategic agenda (a one-page strategy document), the BSC and the forecast. Hence, there was no need to motivate the managers to spend time on the scorecard *as well*, but instead to redirect their attention and present their plans for the coming year in a scorecard.

Helsingborg
An important ambition has been that the introduction of scorecards should not increase administrative work. It is regarded as a tool for more meaningful discussions about city government activities, and so the time and effort spent on budgeting should be halved.

Top management support may follow naturally from the reasons why the project was started. This also makes it easier to consult outside experts:

AMF Pension
At AMF Pension there was strong support from the new CEO and several other members of the management team. A sequence of meetings was organized to arrive at scorecards for the different parts of the company, and consultants were hired to act as seminar leaders.

Political organizations may want to guarantee that the BSC will survive a possible change in political majority.

Helsingborg
The major challenge that Helsingborg faced was making the work politically neutral. Scorecards were introduced in the early part of the mandate period 1999–2002. It was seen as important that the scorecard remained *the*

management tool also after the election in autumn 2002. The scorecard therefore needed to be implemented and considered 'running' before then. They also involved representatives from the opposition parties in the project.

In January 2002, the chief executive and the project manager of its scorecard project used an official visit to Göteborg, Sweden's second-largest city, to reinforce the view that the BSC is a politically 'neutral' method. Göteborg had a different political majority from Helsingborg, and it is the other city in Sweden with an extensive scorecard project. During the visit, in which politicians from Helsingborg's opposition participated, they made sure that Göteborg's majority leader expressed his faith in the BSC. Listening to this from a highly respected fellow party member probably influenced some of the Helsingborg opposition politicians.

Political power plays may take place also in corporations. We saw how 'NADIR's' CIO initiated a scorecard project that was interrupted when the corporate project started.

Extensive resources do not seem to be required for any of these scorecard projects. Except, as we said, one thing: sufficient time. We will come back to this issue in Chapter 8, where we discuss roles. If an organization decides to implement some dedicated software for scorecards, then this will obviously also require resources. We will see in Chapter 11, however, that the cost range is quite wide.

DURING THE CONTINUOUS PROCESS

Why

When projects are under way, how can BSC projects compete successfully with other duties? Leaders of a BSC project in a major European firm who wish to remain anonymous see this as a consequence of continued support from top management:

Anonymous firm

The BSC requires someone in the management team to drive it, making use of the information in it. The tool as such has not emerged as 'the natural' control mechanism in many organizations, so if the management team ceases to discuss the card it will fall out of the loop and no one will pay attention to it.

Unfortunately, this seems to be the case regardless of how thorough the implementation has been. Even if the new concept has been systematically introduced in the organization, and all employees know the ideas behind it, management's agenda defines what is regarded as important in the organization.

Jönköping

To get everyone involved in the work the initiators decided to start from the top in the organization and move down. They thought this was the best way of getting engagement and motivation to work with the tool. The implementation therefore started in one unit, spreading from year to year until everyone worked with the BSC in one way or another. It is now compulsory for all departments to work with the BSC.

Making scorecards compulsory will, however, not entirely solve the issue. There has to be motivation to use scorecards as they are intended, as a way of realizing strategy. To have people 'go through the motions' is not enough. This sometimes is a rather long journey:

Helsingborg

Following the city council's formal decision in June 1999, Helsingborg took several years to reach the stage where scorecards were operative. Seven people participated early on in a series of BSC seminars hosted by the Swedish Association of Local Authorities, and during 2000–2001 Helsingborg itself organized a similar course for 42 of its employees, with an external expert as leader. Some departments took the lead, and one even developed an IT tool of its own for its scorecard work.

Some thought that the process took too long – so far, three years. On the other hand, some felt that having different levels of intensity during these years gave everyone the time they needed to catch up and accept the new ways of working. The most important part after all is the dialogue resulting from using scorecards, involving all employees in the work and making them understand their tasks. 'Documents from superiors cannot control what gets done; in practical life, target levels are set by those working.' And so the scorecard project has triggered local analyses of the users' situation, and a quest for metrics that can capture the complexity without simplifying too much. Measurements are to be published on the Internet for all inhabitants to see, and so metrics have to be meaningful both for employees and citizens.

To work with the tool must become a need for the users themselves. They must see it as a way of understanding why they are there, and a confirmation that what they do and know is important. Otherwise it will not be used.

To 'accept the new ways of working' has to be combined with acceptance from above, as parent companies, boards, or politicians start to trust the model:

Helsingborg

To make sure that the scorecard work became a continuous process it was important to see that it led to positive financial results.

Lund HLC

In introducing the BSC, the new director of the HLC had to prove its value, and also show how it compared with the (continued) traditional budgetary control and the TQM efforts that the hospital expected. If good results had not been shown, then there would have been a risk of lack of engagement in the continuous work. The BSC would have been seen as just another management project – a fading fashion

Early results were crucial in getting continued support for the project. Among these, the most important was to achieve the improvements in collaboration between wards that were the intention of the reorganization. Local improvements concerned things such as absenteeism and psychosocial factors. The work with the BSC has proved to make the organization more efficient. Production has increased and costs have decreased relative to production. In some cases just reporting a low number had immediate effects on performance – or even providing the information that measurement will be introduced. One doctor confirmed that it was the discussions and the activities around the scorecard that were the important part.

The HLC's scorecard project also features prominently in its presentation booklet, and selected measurement data will be published on the Internet. This data will be available not only to the entire hospital, but to all employees in the public health organization in Skåne.

When scorecard projects succeed, they may set going a 'virtuous circle' where they are encouraged as showcases and examples that others should follow. This is one reason for creating networks inside and outside one's corporation:

Helsingborg

Helsingborg also teamed up with cities in Denmark, Finland, and Poland to create additional commitment to its BSC project, and at the same time to provide learning opportunities and boost awareness about what the city does in this area. This involved leading people presenting their experiences in seminars in the other cities, and a joint application for EU funding for continued work.

The Skandia experience reported in Chapter 3 was somewhat similar:

Skandia

All around the world, scholars and practitioners paid attention to how Skandia managed its intellectual capital. Within the organization, the situation looked different – most of the employees had still not worked with the Navigator. Many had not even heard about it. When the new board started their work on the new organizational changes in 1998, it would have been a waste not to get the tool implemented internally. Now, no competing planning and evaluation tools would take time from the employees' usual work, and the Navigator work would thereby be given more attention.

Skandia managed to project a positive external image of its work on intellectual capital, but its initial development of the Navigator, Skandia's scorecard, did not handle all the challenges of motivation, etc. very well. The work that had been done, and the image created, did, however, prove of great value when the project was re-launched in 1998.

When scorecard use has stabilized, it may also be time to think of motivation and rewards in more concrete ways:

Ericsson Enterprise
At Ericsson, scorecards are a language for agreements and responsibilities. Starting in 2000, scorecard performance has had an impact on short-term incentives for managers.

To provide motivation obviously remains an important issue when scorecards are used continuously. As we have seen, some ways to handle this are: to get top-level support; to make scorecards mandatory; to show the good results that have been achieved; to engage people in discussions internally and externally so that the project keeps a high visibility; and to provide financial rewards.

But the important thing is, of course, that people use scorecards in a good way, not that the process survives. We now turn to this challenge: *WHAT* scorecards are to be used for when they have become operational.

What

As scorecards become parts of an ongoing practice in organizations, how do organizations ensure that they are used as intended? In some of the cases this was pointed out to us as a difficulty:

AMF Pension
Really achieving continuous, monthly reporting is a challenge at AMF Pension.

BA Heathrow

It has been difficult to get subunit managers to engage in the evaluation of each other's performance and to create a cross-departmental discussion.

Jönköping

The most difficult part is to capture what is strategically important for the organization. How to move away from short-term thinking and instead link it to long-term. And to actually put the plans into action.

Loss of focus may be the consequence of a change in project leadership, once the BSC is viewed as an established practice. Our anonymous company warned about this:

If the 'owner' of the scorecard in the management team moves on, and no one replaces her as the scorecard advocate, then there is an apparent risk that the scorecard will fade away. In some organizations, the scorecard will just be forgotten when it is replaced with a new set of management principles; for example, more financially oriented goals and metrics. In others, the metrics may survive if they have been implemented in a dedicated management information system that produces a performance report every month. The metrics may then remain and attract some attention. But they will not be used to boost a strategic discussion in the organization, but rather serve as an operational control mechanism to evaluate operational effectiveness rather than strategy realization.

This is part of the most common danger: the 'KPI syndrome' where metrics become an empty ritual, or just the kind of inspection tool 'NADIR' may have tried to develop. Our anonymous company again:

If scorecard metrics are not used correctly, i.e. regarded as indicators of the organization's ability to deliver its strategy, then it is likely that they will grow into an operational management control system. Instead of regarding the outcome as an indicator of the organization's ability to reach its strategic objectives, it may be seen as a process metrics, which may lead to action that is too narrow. If a single metric deviates from plan, they may think that there must be something wrong in the execution. Management becomes too interested in the metrics, rather than the big picture. They may discover that performance is poor in a certain region regarding a certain metric, and then start to take action to correct for this trend. This is, however, not management's responsibility. Typically, they have allocated the operational responsibilities to the decision-makers throughout the organization. Management should not intervene in these operational decisions, but rather allow the subordinate to take the necessary action.

Management's obligation should instead be to challenge the metrics as such – analysing whether or not they are robust indicators of success. But also to understand whether the underlying business model still is valid, or if the strategy needs to be altered. If, for example, delivery precision is monitored, and performance seems to deteriorate, then management's responsibility is to take one step back and relate to the delivery processes as such: analysing the trend and re-inventing the company's attitude to delivery. If management accepts the metrics as 'true' indicators of performance, then it is an apparent risk that they will freeze the organization, focusing its attention on the measured dimensions rather than encouraging agility and ability to change.

Hence, it is paramount that management continuously keeps a strategic focus and considers the metrics as indicators that they must challenge. Unless they pay attention to this, they and the rest of the organization will start perceiving the metrics in the scorecard as traditional KPIs.

The companies we talked to seem aware of this danger. They believe they can avoid it by letting many people have access to scorecards and measurements. This, of course, has consequences for the software they will need (Chapter 11). The major impact, however, is on the dialogues where scorecard information is used (Chapter 7):

AMF Pension

Already the first set of scorecards has been made available over the intranet. The management team used this regularly during their Friday meetings to survey the situation in all different units.

Ericsson Enterprise

Use of scorecards is the key element in what Ericsson Enterprise calls Performance Management Processes. Every month measurements are published on the intranet for every one of 2300 employees to see. For each key performance indicator there should be two or three lines of comments about actions, and the internal board of Enterprise follows this information closely.

The scorecard is now used as the agenda at the management meetings. All subunit managers present their performance according to their scorecards. Still, it is difficult to make them comment on the other departments' performance. The scorecards have not yet created the intended cross-departmental discussion, but rather are used as a framework for each department to describe their performance.

As the organization becomes more mature in its use of scorecards, a challenge is to develop the BSC further: find new applications for it, change strategy maps, scorecards, and metrics, maybe discontinue some parts of the process. Or find more efficient ways of working with scorecards, which leads us to the final part of Table 5.1.

How

As scorecards become part of everyday life in organizations, it is necessary to find resource-efficient ways of working – and yet avoid turning measurement and reporting into stale rituals. There will still be a need to mobilize enough resources: time, knowledge, maybe invest in software if this was not done before:

HP Services
The number 1 pitfall in measurement systems is having too many measures: measures which are irrelevant or not measurable. Other dangers are:

- Disconnection between measures and business objectives, risking *effectiveness*, and processes, risking *efficiency*
- Lack of maintenance of measures, leading to static systems which do not change with the business
- Lack of follow up. If data are not automated, then metrics will be too difficult to collect. If metrics are not perceived as valuable (or maybe are not) then they will not be used. In both cases nobody will act upon them.

HP tries to surmount these problems through a unified, web-based system throughout the corporation. Scorecards are part of compulsory reporting, and the format (including metrics) is unified for all global operations.

HP's system may be considered as top-driven. The corresponding control system at Compaq is locally driven, which now presents interesting challenges for the merger process.

Nordea
The BSC coordinator at Nordea describes his task in terms of facilitating through constantly 'supporting' and 'pushing', allowing time for scorecard practices to mature, and for people to adopt new ways of working.

This support may be needed when the process takes longer than people expect:

Lund HLC
To get the BSC to work continuously, it must be given priority. Some employees were somewhat frustrated because it took longer than expected from the initial announcement of the BSC to the point where the project really

got going. The project managers want to give the initial phase another two
years before any more results are seen. 'When you get to see the measurements, that creates the will to continue', one nurse says. Proof of the link to
the financial outcome is needed for the BSC to establish itself as the new
control method. Therefore, there is now also an effort under way to develop
budgets and accounts to fit better with the new organization and the scorecards.

Our anonymous company points out how different choices during implementation may maintain or endanger the strategic focus for a BSC project:

> Sometimes the design of the scorecard, with its speedometers and traffic
> lights, as well as deviation measured as percentages, may take manage-
> ment's attention away from the strategic issues and direct it to the specifics.
>   Because of this, the performance reports should be verbal rather than
> numerical. And the graphical indicators should be as multi-dimensional as
> possible, in order to promote the strategic utilization of the scorecard. The
> indicators shall not be used to evaluate the specifics, but to boost a dis-
> cussion in the management team on the long-term initiatives in the organ-
> ization.
>   This also has implications for the frequency of reporting. The scorecards
> should normally be presented on a quarterly basis. And they should never be
> presented more often than each month. Otherwise, the scorecards will
> inevitably attract an operational interest, since it is mainly the metrics that
> vary between weeks that will get attention. The initiatives that this will pro-
> mote will hence focus on the small and short-term gains (process improve-
> ments) rather than the more important and strategic initiatives.

Most of the other comments we hear refer to challenges which are common
to all longer projects; for instance, to allow enough time for changes to sink
in. If this succeeds, however, we have seen cases where local units continue
to use scorecards voluntarily even after a new corporate CEO has reverted to
more traditional management control methods.

So, to summarize, the *HOW* challenges once the BSC is established are
continued support and sufficient resources. But also to deploy these wisely.

SUMMARY

In Table 5.1, we identified the general categories of challenges we have
found in scorecard projects. Not all of them have come up in our case
material, but this is partly because these organizations believe they have

avoided most of these dangers. This can be done in different ways, and it also depends on how you want to use the BSC concept.

As in all projects, it is vitally important to prepare for potential difficulties before they arise. Areas such as the scope of the project, whether scorecards will replace traditional budgeting, whether use will be mandatory, need to be addressed at an early stage. The ambitions will vary between organizations – as we saw in Chapter 2 – but whatever they are, they should be well motivated and possible to describe in some detail when people ask. Top management need to get involved. Even if definitive answers may not exist until later, it is important that the BSC project team have strong support from management concerning their ambitions and how they may influence the organization. This should be obvious, since we have stressed the use of scorecards in realizing intended strategies. In several of the organizations we studied, the CEO (or equivalent) personally presented the BSC and its intended benefits – in personal speeches, in company newsletters, or through other internal media.

The design issues we have selected for the remaining part of this book represent some of the areas where tentative answers are needed at an early stage. As we said at the beginning of this chapter, the relations between challenges and issues are not one-to-one. How scorecards are used for dialogues in the organization may primarily be part of *WHAT* is the intended use of scorecards, but how they are used will certainly affect motivation and have an impact on the resources needed.

Because of this, we believe that the challenges discussed in this chapter should be kept in mind throughout Chapters 6–11.

Visualizing Strategies in Maps

6

CREATIVE VISUALIZING

Scorecards are increasingly used as tools for visualizing strategy: communicating strategies as part of control, but also developing and articulating strategies. They help in structuring strategy discussions and deriving concrete targets for all parts of the organization. By providing links to higher-level strategies and aims, they help the entire organization to realize the underlying logic. We believe that a large number of the employees, probably the majority, should know about the scorecards and take part in dialogues about them (see Chapter 7). Otherwise, measuring and monitoring the new metrics will be perceived as a meaningless ritual, a burden or even a threat. Only through involving people in discussions about the intended logic, and how the metrics relate to it, will everyone start taking an interest in the measures. This was well illustrated in the Skandia case in Chapter 3.

The need to bridge strategy and control was one of the original reasons for creating the BSC. In Chapter 1 we connected this to the growing importance of intangibles for corporate success. Closely linked to this is the ambition to explain strategy to almost everyone in the organization. More people are empowered to make their own interpretation of upcoming situations. To act quickly in ways that are desirable for the entire organization, they must comprehend the needs and possibilities of new situations in terms of the intended strategy. This understanding will only occur if people have been involved in discussing strategy, contributing to developing it for their own unit, and having memory-friendly tools at their disposal for remembering strategic intentions, and recognizing how they are met.

One such tool is the strategy map as presented in Figures 2.2 and 2.3. It provides a simplified overview of an organization's strategy and how it is intended to play out over time. At the beginning of Chapter 2 we used a simple example: 'If we have the right staff (Development perspective) doing the right things (Process perspective), then the customers will be delighted (Customer perspective), and we will keep and get more business (Financial perspective).' A business strategy is based on a number of such 'if-then' statements. Each is a hypothesis which management may believe is a statement of fact, or a 'strategic bet'. In a strategy map, these facts and 'bets' are visualized to enable communication about alternative actions and their consequences.

Strategy maps fulfil several purposes:

- They enable discussions about cause-effect relationships when facing strategic decisions, and about possible strategic actions.
- They assist in finding and selecting metrics to monitor activities.
- The completed map can be used to communicate strategies and their inherent logic: 'Why we believe we will succeed.'

Kaplan and Norton (2001) provide a wide range of such maps for many different types of organizations. They also suggest that there are 'generic' parts of such maps, such as the customer perspective being closely linked to the 'value proposition' chosen by the organization. As a starting point for working with one product company within an international corporation, we might, for instance, make a draft consisting of the ellipses and boxes shown in Figure 6.1, and use this to initiate a discussion in the leadership team about the identity of each, and how they relate.

A strategy map should answer two related questions: *How does this organization intend to succeed?* and *How can we recognize whether this organization is succeeding?* Figure 6.1 highlights the links between this company and other parts of the group. The more dependencies there are, such as the common sales organization in our example, the more careful the corporate level has to be in judging this company separately. Strictly speaking, this company can take total responsibility for only its internal processes and development efforts. Revenues, etc. also depend on the degree of success experienced by other parts of the corporation. Yet it will be important to show these shared responsibilities in the company's strategy map.

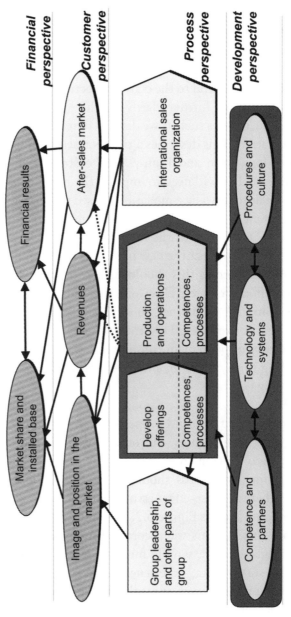

Figure 6.1 Draft of an initial map for discussing the strategy of a product company within an international corporation.

One of the main purposes of the maps is to communicate strategies and their inherent logic in the organization. They should document where the chosen strategy is going to take us and over what timescale, what activities will be needed, and also make the long-term success credible. To achieve this, a good map – and a good strategy – requires huge simplifications. To focus the organization we have to reject a number of tempting possibilities that are not central to the chosen direction.

One way of further clarifying the logic in the map is to emphasize strategic themes such as we discussed in Chapter 2. Figure 6.2 provides an illustration. This describes a transportation company that wants to attract more long-term and high-paying customers. In going for this market segment, they will need to improve their fleet of vehicles. In so doing, they also want to introduce modern IT-based scheduling. Employees will remain important in this, and in highlighting the brand image as a third area in need of development, the intention is as much to strengthen the internal morale as to project the new image externally.

A map such as this should be used to discuss questions like: How do these efforts connect? How long will they take? How do we make sure that they link into each other, so we do not start promising things we will not yet be able to deliver? How much do we really know about the potential for efficiency improvement through improved scheduling? Will customers be willing to pay more for improved service, and enter into more long-term binding contracts?

We prefer such discussions to be fact-based. Some questions will concern matters that can be researched, or for which there is evidence from previous similar cases. But other questions will require assumptions and corporate 'betting on the future'. We suggested in *Performance Drivers* that over time, scorecards should be used to collect more facts and convert hypothetical cause-effect assumptions into fact-based ones. For every link in a figure such as Figure 6.2, we should ask: What knowledge do we have about that? In this way, scorecard discussions sometimes need 'time out' for managers to assemble more evidence: product cost calculations, customer survey data, experiences from past change projects, or quotations from suppliers of new assets that will be needed.

Another important question is: Why us? Any organization should strive to become unique in some way. A strategy map that would suit your competitors will not be right for you. Your situation and resources will always

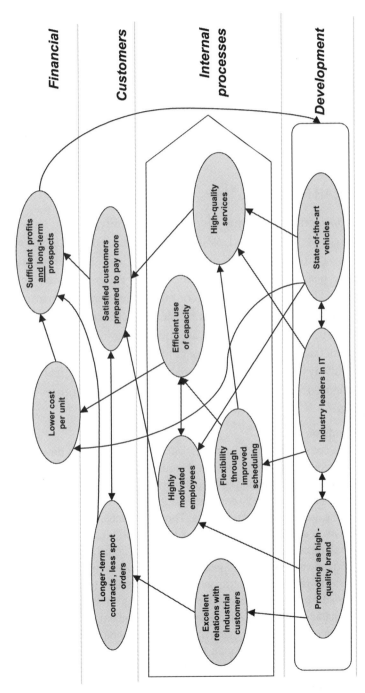

Figure 6.2 Simplified strategy map for a transportation company.

be somewhat different from everyone else's. Strategy maps easily degenerate into wishful thinking. They probably need some element of Shangri-La – a dreamland which may motivate some, while others reject it as... just a pipe dream. They also need an element of steady and patient improvements – incremental changes which will seem reasonable to some, while others reject them as unambitious. But regardless of how visionary or down-to-earth the resulting strategies are, success requires that they suit our talents. We need to accept our heritage as a fact, and make it into an asset.

THE PARTS OF THE MAP

The horizontal building blocks of the strategy map are the four perspectives of the scorecard. Within each, the most important strategic goals and their interconnections are shown. We have also seen strategy maps that display next year's targets, connected in the same way. In practice, the 'bubbles' in the diagram may contain either verbally formulated goals (as in Figure 6.2), critical success factors for achieving them, the metrics that will tell us about how well we are succeeding, or targets or performance for these metrics. As in other formats for presenting scorecard information, it is not always easy to keep these apart, even though logically there should be a sequence from goals to targets and actions – see Figures 2.4 and 2.5, and below.

Oriflame

The cornerstone of Oriflame's initial BSC effort was the development of the strategy maps. When the project group had concluded that scorecards would be a suitable planning and control instrument in the organization, a set of instructions that would serve as a pilot implementation was submitted to each of the seven country managers. These instructions asked each manager to develop a strategy map that would describe his/her business model. The strategy map consisted of four perspectives (from the bottom and up: learning and growth, internal business processes, customer, and financial) that were used to relate different aspects in the operation to one another. The map would show the cause–effect relationships in the operation that would contribute to create the intended business outcomes.

During the process there was some confusion in the units as to what the entities in the strategy map should be: whether it should contain activities, objectives, or measures. The instructions did not stipulate this, but let the local managers decide what they wanted to present in their maps. In this way, the maps turned out to be varied in their details, but still looked remarkably homogeneous in the general construction.

From bottom to top we should be able to trace the most important 'strategic themes' (cf. Chapter 2). These together form the total strategy of the organization. The themes segment the strategy into parts that can be discussed separately. For instance, in Figure 6.2 one such theme concerns service quality. It seems this is to be improved through new technology rather than through people, and that the outcome of this should be an increased willingness among customers to pay.[34] Themes identify the most important paths toward the long-term goals, and more precisely what needs to be done to realize the strategic vision. They also are an aid in remembering the intended business logic, and through this they should assist in daily decision-making.

Themes usually interact, as in Figure 6.2. We may discern a number of additional themes for the transportation company, mainly to improve scheduling and change the image of the organization among customers and employees. The identity and names of these themes is ultimately a matter for top management. Each will be based on facts and assumptions, and may be considered as a hypothesis or 'strategic bet' on what is going to lead to success within this industry.

Kaplan and Norton suggest four general categories of strategic themes:

- *Build the franchise*: achieving growth through creating new business opportunities (products, markets).
- *Increase customer value.* Working closely with customers better to understand their needs and improve one's offerings, thereby strengthening relations and attracting new ones.
- *Achieve operational excellence.* Improving profitability and quality through more efficient use of resources, e.g. utilizing best-practice methods.
- *Be a good corporate citizen.* Managing relations with stakeholders to improve the long-term credibility and stability of the corporation, e.g. in environmental matters.

The themes we found in Figure 6.2 were service quality, improved scheduling, and changing the organization's image. The first is meant to increase customer value, but it seems to be an 'inside-out' attempt since the employees are not involved. Improved scheduling clearly is a matter of achieving operational excellence. Changing the image may be construed as building the franchise by reaching new clients, or as a matter of good corporate citizenship. As described in the figure, the company seems to regard this as more about packaging and promotion than real change. Drawing strategy maps may show the relative emptiness of one's strategic thinking, as well as communicating its brilliance!

One important aspect of deciding strategic themes is to make them interact and support each other over time. Obviously, achieving operational excellence is usually a more short-term and building the franchise a more long-term endeavour, with the others coming somewhere in between. Organizations usually will need a mix of more short-term and more long-term strategic themes.

Nordea

To make shareholder value more concrete and relevant to the financial services industry, Nordea uses the concept of 'Economic profit'. This is defined as in Figure 6.3.

The overall strategic themes are linked to the various components of Economic profit through internal discussions. The three-year target values will reflect a business area's ambition to improve financial performance (i.e. economic profit) by pursuing its strategic themes. Some of the themes in Figure 6.4 have a clear impact on economic profit, while for others the link is more conceptual than mathematical.

Themes should be linked to long-term objectives, e.g. 'economic profit' in Nordea's case. We find it interesting that Nordea presents these themes in its external presentation.

Economic profit =

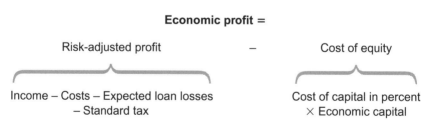

Risk-adjusted profit   −   Cost of equity

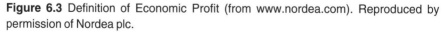

Income – Costs – Expected loan losses   Cost of capital in percent
– Standard tax   × Economic capital

Figure 6.3 Definition of Economic Profit (from www.nordea.com). Reproduced by permission of Nordea plc.

After the themes have been formulated, they need to be translated into action for everyone in the organization who needs to contribute. As we showed in Chapter 2, the basic sequence for this analysis is through CSFs, metrics and targets to actions:

Strategic themes

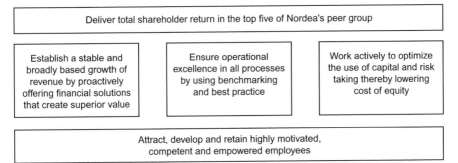

Figure 6.4 Strategic themes for the Nordea group (from www.nordea.com). Reproduced by permission of Nordea plc.

- Formulate the aim for each strategic theme.
- Identify the most important CSFs, taking particular note to remember the customers' viewpoint.
- Identify the most critical internal processes.
- Identify the most critical resources.
- Identify the most critical competences.
- Formulate metrics and target values.
- Decide on the plan of action.

Since themes also need to be linked to vision and business idea, the entire sequence can be visualized as in Figure 6.5. We refer readers to *Performance Drivers* for more views on this. Although the logical sequence is from left to right, in practice we often find it useful to start with a crude draft of the entire strategy map. We often discuss this with managers in terms of a future 'virtuous circle'. By this we mean that financial outcomes, and a growing popularity with other important stakeholders, should make continued renewal and development possible: success breeding success. In Figure 6.2 this is illustrated by the feedback loop from the financial perspective to the development perspective. Obviously, a virtuous circle requires some feasible idea about the business logics that the corporation will pursue.

AMF Pension

The team spent many hours portraying a business logic for AMF Pension in terms of a 'virtuous circle' and strategy map. These built on the fundamental

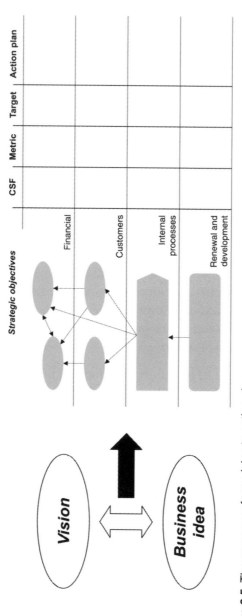

Figure 6.5 The sequence from vision to action plans.

values of the company: 'simple, safe, and human'. They meant that AMF Pension should stick to strategies emphasizing scale economies, openness, and 'no frills', but add closeness to 'normal people'. In the virtuous circle and the strategy map, this translated to cost savings, enabling low premiums, attractive pension solutions for the majority of employees, and reinforced economies of scale. It also meant that certain developments should be resisted, for instance using brokers and offering more specialized pension plans.

We have already introduced Nordea's version of how to derive KPIs, etc. in Figure 2.4, and it is essentially similar to Figure 6.5. Nordea is an example of a company using the model and process more or less 'by the book'. It also seems the corporate leadership actively stimulates strategic thinking in all follow-up work, and in discussions about deviations from targets:

Nordea

In deciding KPIs, targets, and initiatives, Nordea uses a three-year perspective. As in most corporations, the focus used to be on financial commitments, and the attitude from top management was to squeeze costs. With scorecard planning, this has been replaced by a much more future-oriented questioning: 'What strategies do you have? How are your ideas – what initiatives are you taking?' This has led to good discussions, and, of course, raised interesting questions about where the ideas linking strategic goals (or, as they are called in Nordea, focus areas) to KPIs, targets, and initiatives should come from.

So far, these discussions have been with the business areas, and they have appreciated getting involved in this way. They were asked to identify and motivate one KPI for each of their maybe 15–20 strategic goals. There was an interesting dialogue concerning to what extent these should be similar across business areas. Further down in the organization there may be unease about committing oneself, and a perception that higher levels should decide. This will only be tested as scorecard work progresses in Nordea.

Strategy maps have been drawn also for support units. For instance, the Finance Area has two strategic themes: cost efficiency and value creation.

Sometimes one strategic objective per perspective will function almost as a theme:

Lund HLC

In HLC's new promotional brochure, a high-level scorecard figures prominently as 'our navigational instrument'. The path from vision through strategic objectives and success factors to indicators and action plans is described. The objectives are stated as in Figure 6.6.

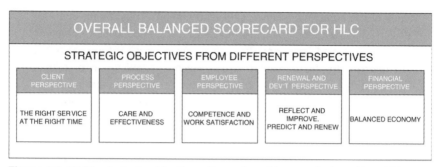

Figure 6.6 HLC's strategic objectives. Reproduced by permission of Lund Heart and Lung Centre.

It is probably rather common that strategy maps are drawn without using strategic themes. Still, there may be implicit use of them, as when BA discussed what desirable performance *really* is:

BA Heathrow

When the scorecard project was launched at BA Heathrow, no strategy maps were created. Instead, the subunit managers were asked to describe how they thought the customers were evaluating them, and how this 'evaluation scheme' could be translated into operational metrics.

Even though strategy maps were not modelled at the beginning of the scorecard project, the importance of leading and lagging factors has always been addressed. The manager refers to the process of identifying relationships as 'the intellectual challenge for managers'. It is not only the manager's responsibility to figure out the relationships, but also to communicate these in the organization. For example, 'on-time departure' is a very important outcome for BA, therefore it is important to understand what factors might influence this outcome negatively. Describing cause-and-effect links to all members in the organization will thus make it obvious that, e.g. 'late check-in' (which might be perceived as an effort to increase customer service) will generate delays throughout the whole system, which will create more dissatisfaction to the customers in total, outweighing the satisfaction of the one customer who is allowed to check-in after the stipulated last check-in time. Describing the cause-and-effect links in a strategy map will make the effects of certain decisions explicit. Even if an initiative is taken to increase customer satisfaction, it may lead to decreasing customer satisfaction on the aggregate level.

Companies not making use of themes still may work very conscientiously to link strategic objectives to KPIs, targets, and actions. Here is how Ericsson Enterprise's 'grid' (Figure 2.4) was developed:

Ericsson Enterprise

Ericsson Enterprise had extensive discussions about the way scorecard measures should be linked. The scorecard is used for the one-year perspective, and based on the Ericsson Strategic Plan which represents a three to five year perspective, and the Business/Product Plan for the next one to two years.

Enterprise's scorecard was developed very systematically during three meetings (cf. Chapter 7). The model used was the basic Kaplan–Norton one, but with five perspectives (employee is the fifth one). The starting point was the Vision/Mission of Enterprise. It was decided not to revise this before work on the scorecard started, but at a later stage of the process it was changed slightly.

The next step was to decide on strategic objectives for all perspectives. An alternative could have been to continue with KSFs, etc. for each perspective before going on to the next one, but the group made a point of completing the objectives before going on the next lower level, the KSFs. Likewise, they here decided on all KSFs before embarking on the next level, the KPIs. Here, however, discussion of the next level: strategic (or high-level) actions and KPIs became intertwined.

For all of these, a discussion format was used which involved the 'facilitators' and the use of 'post-it' notes. When everyone had noted down his suggestions, these would be *read* by everyone, and *clarification* would be requested if necessary. Following this, similar ideas were *synthesized*, i.e. the number of items was reduced. Then the question would be put as to whether the set of suggested KSFs, KPIs or actions should be considered *complete*, or whether some additional ones should be added. The group would then take a formal *vote* about which items should be eliminated. For items with few proponents, they would be asked whether they could 'live without them' before they were removed. In this way they arrived at a final set of 16 KSFs, with between one and seven actions for each of them.

It was easy to identify candidate actions – but the essential question was whether it was possible to link or 'map' them to the objectives and KSFs. Many measures (KPIs) came from questionnaires already in use.

It is apparent that this process was in no way a 'mathematical' exercise, and did not involve explicit assumptions about the strength of relationships, lead times, etc. But in spite of this, it provided a shared and clear view of strategic necessities, and the business logic inherent in Enterprise's plans for 2002.

Ericsson found it difficult to 'cascade' goals down to metrics and action plans, and found that this had to be more of a back-and-forth exercise. Several organizations had similar difficulties:

Jönköping

In Jönköping's county council the management board have spent an extensive amount of time on developing goals and measures for the different perspectives. From the beginning, the balance between the number of measures in the different perspectives was not very good, but over time the groups have become better at balancing the perspectives. The management board has also set a vision for the organization that is meant to permeate all the organizational scorecards.

In the different organizational units the work with the BSC has most often started with what measures they would like to visualize in the different scorecard perspectives. From there they have moved on and worked themselves 'upward' in the scorecard determining the CSFs, goals, and vision. Extensive work is done on these parts of the scorecard, where careful definitions are made and documented. The ambition is that everyone in the group is to feel that the scorecard represents their view of the organization.

Lund HLC

The work of developing the scorecards has changed somewhat over time. Initially, the work started with the definitions of strategic goals for each of the five perspectives (the centre had made the decision to have a separate human perspective because of the central role the employees' skills played in the organization). This was, however, considered too difficult – the process did not get concrete quickly enough. Therefore, today, the centre works with one perspective at a time, beginning with strategic goals, and then moving on to success factors and measures. This way of working is found efficient to improve the understanding of the work and make it more hands-on. The activity plan, which embraces all perspectives, is the final step in the process.

In some cases, causes and effects were discussed in a more short-term way:

Helsingborg

In general, the culture in Helsingborg's city administration has not emphasized strategic thinking. Instead, the tradition has been to accept rather different directions in different departments and reach decisions ad hoc. In the 1990s, a verbal vision document for the city was developed, but this turned out to be of limited value in guiding the scorecard project.

This has made work with the scorecard operational rather than strategic. BSC work has had a pragmatic focus on finding a balance between the measures in the different perspectives. The positive outcome of this is that the actors see quickly the results of what they do, which has become an incentive to continue to work with the tool.

An example of this was when the social services unit developed their scorecard. Through their measures they soon discovered that they got the lowest grade among the compared units. This triggered them to take action and try to change the situation. The unit's clients get to fill in a form after each meeting and, based on the results from that, action is taken. Today, the customer satisfaction goal has been reached and this has also created satisfaction and motivation among the employees.

Another example involved the integration of ethnical minorities. At first, everyone was satisfied with a measure of this that focused on the share of people who held jobs. But then a discussion developed where some employees pointed out that this would miss out on the social dimension: isolation, linguistic skills, their perception of how they are treated, etc.

This experience leads on to a rather common one: when concrete measures are proposed, this may lead back to a renewed discussion of the logic behind them. Let us take a closer look at this.

LEADING AND LAGGING METRICS: 'DRIVERS' AND 'OUTCOME MEASURES'

Deciding on the metrics (KPIs) to use is often experienced as one of the most difficult parts of a scorecard project. This is probably because at this stage the project becomes 'real' for its participants: these will be the measures used to set targets, and there are often discussions as to whether a specific metric captures the intention behind it. We saw good examples of this in the Skandia case in Chapter 3 as the business support group discussed its tasks and linking metrics to bonuses.

Metrics should be regarded as compact descriptions of those aspects of the organization's activities that are the most critical for long-term success. Through the process just described the organization arrives at which aspects these are, but often there are alternative ways to measure them.

What to measure, and how, may need to vary over time. Some companies such as Nordea expect their long-term strategy map to remain essentially unchanged for several years, with only the target levels changing. But changes may occur in the market-place that motivate strategy reviews, and a company may sometimes reach its targets, so it becomes more important to focus on some other success factor and metric.

A good scorecard will have a mixture of leading and lagging indicators. These are sometimes called 'performance drivers' and 'outcome measures', but it is not always possible to make a clear distinction. A marketing campaign may have as its outcome increased brand awareness in a targeted group of customers. This, in turn, is a driver of future sales. As in all causal chains, one person's ends is another person's means. In general, however, all lower parts of the scorecard or strategy map will consist of drivers if we think of the relationship between these measures and long-term success as measured in the financial perspective. We need measures that can indicate whether the organization is changing its behaviour in the direction that is desired.

It is commonly said that behavioural changes come about mostly through new experiences. Experiences shape our attitudes, and through these our behaviour. We are unable to experience directly all important aspects of what goes on around us. Various measurements supplement our own observations, and provide us with experiences that will influence our interpretation of what we should do. This is particularly true in an organization whose managers and employees need also to monitor events outside the company. Information provided through the BSC process can be viewed as designed interventions in how people will experience what goes on. For instance, we learnt in Figure 2.4 that Ericsson Enterprise include 'partner satisfaction', 'employee empowerment' and 'time to market precision' among its KPIs. By regularly reporting and discussing these metrics, which are indicators of attitudes and behaviour rather than effects or outcomes, managers will experience differently what goes on in the organization. Figure 6.7 describes this 'intervention'. By measuring performance drivers that are logically 'earlier' than outcome measures, an organization should be able to move more quickly.

Outcome measures normally capture just the end results of processes. This is natural because end results are what stakeholders are ultimately interested in, and so far most of them have taken little interest in indicators of future performance. But an organization also needs to monitor what is happening now, e.g. process efficiency, and emerging changes in customer and employee perceptions. Strategy maps should lead to an appropriate selection of what should be the most important 'interventions' that the BSC process should provide.

One of the few companies where we have seen an effort to label both types of metrics clearly is Ricoh (Figure 6.8):

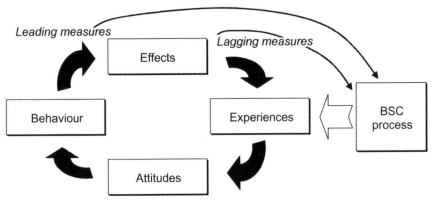
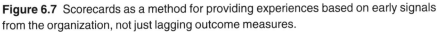

Figure 6.7 Scorecards as a method for providing experiences based on early signals from the organization, not just lagging outcome measures.

Ricoh

As shown in Figure 6.8, Ricoh has introduced two particular features in their scorecard. One is the addition of a fifth perspective: safeguarding the environment. Another is a clear distinction between lead and lag indicators.

An important dimension of using earlier or later indicators (cf. Figure 6.8) concerns risks and responsibilities. How certain are we of the link between 'driver' and 'outcome'? In encouraging employees to react on early signals, and even holding them accountable for the drivers, should we then also reward them if targets for the drivers are met, but the final outcome does not materialize, since the link did not hold? We will come back to this in Chapter 10.

MODELLING

Drawing strategy maps is an attempt at informal 'business modelling'. Various forms of this have been proposed at least since the 1960s. Early developments were closely linked with the aspiration to create management information systems that would prove valuable for managers' decision-making, or even automate part of it through being able to simulate various alternative actions and their effects. Developments have been much slower than expected, at least concerning more long-term and high-level management tasks. Models are seldom trusted if they become too complex to understand, and changes inside and outside the organization tend to make

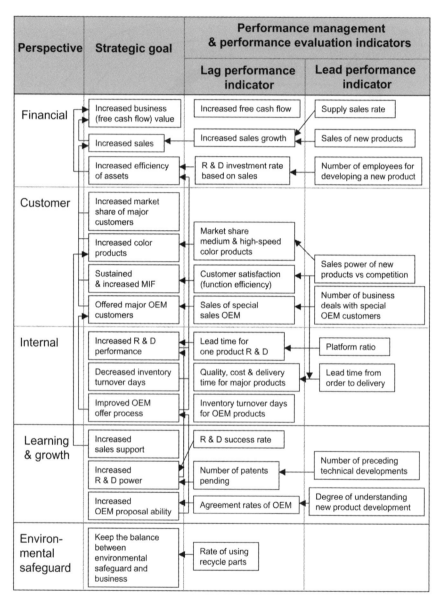

Figure 6.8 Scorecard from Ricoh; it has since been somewhat modified. Reproduced by permission of Ricoh Co. Ltd.

the models too rigid and time-consuming to construct. Yet, finding combinations of managers' intuition and formalized modelling remains important. Books such as Senge's *The Fifth Discipline* have again popularized this quest in recent years, and refuelled interest in 'systems thinking' and the discipline now often known as system dynamics.

What characterizes system dynamics is that in order to understand how a system behaves and develops over time, one tries to understand its underlying structure by modelling it. The structure can be described in terms of stocks and flows. Stocks are the accumulated resources (cf. the balance sheet in financial reporting); flows, the changes in these (cf. the income statement). With some training, business strategies like those discussed in this chapter can be modelled along these lines. To model customer relations, we may, for instance, categorize customers and define the current stocks of the different categories. Examples of flows could then be customers being added – or subtracted – from these categories. Flows would have to be associated with some rule, and often with some action being taken. A customer might, for instance move into a category representing more frequent purchases, due to a marketing campaign. In Figure 6.9, this is called a 'converter'. But as the campaign is unlikely to have an absolutely certain effect, we would soon have to introduce an element of chance into our model.

System dynamics provides a language for developing strategy maps more systematically. In the cases we have observed this has not yet been utilized, but we recommend those who want to discuss, for instance, lead times and strengths of dependencies in a systematic way to try to learn from this body of thought, rather than re-inventing some method which is likely to be rather similar.

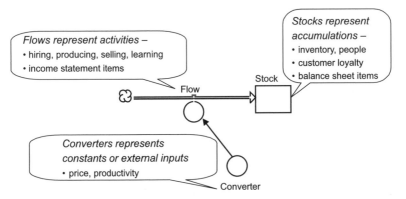

Figure 6.9 An illustration of stock and flow in System Dynamics.

There are situations where formal modelling has proved an interesting and efficient tool but it requires training to use the methods for identifying components in a system, elucidate relationships, and enter the information into an appropriate software model. It is, of course, also possible to enrol modelling experts as consultants in strategy map discussions.[35]

Further examples of 'stocks' and 'flows' relating to different strategic themes in strategy maps could be as shown in Table 6.1:

Table 6.1 Examples of stocks and flows relating to strategic themes in strategy maps

Theme	Stock	Flow
Build the franchise	Share of new products in our sales	R&D spending
Increase customer value	Number of customers needing help-desk advice	Use of focus groups and other feedback
Achieve operational efficiency	Delivery time	Number of rush orders
Be a good corporate citizen	Share of general public who consider company environment-friendly	Product design

If we define measures for the stocks and flows, we will arrive at something similar to Ricoh (Figure 6.8) – proving that the cause–effect patterns in a strategy map or a scorecard are quite similar to the logical patterns in a system dynamics model.

It is, however, quite important how the connection between formal models and the more intuitive discussions about scorecards and maps is handled. Let us go back to Skandia for an illustration.

Skandia

To ensure a uniform implementation of scorecards, Skandia introduced a model (see Figure 1.2) which was also combined with a supporting IT-tool. This took a long time to spread in the organization, since employees found it hard to understand the underlying ideas. Some even had to dissociate from the tool and to work themselves with the processes in order to get satisfied and convinced about the results. Doing this, they developed their own process model, resulting in a strategy map (Figures 3.5 and 3.6). These have a different order of steps compared with the 'official' model, and the idea of using a map was not part of Skandia's original way of working.

WHO DECIDES?

Skandia's experiences illustrate that it is, of course, not unproblematic to arrive at scorecards or strategy maps. In this chapter we have more or less assumed that when managers or employees have come together to agree on and model their strategies, and everyone has shared their insights, the new strategy will emerge by itself. This is obviously not always true:

- There are risky choices to be made. We talked of 'strategic betting', and it will be the CEO, unit manager, or sometimes the board that decides on these. How large an exposure to risk is right for this company?
- There will be assumptions to be made about external and internal conditions and events. As in any planning, managers will need to decide whom they believe in terms of customer spending, dollar rates, etc.
- There may be an element of 'gaming'. Targets involve deciding on ambition levels. We saw in Chapter 3 that employees in Skandia seem to have a lot of influence on this. In more traditional corporations, these may be set as tough benchmarks from above, inviting tactical behaviour.

In making these choices, we have stressed the use of facts. The process should take advantage of all available knowledge in the organization. In our experience, this is one of the benefits from working with strategy maps and scorecards: employees start to understand the 'big picture', and it turns out that they have many insights and ideas – for instance about customers and potential improvements in processes – that were unknown to management.[36] This has clear connections with how scorecards are used for dialogues throughout the organization, which will be discussed in Chapter 7.

RECOMMENDATIONS AND IMPLICATIONS

We have discussed strategy maps, a method for visualizing the intended strategic logic which we find very useful. Most of our cases use various types of 'grids' as in Figure 2.4 rather than strategy maps, but we find that drawing the connections in a map adds to understanding and makes for more productive discussions. Either maps are drawn, or discussions take place using other ways to illustrate strategies and link objectives. Whichever method is adopted, we believe the following should be kept in mind:

- The group of people who should contribute their views of strategy may be fairly large. As we discuss more in Chapter 10, to get a coherent set of scorecards for a larger organization it may be necessary to start at the top. But, even so, we advise that people on all levels should get invited into discussing their unit's strategy maps, and we have found the tool easy to understand for almost everyone.

- One purpose of such maps, which we stated at the beginning of this chapter, was that the completed map can be used to communicate strategies and their inherent logic: 'Why we believe we will succeed.' This will work only if the map is kept simple, and the terms used for objectives, etc. are easy to remember. We do not believe that our cases, nor our textbook examples, are exemplary in this regard, but it is important to strive for this goal.

- A map is a collection of cause-and-effect linkages. These 'if-then' statements are hypotheses about how the strategies of the organization will play out in reality. Some of them will be based on experience and facts, while others will be 'strategic bets' about customer tastes, achieveable internal efficiencies, etc.

- Modelling strategy in this way can be seen as a primitive form of system dynamics, and such models might be considered as an aid. However, as in the Skandia case, it is the discussions rather than the precision in the models that matters.

- Strategic themes may be useful in identifying different 'paths' through strategy maps, and in communicating to other parts of a corporation the major strategies that should be pursued by everyone.

- The strategic objectives exhibited in a strategy map need to be developed into metrics and action plans. We have not discussed this extensively, since it is described in *Performance Drivers* and elsewhere. It is, however, vital that metrics are balanced in the sense that they 'cover' the most important parts of the strategy map. Both leading and lagging indicators (drivers and outcomes) need to be included.

We often find that a valuable role for us as consultants, or for in-house process moderators, is to assist in challenging and simplifying cause–effect patterns, to help identify strategic themes, and to put names on objectives and success factors. It is somewhat similar to translating a poem from a remote language like Chinese. To understand the meaning of the poem you need a good understanding of Chinese. But this is usually not enough for rewriting it into an English poem. This requires the assistance of a poet who is highly skilled in English. He may not understand much Chinese but should be skilled at creating a memorable English text. In a similar way, managers discussing their strategic logic may not be able to express it in the most communicative way. The process of formulating scorecards or strategy maps often benefits from having an experienced scorecard process leader – an in-house expert or an outside consultant. But managers must be able themselves to arrive at a good strategy – no consultant can provide this for them.

Using Scorecards to Boost a Strategy-Grounded Dialogue

7

Scorecards should be used on various levels in the organization to enable strategic discussions to take place between different stakeholders. Such discussions, of course, take place within the management team, but should also be extended to strategy-grounded discussions between management and employees, as well as between management and other units in the organization and superior management. In what follows, we elaborate on the different participants in these 'dialogues'. Ordered sequentially, we also describe how the intentions in the strategy maps can be covered in these dialogues, how targets and outcome can be discussed, as well as how these discussions contribute to realizing the intended strategy.

- Discussing the strategy map
- Validating the conjectured links
- Setting targets together
- Analysing results
- Using outcome metrics to spur action

But first, we turn to the different dialogues that may take place in the organization – between different stakeholders at different organizational levels.

A MULTITUDE OF DIALOGUES

If scorecards are to play an important role throughout the organization, then they must be discussed and embraced by all employees. Preferably, the scorecards should not only be used within the management team, but also in every discussion in the organization on strategic intentions and past achievements. Figure 7.1 addresses some of the potential dialogues that the scorecards may stimulate, illustrated from a management perspective.

Addressing dialogues from a management perspective also points up management's responsibility in making the scorecards actionable. Unless management ensures that the scorecards are given due consideration in its work, it is unlikely that the concept will diffuse into the organization.

Dialogues within the management team

Even though scorecards should be used to keep all employees in the organization up to date on the organization's ambitions and achievements, utilization should start within the management team. Unless the managers relate to the scorecard as the natural planning and evaluation tool, it is unlikely that the scorecard(s) will gain any credibility among the employees in the organization.

In previous books we have described how KappAhl, a Swedish retail store, implemented scorecards. To signal the importance of the scorecards in the management processes, the CEO stated, 'Scorecards should not be put on management's agenda. Scorecards should be management's agenda.'

Hence, the management agenda should be organized along the perspectives in the scorecard, making sure that the relevant aspects of the business receive due consideration during the meetings. Using scorecards in these discussions will make sure that the organization's vision and its strategic goals will be 'kept alive', since they are continuously discussed by the management team.[37] Evaluating performance according to the differ-

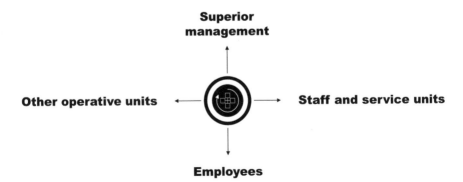

Figure 7.1 Using scorecards in multiple dialogues throughout the company.

ent metrics in the scorecard also allows the management team to assess whether or not they are realizing the intended strategy.

In some organizations, the management team has decided to allocate the responsibility for the different perspectives to respective functional stakeholders in the group, such that the sales and marketing manager is responsible for the customer perspective, the administrative manager is responsible for internal processes, the CFO for the financial perspective and the R&D or HR manager for the learning and growth perspective. In our opinion, this is contradictory to the purpose of the scorecard. Rather than isolating the responsibilities – treating them as independent entities – we believe that the scorecard should be considered a shared responsibility for the management team as a whole. Regardless of functional background, all members in the management team must engage in the discussion on customer expectations, internal efficiencies, future investments, and financial results.

Dialogues between management and superior managers

Management is always accountable to some superior body in the organization. If the unit is a separate company, then the CEO and the management team report to a board and if the unit is a department within a larger organization, then it reports to the next management level. Whichever it is, the management team can rely on its scorecard in its dialogue with its superior managers. In BA, for example, the manager at Heathrow voluntarily uses his scorecard when he discusses the unit's intentions and achievements with his boss.

BA Heathrow

The manager at BA's operation at Heathrow reports to the manager of Customer Service and Operations in BA. All managers who report to the manager of Customer Service and Operations meet once a month. In advance of these management meetings each separate unit submits a performance report. While all other members in the management team submit a typical financial report, the manager at Heathrow has chosen to submit his scorecard to his manager. In the scorecard he points out the unit's spotlight areas – i.e. where improvements are required – to inform his boss about the state of the operation and maybe get some suggestions from his fellow managers. The Customer Service and Operations manager at BA has

not asked the manager at Heathrow to produce this kind of performance
report. The manager at Heathrow does it because he thinks it is the best way
to inform his superior about his unit's performance.

When managers at different levels in the organization use scorecards to
discuss performance, it is important to make sure that the scorecards do not
develop into inspection devices. Rather, the manager should feel that the
scorecard presents a valid image of his or her business – for better or for
worse – much in the same way as the manager at BA uses his scorecard to
inform his superior about aspirations and performance. If, on the other
hand, the scorecard turns into an inspection device, then it is likely that
those who are 'described' in the scorecard will try to make the scorecard
look as favourable as possible, instead of presenting the actual achievements or interesting challenges. The only way to ensure that the subordinate managers perceive the scorecards as 'their' description of their
performance is to encourage them to develop the scorecard and the strategy
maps themselves. If, instead, someone else has developed the scorecard –
somewhere else in the organization – then it will probably not be regarded
as a valid representation of what is important in the business. And the unit
managers will not pay any attention to the scorecard.

Dialogues between management and other units in the organization

Typically, we have seen how scorecards and strategy maps have been used
to discuss ambitions and responsibilities in the organization's hierarchical
dimension. As we saw in the Skandia case, senior management has encouraged unit managers to describe how their business logic and vision relate to
the corporate vision. In the Skandia case, for example, the departments
spent numerous days in workshops deriving their vision and strategy from
the corporate strategy. Then they had to present their intentions for
management.

Lately, however, we have also seen how scorecards have been used to
coordinate relationships between units on the same hierarchical level in an
organization, in the business processes or supply chains. In such horizontal
dialogues, all units that participate in the process or supply chain come
together and define a shared scorecard, which addresses the ambitions of
the process, transcending the responsibilities of the functional units (cf.
Chapter 9). By setting targets for the whole process, the units focus on their

joint value creation, rather than narrowing their attention to their functional responsibilities. Just monitoring process performance and comparing results with targets will create a better understanding of the company's value creation, and contribute to more aligned processes.

An even more formalized utilization of scorecards, or at least of multidimensional contracting, is the use of SLAs in many organizations. Such contracts may be designed and agreed upon between internal providers of different services (usually internal support services such as IT, HR, finance, legal) and the units relying on them. Whereas the examples above aimed at creating a shared understanding of the business processes in general (reaching alignment through extended understanding of the process), SLAs are formalized contracts that define rights and responsibilities in a multidimensional structure. Typically, the contracts also indicate how to handle deviation from targets, i.e. how the internal service provider will be rewarded if it exceeds the expectation or how it will be punished if it fails to deliver what it has promised.

Nordea

To provide a clear understanding of the services to be provided by internal service providers, such as IT, or HR, to service receivers (mainly the business areas), SLAs have been introduced that consist of four key components:

- Clear definitions of the scope of services provided.
- Defined measures in order to track quality, costs, content, and timeliness of services delivered.
- A governance structure establishing decision processes and clear responsibilities.
- A structured process for building and maintaining the SLAs.

Dialogues between management and employees

Unless the scorecards are used and discussed by the management team they will not make any difference in the organization. Of course, management can restrict its use of scorecards to serve only as an extended performance report, which it can consult (and discuss with its superiors). However, the aspirations captured in the strategy maps and the need for action (indicated when the results deviate from targets) will not reach the employees – those who, in their daily decision making, determine whether or not the organization realizes its intended strategy.

Hence, we argue that the most important dialogue regarding scorecards is when the employees are invited to take part in the creation of the strategy map, when they understand and subscribe to the targets, and when they get to know the results compared with the goals. And, maybe most important, when they can take action if they see that the intended strategy is not materializing.

Scorecards may be used by management to discuss intentions and results with its superiors, and scorecards may be used to align the units' efforts with other units in the organization, but if management does not use the scorecards to engage all employees in a continuous discussion on aspirations and achievements, then the scorecards are not likely to yield any significant results. Rather, the scorecard may grow into a performance measurement system, with little significance to the employees and on what they decide to focus their attention, which was apparent in the Skandia case:

Skandia

The group Navigator doesn't have any function. I can't relate to it. It has been developed by our group manager and I don't even understand what's in it. (Employee, Skandia Connection)

The current Navigator doesn't make sense. We haven't been involved in the process and therefore the variables in it don't have any practical implications for us. We must be involved in the process to be able to act accordingly. (Employee, Skandia Connection)

If the scorecards are intended to engage all employees in the continuous development of the business – not just the management team – then we believe that the employees must be invited to take part in the development of the strategy maps as well as in the analytical effort to understand why and how performance deviates from targets.

THE DIALOGUE PROCESS

We regard all four dialogues mentioned above as important, but based on the observations in the Skandia case, it is apparent that the way scorecards are discussed and used among the employees will influence whether or not the organization will succeed in its scorecard effort. Still, we find it generally interesting to discuss how management shall use scorecards in the dialogue throughout the company – with its superiors as well as with other peer units in the organization. However, much of what we say below may be more relevant when engaging all employees in a strategic dialogue about the organization's future and its achievements.

Discussing the strategy map

The strategy map is the foundation for the scorecard, and it is usually developed in the early phases of a BSC project. The project group typically consists of different stakeholders from different parts of the organization. Even though the group consists of representatives from different units, all employees in the organization rarely take part in the final design of the map (they may participate in different workshops along the project, but the map is typically finalized by a small group). Therefore, it is important to introduce the final strategy map to the organization and explain the logic behind it, i.e. the links between the components in the different perspectives.

Sometimes the employees are fooled by the simplicity of the model – that the links and relationships seem trivial and self-evident. But, as important as the components that are in the map are the components that have been left out. Michel Porter has said that strategy is 'management of trade-offs',[38] i.e. that the strength of the strategy is defined by its capacity to reject alternative courses of action. In the same way, a good strategy map both describes the relationships that the organization believes in, and indicates what businesses the organization should not be in. Compare, for example, Oriflame's decision to position itself as a cosmetics company selling direct. Over the years they have had many opportunities to bypass their sales organization – directly over the net or via other outlets – but they have always rejected these opportunities because it lies outside their business model. Hence, the strategy map and the vision statement have guided Oriflame in deciding, for example, what distribution channels to use.

Oriflame

The scorecards in Oriflame have initially been used as a means of interaction between corporate head office and local sales organizations (in each country). The country managers have used the strategy maps to illustrate how they plan to reach their goals. And the strategy documents have included presentations on more strategic initiatives, as well as the financial goals for the coming year.

The country managers spent the summer of 2001 designing their strategy maps to present them to the regional directors during the extended financial forecast review in the autumn. The year 2001 was, however, the first year that the country managers had been asked to present their ambitions in this format. Since no time series or measurement data existed, it was somewhat difficult to discuss what the appropriate targets should be. However, an important decision was made regarding the metrics and the targets. Rather than perceiving the targets as forecasts or estimates, they would serve as a level of ambition. The targets were set to serve as goals, which the organization would try to reach.

Since the purpose of the targets is not to be forecasts, there is no need to change/update them when circumstances change. The target values will be kept, even if it becomes obvious that they will not be met. They can, however, be changed under exceptional circumstances. As such, they will show what the ambition was for the period, rather than what the result was expected to be. One of the problems with the former budget process was that it was supposed to be an estimate of future results, and when it was apparent that circumstances had changed, the budget also needed to be changed. This is not the case in Oriflame's utilization of targets in their BSCs.

The scorecards and the strategy maps are mainly used as *ex ante* instruments to discuss future directions between corporate management and the management team in each country. The continuous monitoring and evaluation of performance is, on the other hand, a responsibility of the country manager.

The initial dialogue about the strategy map and the scorecard most often resembles education rather than reflection. The project team typically explains the map by telling the story: this is how we believe we will be successful. The aggregate strategy map indicates the aspirations of the whole company, which serves as a common denominator for future development of local strategy maps and scorecards.

Helsingborg

From the beginning, the ambition with the BSC work in Helsingborg has been that everyone in the organization must be involved in the work. This is seen as the only way to improve communication in the organization and to enable change. A few key words were defined as crucial to enable everyone to be involved. These words were dialogue, engagement, understanding, openness, and management. A subnurse and a member of the city council should have the same information about city services.

The most important success factor of these words has been to have a continuous dialogue throughout the organization. To make a scorecard natural for the employees, they need continuously to hear about it and see it. The BSC is therefore constantly put on the agenda during meetings. The presentations of the tool are also ensured to be short and simple. It should be easy to get an overview of what is going on in the organization.

Indices and other measures have to be simple, but not over-simplified, in order to be understandable both for employees and citizens. They also have to be rather few. There will always be other, more detailed measures taken which will remain outside the scorecards. There are no formal requirements about how measures are to be taken, except that, where possible, they should be supported by IT systems. In some cases, employees who are present during the service process being studied may even be asked to rate the experience as participators.

However, it is not the BSC model itself that is considered important. It is the process during which it is developed. As many people as possible should be involved in developing a scorecard to reach acceptance throughout the organization. Everyone should be able to make his or her voice heard. The BSC should thereby become part of a democratic organization. Any person who holds a political office on a part-time basis should be able to understand and accept a scorecard as a valuable and valid description of a city department's performance after discussing it for 30 minutes with the civil servants in charge of it.

Also, in the Skandia case it was obvious that the employees must participate in the development of the strategy map as well as the scorecard from the beginning. Otherwise, the maps and the metrics will not have any apparent meaning for the employees:

Skandia

Finally I understand why I should use the Navigator. Before, someone else has just put numbers into the focus areas and we have seen how they change, but never understood why. I'm glad to be able to be in the discussion from the beginning (Employee, Telephone Support).

I agree with [previous employee]. It is really important to follow the process from the beginning. Otherwise, everyone sits there with his or her own definitions and don't understand what the others are saying. How do we integrate newcomers in this process? We can't go through this every time someone is recruited (Employee, Telephone Support).

Validating the conjectured links

The strategy map is the organization's bet on the future. The links must therefore be seen as hypotheses, rather than indisputable facts. Over time, however, as the scorecard is used, some links will emerge as more robust than others. They might even prove to be statistically valid, whereas others will remain mere speculations – hence they should rather be regarded as strategic investments the company is making because it believes they will yield positive results in the future.

It is important that all members in the organization discuss the relationships in the strategy map. The more robust a specific relationship, the more management can turn its attention to the leading indicators rather than their financial effects. When management tries to control the leading indicators, they may stand a better chance of affecting the lagging results. Managing leading indicators means that they are regarded as equally important as the lagging results, if not even more important. Incentives may, for example, be tied to the leading indicators rather than their lagging outcome. Similarly, the leading indicators should attract considerable attention in the business planning process, for example, when setting targets or when deciding on future investments.

Weaker links, on the other hand, should instead be observed and analysed to see whether they carry any predicative value. Instead of controlling these dimensions, they may be used as information providers, signalling trends and possible changes in the environment. When the scorecard is discussed and scrutinized in the monthly meeting, these relationships (and their indicators) must only be kept as long as they are believed to illuminate some important aspect of the operation. If they do not pass this test, they should rapidly be removed from the map, so that the map always represents the company's current knowledge about the logic of their operation.

Setting targets together

The way an organization structures the target-setting exercise reveals much about its approach to scorecards. If targets are set by a small group of scorecard specialists or controllers – or even by managers on the level above the one which the scorecard covers – then the scorecard is likely to be viewed as a surveillance mechanism. Under such circumstances, it is often in the interest of the controlled unit to be able to beat the targets, hence it will try to negotiate targets to be as low as possible. Target setting thus becomes a negotiation process between superior and subordinate units, with an apparent risk that the parties kick off the process with hidden agendas. If, on the other hand, the scorecards are primarily used by management in the unit they describe, then it is much more likely that the targets will serve as ambitious goals – as levels of ambition – that will not be trivial to meet. These ambitious targets will serve as challenges that all members in the organization will have to stretch to reach.

Skandia

In the Skandia case presented earlier in this book this is exemplified, since the unit decided to set the target to answer 4000 incoming calls. This was not a forecast, since the unit did not expect to receive more than some 3000 calls at the time. Instead, the target embedded an ambition deliberately to increase the volume of incoming calls. In a different situation, if targets were set by the superior level, then we could expect the subordinate unit to defend existing volumes (equivalent to the 3000 calls), refusing to take on a heavier burden.

When setting targets for a scorecard, much can be learned from the traditional literature on budgeting. For some years now, budgets have been widely criticized in Sweden and elsewhere, because they are rarely accurate, because the process is very resource consuming and because they tend to foster a bureaucratic atmosphere in the company. To some extent we agree with the critics – that the quality of many budgets is not as good as it could be. But we do not agree with some authors' suggestion to quit budgeting. Rather, we find that the most successful companies we know of have elaborate 'budgeting' and planning processes that help them to stay on top of their future.[39] Not only do these budgets help the companies to prepare for the future (for the different possible futures that may materialize) but also to challenge every unit in the organization to perform at its peak capacity.

Jönköping

The county council of Jönköping has developed a connection between the planning processes and the follow-up processes. The yearly planning process in each unit is seen as a long-term strategic plan for what the unit wants to achieve. On the administrative level the budget is produced on the basis of the overall scorecards. Budgets are then communicated to management and down to the different departments in the administrative unit.

At management level, the budgets are collected and summarized. Being a politically controlled organization, the budget needs to be approved by the politicians before the organization can act upon it. An official document is therefore created, making it accessible to all interested parties.

> After the budgets have been set, approved, and made official they become operational in the BSC format. Concrete plans are made on how to reach the goals within the different perspectives. Targets are set and communicated through another official document. The planning reports are then followed up three times a year to ensure that the organization is on track towards its goals. If a unit or clinic is off target they have to take action. The administrative unit continuously checks what efforts are made to improve the situation.

Budgeting literature usually simplifies the different approaches to budgeting as either top-down or bottom-up. The top-down approach is most often used as a mechanism to allocate quantified responsibilities to sub-units, based on an overall goal.

Retail company

In a client company, one goal in the scorecard was the number of goods sold. The target for the whole organization was calculated as a market-share percentage multiplied by the industry forecast for the total volume of sold goods in the market. Market share times estimated number of sold goods equalled the company's target (number of sold goods). This aggregate sum was then split (top-down) among the sales units, in proportion to the size of each district, compared with the whole market (calculated as the number of citizens in the district compared with the number of citizens in the country). From the sales units' point of view the target was given, based on a numerical equation. This equation did not take into account any specifics of the districts. Some units hence met their targets without any difficulties, whereas others had no chance of reaching them.

Only if common metrics are used across hierarchical levels is it possible to define aggregate goals that can be broken down throughout the organization. If, on the other hand, unit-specific metrics are used, targets are most likely set in a bottom-up fashion, since it requires deep understanding of the local circumstances. Setting targets from bottom and up also embeds some challenges, especially during the first year when the scorecard is 'new', when there are no past statistics to draw from. 'Number of customer visits', for example, is often a leading indicator in the customer perspective – but what would be the appropriate level? A typical approach is to run the first year without targets, just to monitor the outcome. The first year's result then serves as the basis for the next period's target.

One organization we know has implemented a common scorecard for all their units, and also developed a web-based scorecard system that allows the managers to see the outcome for the best dealer in the network for each metric. Since most metrics are normalized, the figures can serve as best-practice benchmarks within the organization. Hence, any manager can browse through the system to find the best outcome for each metric, and use this as a starting point when establishing his own targets: whether to aim higher than the best unit in the organization or to choose a more moderate target. The strength of the best-practice metrics, as opposed to those derived from guesswork, is that they are true and have actually been reached by another unit.

In our experience, the bottom-up target-setting approach is much more effective in creating commitment for the targets than the top-down alternative. If someone else sets the targets, then it is possible that deviation from the plan may be referred to the level of the targets, rather than the unit's actual performance. Instead, we find the most intriguing scorecards, those that contain targets that have been set through a collective bottom-up process where the targets are perceived as goals to stretch for by the employees.

BA Heathrow

Half of the metrics are robust over time – as indicators that the unit will always have to follow. The other half, however, are metrics that vary over time to focus management's attention on issues that have to be improved. As soon as one of these issues is under control, 'the spotlight indicator' is changed for a new indicator that grasps another area of interest.

Performance is not just monitored *ex post* – goals are also set for each metric. The goals are not, however, considered to be forecasts or estimates; what the unit is expected to reach. The goals are set as targets to stretch for. As one example, the manager mentions a failure-rate target that is set to 65 units per 1000. If the goal were to be set according to the expected outcome, then the level would be around 85. The manager's opinion is, however, that the target must signal the level of ambition. In this particular case, it has also been proved that it is realistic to reach as low as 65 on a yearly basis. The best outcome for a single day has been as low as 35, so 65 is not impossible. Hence, targets are set to stretch for, not to be reached without effort.

The target-setting exercise does not need to be very extensive or complicated. It is normally enough to gather the employees for a day or so to discuss the ambitions for the coming year. The process should start with some brief orientation on past performance, the general goals for the company, some information on which links in the scorecard are proven and which are still hypothetical, etc. The team may then break up into smaller groups and discuss the dynamics in the strategy map, and estimate what to aim for in each perspective, for each metric. The groups may then meet in a plenary session again, comparing each group's proposition. Following on from this, the team together may define appropriate targets based on the collective knowledge in the room.

Ericsson Enterprise

An interesting illustration of a BSC planning process is provided by Ericsson Enterprise. Scorecard work is closely linked with other plans and reports – see Figure 7.2, 'Business planning and performance management'. The scorecard for Enterprise is used to set one-year targets, based on longer-term plans.

In Figure 7.3 the seven units within Enterprise are shown as horizontal bars, and the process between them over time is indicated as they prepared the scorecard and goals for 2002.

The management team ('Enterprise MT' in the figure) held three four-hour-long scorecard meetings. Input for the initial one on 18 October came from preliminary financial goals and the strategic planning that had taken place

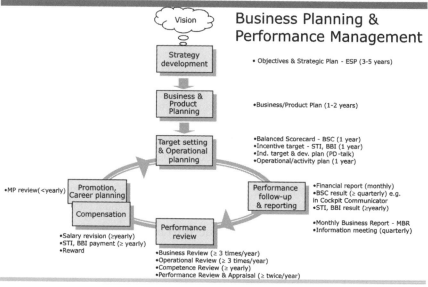

Figure 7.2 Ericsson Enterprise's business planning and performance management. Reproduced by permission of Ericsson Enterprises AB.

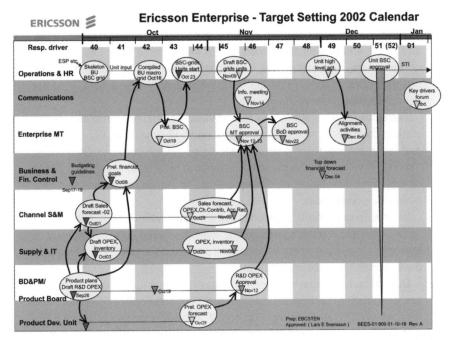

Figure 7.3 Ericsson Enterprise's target setting calendar. Reproduced by permission of Ericsson Enterprise AB.

during the spring. From the latter an extract was made which determined the overarching ambitions for Ericsson Enterprise.

The financial goals were determined during weeks 40 and 41. This was a traditional budgeting type of exercise, where sales targets and product plans were reconciled. During the 18 October meeting, an important ambition was to use scorecards to achieve a deeper common understanding of the situation.

The meeting consisted of the seven unit heads – four operating units and three staff – plus the managing director. In addition, two people representing the scorecard process were invited to guide the process. One of these, Sten Olsson, had been heading Enterprise's scorecard work since its inception. The other, Kerstin Lilje-brinck had a background in executive development and HR and took an interest in how scorecards could be used to clarify intentions. During this first scorecard meeting, strategic goals and the 'wanted position' for Enterprise in each of Ericsson's five scorecard perspectives were discussed, as were KSFs. The intention had been to cover also KPIs, but the time was not sufficient.

The discussion was structured through use of 'post-it' notes. Goals and KSFs that were similar were merged, and the number of items gradually reduced through voting about what should remain as part of Enterprise's scorecard. In this way, the participants in the meeting also came to act more as a team, and less as spokespersons for their units. If some item received only one vote, then that person was asked if he could live without that item being included. In some cases that led to the inclusion of items which were not considered important by the majority.

The final number of KSFs was 16, and these were numbered to provide the starting-point for the next scorecard meeting on 13 November. For each KSF, one in the management team was appointed 'driver' (also see Chapter 8). The intention was that this person, in addition to his duties as unit head, would devote particular attention to Enterprise's performance concerning that KSF during the coming year.

In the following weeks, most units started work on their own scorecards. In some, Sten and Kerstin contributed facilitation, whereas others managed at their own. The requirement was that unit scorecards should be approved by the Enterprise head before Christmas.

During the November management meeting and a further one in December, each lasting four hours and assisted by Sten and Kerstin, agreement was reached on KPIs and strategic actions. These were derived for each KSF, and ultimately there were between one and seven actions linked to each KSF (also see Chapter 9). In Figure 2.4 we provided a summary of the entire scorecard grid.

Analysing results

The targets in the scorecard should be perceived as goals – not forecasts. Using this approach, it is obvious that some outcome measures will deviate from their targets. And this is not alarming. On the contrary, deviation is probably more common than not. And deviation should be regarded as a trigger for action.

Management's responsibility is to spot these deviations and analyse why they occur – both when the result is better than anticipated and when it is worse. The simplest way to do this is to monitor performance according to each metric separately. This evaluation should be carried out instantly when the monthly (or any other period) scorecard is presented. Since targets have been set, it will be obvious whether or not performance has been on a par with expectations. If not, the management should spend some time discussing why the outcome has deviated from expectations. Sometimes, the analysis is simple and it is easy to understand why the deviation has occurred, and no action is needed. At other times, a problem may be identified and the deviation should hence trigger some action. Under yet other circumstances, it may be difficult to understand the reasons behind a certain value, which calls for some deeper analysis. Sometimes, the management team will have allocated the responsibility for specific metrics to different persons in the group (in Ericsson they refer to this as KPI drivers, see Chapter 8), and then it is usually up to that person to investigate the reason for the deviation and come back to the management team with a suggestion on what to do.

The second order of analysis is more complex and deals with the underlying design of the scorecard and the strategy map. A typical trigger for such an analysis might be that the results are satisfying for a number of leading indicators, but no visible effects can be seen in the connected lagging indicators. If this is the case, then the outcome signals that the strategy map (the links between the metrics in the scorecard) may need revision. If the assumed links between means and ends do not seem to work, then the model must be adjusted for these inconsistencies.

A metric does not embed any meaning in itself. It does not offer any insight into the specific matter unless the receiver is educated to understand the metric, and perhaps also knows something about the procedures required to provide information for the metric. We have seen many examples where even the 'simplest' metric has proved to be more ambiguous than anyone could imagine. One company we worked with, for example, used *delivery precision* as an important indicator. When studying how this metric was used in different parts of the organization, the definition of the metric and how it was measured varied a great deal. These emerging differences not only prevented comparison between units, but also eroded the trust in the metric, '*Unless it is clear what the metric means, why should we bother to study it at all?*'

BA Heathrow
Scorecards constitute BA Heathrow's management control system. They are used to set targets for the coming year; they are used to evaluate performance; and they are used to focus the management team's discussion on what needs to be done to develop the operation.

Their use is encouraged by the manager's interest in scorecards. He brought the concept into the organization, and he expects the unit managers to inform him about their performance, based on what they have defined as important in their scorecards. In the beginning there was a slight tendency in the organization to hide metrics that did not indicate successful performance. The manager has, however, made an effort to encourage the unit managers to show metrics that are possible to improve (i.e. do not look too favourable). Hence, it has become more important to show indicators that have not reached their targets. Instead of hiding performance, the scorecards have been used to highlight areas that need further attention. In the scorecard, these areas are labelled 'spotlights' – areas that are of special interest, which the management team should spend some time discussing in order to work out ideas as to how to improve the operation.

The scorecards are used as the agenda for the monthly management meetings. In advance of the meeting, each scorecard is circulated to the respective unit manager who is asked to comment on the report. The comments are then included in the scorecard, and all scorecards are compiled in a binder, which is submitted to all members in the management team some days before the management meeting. During the meeting, each unit gets some 20-30 minutes to comment on past performance and describe future plans. Creative discussion is encouraged where the members can give each other feedback and suggestions on initiatives.

In addition to the monthly compilation of metrics, some key indicators are measured on a continuous basis and communicated instantaneously throughout the organization. 'On-time departure' is, for example, an important indicator, and its outcome is continuously displayed on internal screens in the office buildings.

The scorecard has also been used to indicate BA's intentions on a longitudinal basis. All strategic investments have been compiled on one page and related to the metrics in the scorecard. In the left-most column, the metrics in the scorecard are listed. Next to the measures, the targets for the coming five years are listed (one column per year). On the other half of the page, all strategic initiatives are listed in columns, where the projects are grouped into programmes. Using this one page, it is possible for the manager to ensure that all programmes, and all separate projects (that constitute the programmes), add up to the dimensions that have been defined in the scorecard. Unless a project, or a programme for that matter, obviously adds up to all the perspectives in the scorecard (or adds up fundamentally to a specific perspective), it is not apparent that it is worth investing scarce resources in that particular effort.

Hence, the manager at BA Heathrow uses scorecards both on a monthly basis to ensure that the unit is performing satisfactorily, and also as a strategic tool to communicate the long-term goals as well as the strategic initiatives taken to reach these goals.

SAS

At the SAS Group, scorecards are sure to receive group management attention, since they are compact and easy to understand. They play an important role in the assessment of each company. The format is shown in Figure 7.4.

To instil some meaning into the measures, we believe that the metrics must be used in the company's daily discourse. Differently from the metrics in the external financial reporting, these internal metrics do not have to follow any externally standardized format. The purpose of the scorecard is, as mentioned, to ensure that the intended strategy is realized, thus the metrics should be designed to fit the scorecard's purpose within the organization, not to present a standardized picture of the operation externally.

Lund HLC

Scorecard implementation led to discussions about financial outcomes among the employees who previously had been more or less unaware of these. These discussions immediately led to some cost reductions. 'We were not aware of how much our ward cost – becoming aware of it made us think about all the money we were spending.' This was seen as somewhat paradoxical. Scorecards were introduced because traditional financial measures were seen as less relevant. But one effect was an increased attention to finances! On the other hand, it can be seen as proof that links are perceived between the perspectives in the scorecard, although they have not been stressed or documented in a formal way.

Seeing the positive changes at the centre has also had an effect on things such as employee turnover. More people tend to stay in the organization – the turnover has decreased by 38%. The number of sickleaves has also decreased, which is seen as a positive outcome of the work that has been done with the BSC. This is also obvious when comparing the employee survey from autumn 2001 with the survey from spring 2000. It clearly indicates improved management and stimulation among the employees.

Another positive outcome of the discussions around the scorecards was an increased cooperation across borders. The employees see the need, or opportunities, to improve their performance by talking to others at the centre – not just those on their own ward. The natural meetings between the employees have thus increased and will hopefully have further positive effects.

The principal occasion on which to discuss performance according to the scorecard is the monthly company or group meetings. By following the scorecard's structure during these meetings, the perspectives as well as

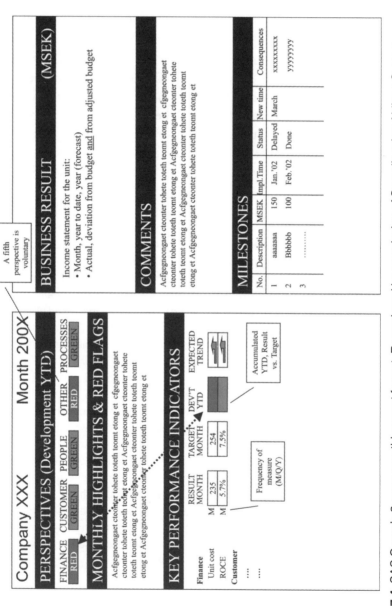

Figure 7.4 SAS Group's 2-page monthly report format. Reproduced by permission of Scandinavian Airlines System.

metrics gain credibility. Relying on the structure in the scorecard also enables management to show the continuity of the business, since it may be proved that initiatives taken in the *today*- and *tomorrow*-perspectives, yield results in *yesterday*'s financial perspective. As mentioned earlier, the outcome in the scorecard boosts a discussion in the meeting room, where some people try to explain why one specific metric shows performance below target while some others show better results than anticipated. When the same metrics are used in different units in the company, most employees will also be curious to know how their unit performs relative to those of their peer groups in the organization.

In addition to the discussions in the monthly company meetings, information about performance must also be available over the intranet. It is, however, important to remember that this type of performance statistic is seldom a blockbuster on the corporate intranet. Therefore, management has to promote and market the information in such a way that the members in the organization gradually acquire an interest in it. One obvious way of doing this is to connect the incentive systems to the scorecard. We, however, do not believe that the organization must 'bribe' the employees to develop an interest in the performance indicators. Just by paying attention to the scorecard and illustrating its 'predictive' capability, most employees will eventually turn to this section on the intranet just out of curiosity.

In organizations that use common metrics across several units, the competitive spirit may also help to fuel an interest in the outcome. In some organizations, the race itself has been catalyst enough, whereas others have introduced inexpensive funny games such as pizza-for-all if the unit exceeds past performance or beats its peers on a selected number of indicators.

Using outcome metrics to spur action

At the end of each period (usually once a month or every quarter) the scorecard should be presented to the organization. Preferably this presentation should be made during the monthly company or group meeting. If the company or unit does not arrange such meetings on a regular basis, then the scorecard project could be a suitable reason to establish such a recurring event.

It is not only the comparison between outcome and target that may fuel a discussion on improvements. One retailer we worked with implemented a common scorecard throughout the organization. On the intranet, each unit could see their performance in total. In the graphical presentation of each metric, it was also possible to monitor the unit's development over time and compared with the target, as well as compared with the country average and with the best unit in the organization. Even if the unit in question exceeded its target, the comparison between units could fuel a creative discussion: 'How is it possible that the best unit sells 300 products per employee, while we are only delivering 230? We have to find out what they are doing, and see if that is applicable in our region as well!' The presentation of performance during these monthly meetings thus created a discussion on what could be done to improve the business as a result of the comparison between outcome and target, as well as between the unit's results and the results of the best unit in the organization.

Ericsson Enterprise

During 2002, unit performance in Ericsson Enterprise has been presented on the intranet for every employee to see, at quarterly information meetings for all employees, and in the monthly business reports. It has also been followed up regularly in each of the management teams. At Enterprise level the intention was to do this quarterly, but in practice, however, this performance review has been done monthly on request by the Enterprise head. In addition to presenting their own unit's performance, the team members have also had to present Enterprise's performance concerning the KSF for which they are the 'driver' – its status and how its strategic actions are shaping up. They have also had to present forecasts, and in preparing for this they have acted as the managing director's right hand with a special responsibility for this factor. For this report, a new appendix to the monthly report has been added. Focus during the monthly reviews has been on strategic actions, since not all metrics are measured every month. (This was also a reason why it was intended originally to discuss the scorecards only quarterly.)

When the scorecard is presented, some metrics will inevitably attract more attention than others. Typically, measures that are way under the anticipated level will get attention, and almost certainly the group will discuss why the outcome is worse than planned. Suggestions will be brought forth on what could be done to correct the trend. This group-based problem-solving process is a valuable resource for the organization. Among the employees, all the answers the organization could ever ask for can be found. The challenge is to mobilize this creativity and turn it into action – to fuel the organization's continuous development. If, for example, lead time is an important metric in the process perspective, and the outcome for the last period shows poor performance, then the observation will promote reflection. In the meeting, some voices will probably be raised arguing that the poor performance depends on exogenous factors that are out of the company's control – and that the next period's result will get back on track again. Hence, there is no need to intervene. Others will argue that this is an early warning signal that must be taken seriously. Unless action is taken now – immediately – the process will deteriorate, and the internal performance will affect customer satisfaction. Hence, some action must be taken at once.

As mentioned, when an outcome deviates from plan in the scorecard, it inevitably boosts a discussion in the group on why this happened and what can be done to correct it. Companies that manage to capture these suggestions and – more importantly – manage to execute them are more competitive than those who do not. Capturing ideas for improvements is not complicated in principle, but still takes some effort in practice. More than anything, it is a question of discipline and rigour. The creative process is the idea-generation phase, which typically comes as a consequence of the monthly meetings where the scorecard is presented and discussed. Capturing and managing the ideas, on the other hand, just takes some administrative effort systematically to record the ideas and allocate the responsibility to execute the initiatives.

BA Heathrow

In addition to the separate scorecards in BA's different operations at Heathrow, the performance report binder also includes to-do items decided on at prior meetings. These activities are compiled on the first pages in the binder so that the group can browse through them at the beginning of the meeting and inform each other on what has happened since the last meeting. When an item is completed it is removed from the list, so the list will only contain items in progress.

Suggestions for improvements, which are generated as a result of the outcome in the scorecard, focus on a specific perspective or even a specific metric. For every action that is taken, a review should be made after the action is completed. This is an important characteristic of a learning organization – to learn from its own actions and reflect on its past performance. If an activity is carried out for a particular reason, it is important to verify whether or not that activity has yielded the intended results. Such reviews can, of course, be manually assured, but it eases the administrative burden to have them implemented in the BSC software (this will be further elaborated in Chapter 11). When an activity has been completed, a date can be set when the review will be performed and the system will automatically check whether the performance has improved (according to the metric) or not.

TAKING SCORECARDS TO THE NEXT LEVEL: WORKING WITH PLAYBOOKS TO RECOGNIZE PATTERNS OF OPPORTUNITY

Companies occasionally face situations that have occurred before, that they should be familiar with, and, more importantly, that they can prepare for. In a football game, the equivalent situation would be the free kick or the corner. Given the specific circumstances – who are playing, where on the field the free kick is ruled, when in the game it is rewarded, etc. – the team has practiced what to do in such a steady state. The team has practised several alternative tactics to use and all the players know exactly what their responsibilities are in the given configuration.

As consultants we have helped companies develop such tactics, or 'plays', to take advantage of different recurring patterns in our clients' business environment. These plays are similar to scenarios, but on a narrower level. Whereas scenarios focus on the grand schemes – and are limited in number – the plays focus on the tactical dimension. As such, the play is like a script of proven and tested actions that are known to suit a specific situation. If the environment develops in a certain direction, then the organization can prepare what to do. Thinking ahead like this not only develops the company's ability to execute pre-defined initiatives, but also to accept that the organization's actions should be contingent upon the situations they face. Under certain circumstances, for example, it might be the right tactic to expand the customer base and attract new customers, whereas other circumstances might favour increased customer share (i.e. focusing on the company's share of the customer's purchases, addressing existing customers and expanding the offer to them).

We develop the playbook from a set of macro what-if questions, in a scenario-like approach. Each play, or script, is thus an answer to a specific opportunity or a threat as it would be perceived through the scorecard's lenses. The script contains ideas that the organization has had some time to play around with, before they actually execute them in real life. Discussing these plays in seminars, having them exposed to strategy-hacking sessions, running them through 'quality audits', etc. before they are executed in a real setting, will allow the organization to perform them more efficiently than they otherwise would. Using 'plays' also offers the decision-makers the opportunity to get 'a second opinion' on the initiatives they plan to put into operation. Before a strategic decision is made, the members in the organization can consult the playbook and see what they thought (previously) they would do if a certain situation emerged. The playbook does not offer *the* solution, but rather serves as a memory where potential ideas that have been thought through and 'logically' tested are stored.

A challenge when using a playbook is to recognize the emerging situations in reality. It is one thing to dream up a set of possible scenarios, but it is another to recognize the direction of the development in the environment. Using the playbook, the scenarios that were formed at the beginning of the scorecard project can now be specified into clusters of patterns. All scenarios from the early stages in the project should be analysed and specified into plays, containing both the pattern (which is used to recognize whether a trend is emerging, based on what it would look like in the scorecard) and a suggested script of actions. The playbook thus serves as a corporate memory, reminding the members in the organization about the intellectual capital that was developed during the initial strategy process.

The patterns or the plays will not make any difference unless the members in the organization participate in their development. It is necessary that all employees understand the scorecard and the outcome, and that they participate in the pattern-recognition process. When a pattern emerges, the employees must understand the scorecard so that they see how the circumstances are changing and what actions are needed. It is also important that they participate in the development of the plays, so that they

1. are familiar with the scripts (what to do and why)
2. trust the scripts as such (that they contain a valid set of initiatives)
3. trust the connection (that the play is relevant given the particular circumstances).

RECOMMENDATIONS AND IMPLICATIONS

Making scorecards truly actionable requires attention and interest from employees throughout the company. This requires deliberate attention from management to promote scorecards as the preferred structure, according to which performance is planned and evaluated. Therefore, it is important to:

- Make sure that the management team subscribes to the content of the scorecard and the strategy map. Unless management believe in the scorecard, it will be very difficult to build an interest for the scorecard among the employees.
- Ensure that the scorecard represents the unit's view of their business model, strategies, and success factors. Hence, the scorecard should not be developed by the superior level and forced upon the units.
- Ensure that the scorecard is used to challenge the hypotheses in the strategy map. When the scorecard is provided with performance information, it is possible to analyse whether or not the hypothesized links and relationships in the strategy map are valid.
- Communicate outcome regularly. Unless the scores are communicated, the members in the organization will not know how they have performed. Hence, it is important that the performance information is presented so that the employees can take action when the outcome deviates from the target.

Organizations that manage to keep their employees up to date regarding the strategy map and the scorecard stand a better chance of realizing their intended strategy, because

- The employees become more strategy-minded, since they understand the business model and participate in the evaluation of the drivers and outcomes (leading and lagging indicators).
- The organization becomes more agile since it may seize opportunities or respond to threats before they harm the business.
- The organization becomes less hierarchical as more employees participate in the intellectual effort to analyse cause and effect.

Assigning Roles and Responsibilities for Operating Scorecards

8

ASSIGNING RESPONSIBILITIES FOR YOUR SCORECARD PROJECT

To get a scorecard project going, responsibilities need to be assigned. These should cover a variety of aspects of 'living with scorecards'. Every manager whose unit now has a scorecard will be accountable for using it. Scorecard 'technology' (definitions, formats, timetable, handling of measurements) needs to be the responsibility of someone, usually in the controller's department. Promoting scorecard use and training people will need someone's attention during the first year or two. This responsibility may require a special task-force near top management. If software is introduced, then usually someone in the IS department will be accountable for its functioning. As data is collected about the various metrics, someone should periodically analyse it in order to learn about cause-and-effect relationships – did the patterns play out as expected, or should previous assumptions be reconsidered?

How these responsibilities are identified and allocated will have an impact on the success and cost of a scorecard project. A KSF is that top management is clear about these roles. People to whom they are assigned need to have sufficient knowledge and organizational status. Most of them will not be working full-time on scorecards, and so management has to make sure that the persons involved have enough time and perceive their tasks as important. It may take a long time before the entire organization understands the ideas involved in the concept and how they should enter the daily work of individual employees. During this time, it is of utmost importance for the entire organization to feel that management unreservedly endorses the values, ideas, and management philosophy inherent in the concept. People playing the roles we are discussing here need to act as their missionaries.

Early on, a priority will be to establish participation and communication concerning a company's vision and strategic aims. In most modern companies introducing scorecards, the emphasis is on creating agreement about directions, rather than checking compliance with top management's orders. It is therefore important that a large part of the company participate in the actual process of developing the BSC, a process that begins with the company's comprehensive vision. In this way, the company can reach a consensus on how each individual can help to achieve its strategic objectives. Additionally, much time will be saved later in the process if resources and time are set aside at an early stage to discuss the ideas and involve people. If the concept is improperly applied, then people in the organization will come to regard it as a tool to check on them, rather than as a way to ensure that the company is making progress toward its established goals.

It is also critical that top management is able to explain the purpose of the project and its relationship to other control methods, and to previous change projects. For example, if the company has already worked with multi-dimensional measures as part of a TQM effort, then management should build on this experience and show what scorecards can add. If scorecards are introduced together with rolling forecasts, like they were in some of our cases, then the need for clarity obviously extends to the whole 'package'. See the long quotation from Nordea's annual report in Chapter 2.

For larger corporations, the launch of the BSC requires well-coordinated internal marketing. To reach agreement on its message, the persons assigned responsibilities for what we just called scorecard 'technology' will need to cooperate as a project team, learning from each other and gradually reaching agreement on how the BSC concepts shall be applied. It is impossible to generalize about an optimal size of this group. While it is important not to let the group grow so large that efficiency and freedom of action are impaired, the team should not be so small that certain parts of the organization have no voice in the process. The team will also have information and training as one of its tasks. It is essential that information on the BSC concept be readily available and easily understood. Training and information can be provided with the help of manuals, an intranet, or seminars. Experience has shown that information is transmitted most easily to groups of 20 people or less. In larger groups, people are often reluctant to ask questions and to examine critically the ideas underlying the concept, as they will need to in order to accept it.

Many companies use consultants to guide them through the initial stage. They can provide experience from other companies' scorecard projects, challenge received wisdom about strategies and business logics, and add capacity for handling the workload. It is, however, important to realize that – even more than with other management methods – scorecard projects have to reflect local conditions and be 'owned' by people in the company. Consultants should act as facilitators and not submit to the demand for ready-made models.

The five primary responsibilities we have identified are the following.[40] In smaller organizations, it is obviously possible to combine these in different ways. In reading about the experiences of our case companies below, it may be useful to look for these roles:

1. *Business stakeholders* whose units use scorecards. A scorecard should be *the* format used whenever the intended or achieved performance of a unit is discussed. The person who can make sure this happens is the head of the unit in question, or sometimes its management team.
2. *Scorecard designers* who are responsible for the design and content of the scorecard. This responsibility concerns scorecard terminology, graphical format etc. which are fundamental parts of scorecard technology. These are not just practical matters but may have a strong influence on how scorecards are perceived and used. They often have an impact on the specifications for scorecard software. It is important to establish common terms, particularly when scorecards are used throughout the company. During the initial phase of a project, there often is a project leader with extensive authority – a 'scorecard czar' – or a team with similar authority.
3. *Information providers* who are responsible for performing measurements and ensuring that the results are made available. Measuring and providing data sooner or later will call for IT solutions – a subject we discuss in Chapter 11. Part of this duty, then, will be assigned to those who operate the information systems. However, employee action is often needed to collect measurements and sometimes to 'edit' them so that they can be understood and used. Creating the necessary interest and involvement here is an important part of the scorecard process. It

may also be considered a part of controllership, since controllers extend their role to include non-financial information.

4. *Scorecard analysts* who are responsible for giving proper consideration to scorecards in management control. Having measurements available is not enough. Whether scorecards will actually be used depends on the incentives to do so. Success no longer is simply meeting the financial budget, and managers constantly need to remind employees – and themselves – that now the scorecard is their shared view of the unit's tasks and achievements. Sometimes the bonus system should be changed – see Chapter 10.

5. *Learning pilots* who are responsible for scorecard measurements being used for learning. In *Performance Drivers*, we claimed that this should be the ultimate aim of a scorecard process. Over time, the strategic themes of a scorecard are put to the test, and verified or refuted. Reflecting on this experience needs to be defined as an area of responsibility.

The five responsibilities we introduced above may be related as in Figure 8.1.

In the figure, we identify a number of important contacts that need to be made:

• Scorecard analysts and business stakeholders obviously need to discuss business performance, but also whether the scorecard works, or should

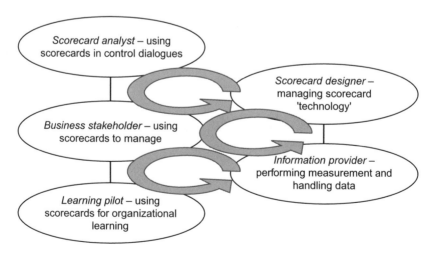

Figure 8.1 Relations between the five responsibilities discussed in this chapter.

be improved. In doing this, their dialogue may extend to scorecard designers, who also need to monitor how scorecard use for business dialogues is developing.

- Business stakeholders and learning pilots need to discuss what can be learnt about the assumptions in scorecards and strategy maps as experience is gained over time. In doing this, their dialogue may extend to information providers, since they need to access other data for comparisons.

- Scorecard designers and information providers need to find practical ways of ensuring data capture and dissemination. They must observe and influence how people perform and access measurements, and so this dialogue may extend also to business stakeholders.

The need for these contacts has to be considered when roles are assigned and teams are organized. For smaller organizations, it is tempting to combine all the roles, except the business stakeholder, to a business controller. This person then designs the system, collects and distributes data, discusses what it means, and tries to learn from it. With an enthusiastic controller, this may work for some time. But there is a big danger that soon it will be a private crusade without much connection with what gets discussed among managers and employees, since the controller cannot be present at all the times and in all places where scorecards should be discussed. Some companies have also been concerned that a financially oriented controller will not be the right person to introduce scorecards, which to some extent challenge the controller's traditional tools.

In a similar way, in some of our case companies it seemed natural for the small team leading the scorecard effort to assume many of these roles. But there have also been scattered attempts to assign more specific roles. Next, we take a look at how they have done this. We first discuss the driving force in the BSC process: who owns the scorecard? Then we turn to how the process is handled in local units.

THE DRIVING FORCE IN A SCORECARD PROCESS

A CEO or other unit head is often the driving force behind successful scorecard work. We learnt in Chapter 3 how different units in Skandia applied themselves to scorecard work with varying intensity, largely depending on how managers engaged themselves:

Skandia

In September 2000, Skandia Connection's manager decided to change the situation and set aside plenty of time to restart the Navigator work. He was determined to make the tool understood and used by everyone.

Ericsson Enterprise

The head of Ericsson Enterprise and the unit heads have the main responsibility for Enterprise's scorecards. One person in the staff unit, Operations and HR, was appointed to make sure that the process moved forward, and to take a critical stance: 'Why do you suggest this?' During the seminars where scorecards were developed, he and a colleague acted as catalysts or supplied advice on the process.

Oriflame

It has been clearly defined in the instruction package that the owner of the scorecard is the managing director: the local managing director owns the local scorecard and the CEO owns the corporate scorecard. When the pilot project came to an end and the project group was dissolved, the business controller became responsible for the roll-out of the new management concept. He assumed responsibility for the scorecard-related responsibilities, such as promoting the use of the scorecard, ensuring that the tools and instruments were available as well as making sure that the local managers monitored and recorded their operation according to the metrics in their respective scorecards.

It will be seen that these later two cases are rather similar. A difference that we will come back to is that Ericsson Enterprise's scorecard responsibility comes from Operations and HR, not the controller's department as in Oriflame. But sometimes the chief executive himself assumes the leading role also in developing scorecards and making sure they are used continuously.

BA Heathrow

The manager at Heathrow introduced the BSC concept when he joined the organization from another part of BA. The choice of control instrument was based on his experience from working with it in another internal change effort. Bringing the concept into the organization, he also became associated with it. He also made the control instrument visible by mandating his subordinate unit managers to use it. Even though he mandated the use of the concept, he allowed each unit to decide how to design their own scorecards.

When this happens, he or she may need the assistance of someone else, and it happens that new positions are created. The background needed for these then becomes an interesting matter:

Lund HLC

The division of roles has been rather clear during the whole implementation process. When the initial initiative was taken to work with the scorecard, the head of HLC felt a need to have one or two people who made sure that the work would become continuous. He therefore recruited two nurses from other parts of the hospital, Anna-Karin Bryder and Ann Gyllenberg, whose main task was to make sure the organization persevered in its BSC process.

Bryder and Gyllenberg have been central figures both in the implementation and in the continuous work with the scorecard. Although they did not have any formal background in management, let alone scorecards, they were instrumental in procuring a software solution, about which they found information on the web site of the company selling it. Now they are very active in supporting work in the local units. In this, it is essential that they are nurses themselves, although not with a background in heart and lung diseases.

Nordea

At Nordea, strong support from the top has been vital in getting scorecard work going. Thorleif Krarup had held the same position in Unibank, the Danish bank which was one of the partners in creating Nordea. The group leadership constantly signals the importance they attach to scorecards by bringing up 'focus areas', etc. in conversations. The group's management team monitors business area performance through their scorecards.

PPMM work at Nordea is led by Group Planning and Control. In addition to the three business areas, there are a number of functions belonging either to the 'Group Corporate Centre' or the 'Group Staff'. Both Group Finance and Group Planning and Control belong to the former, which is headed by the group's CFO. Within Group Planning and Control, it is the head of Group Planning who is coordinating Nordea's BSC effort. Group Planning consists of four people. It will be seen that although they work in parallel with Finance, the scorecard project has not been seen as a task for the finance staff. The head of Group Planning says that he is currently working full-time with the BSC.

It is, of course, also important to have support 'from above'. In a political organization, this makes it advisable for the project owner to anchor the BSC effort in a broader way:

Helsingborg

Focus in Helsingborg's city government had been on pragmatic decisions in the different departments, rather than on the formal hierarchy and strategic decisions in the city council. In a way, the scorecard project aimed to reinforce this local commitment, but also to create a greater coherence and a holistic view of city services that could be shared by citizens, politicians, and city employees. This meant that all of these needed to get involved with the BSC in various ways.

To legitimize the work with the BSC in Helsingborg, it was important to get full support from the political organization at an early stage. It was important to get the politicians involved and to get them to feel an ownership for the scorecards, at the same time making sure that they would not become identified with the majority parties but rather be perceived as a permanent, non-political control tool. Politicians needed to see the changes over time, improvements that triggered their motivation to work with the BSC. This was the only way of getting them to work with the tool – if they felt part of the process, if they felt that they owned it and could affect it. The politician needed to get enthusiastic about the work so that the traditional way of thinking about budgeting could be abandoned.

A steering committee for the scorecard project was created early on, and is considered to have the ownership of the project. When measurements were made available over the city administration's intranet in June 2002, they were among the first to gain access.

The project organization is shown in Figure 8.2. It included a political management group that was to ensure political neutrality and drive the process. This group was supported by a project group consisting of project managers who were members of the five different fields of activities within the organization. These project managers were to be responsible for the score-cards within each field. To ensure legitimacy, a reference group consisting of administrators was also appointed. A group consisting of the central project management group and some of the project managers from the different project groups became the driving force in the project.

The BSC project managers in the anonymous firm we quoted in Chapter 5 also have views on this. They stress that the concept requires someone in the management team to drive it, making use of the information in it. Their view is that the BSC as a tool has not yet emerged as the 'natural' control mechanism in most organizations, so if the management team ceases to discuss scorecards they will 'fall out of the loop' and no one will pay attention to them.

Unfortunately, this seems to be the case regardless of how thorough the implementation has been. Even if the new concept has been systematically introduced in the organization, and all employees know the ideas behind

SUBPROJECTS

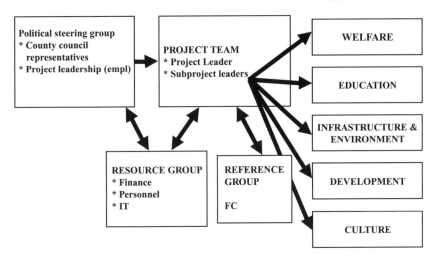

Figure 8.2 The organization of the BSC work in Helsingborg. Reproduced by permission of the city of Helsingborg.

it, management's agenda defines what is regarded as important in the organization.

If the owner of the scorecard in the management team moves on, and no one replaces her as the scorecard advocate, then there is an apparent risk that the scorecard will fade away. In some organizations, the scorecard will just be forgotten when it is replaced by a new set of management principles; for example, more financially oriented goals and metrics. In others, the metrics may survive if they have been implemented in a dedicated management information system that produces a performance report every month. The metrics may then remain and attract some attention. However, they will not be used to boost a strategic discussion in the organization, but rather serve as an operational control mechanism: evaluation of operational effectiveness rather than strategy realization.

HANDLING OF SCORECARD TASKS IN LOCAL UNITS

In Chapter 3 we described how Skandia arranged workshops at various stages of its Navigator project:

Skandia
In some units, three-day computerized business games, built on the Navigator concept, were arranged so that the ideas behind the tools really would sink in. Management and the group responsible for the implementation of the tool emphasized the importance of both understanding the system and the concept to make the work successful.

For each unit, an 'ambassador' was appointed who represented the Navigator team and interacted with it. This has now been going on for several years, showing that a central project team has a role in reaching out into local units, but also that various roles may be assigned or required in these units.

In each local organizational unit, responsibilities similar to those discussed above have to be assigned. The manager may call for people engaged in the company-wide project to come and assist in this, or assign tasks within the group, or perform them himself. In our case companies, some have developed such distinct roles. An interesting case is Ericsson Enterprise, where management felt a need to allocate responsibility for individual metrics:

Ericsson Enterprise
Each of the seven unit heads has responsibility for his own unit's scorecard. In addition, a new role of 'KSF driver' has been introduced, through which each of the seven follow and influence performance for one or a few among the 16 KSFs for *all* seven units. Each quarter, they were supposed to follow up and present 'their' KSFs in the management team's meeting. In practice, however, this performance review has been done monthly on request by the Enterprise head. It also involves providing forecasts for the rest of the year.

The role of 'driver' involves a change of mindset for the unit heads since it forces them to act more as members of the management team for Enterprise, and more in the interest of the entire company.

Where local units are small, at least in terms of administrative staff, their scorecards are usually handled quite informally:

BA Heathrow
When all scorecards had been defined, an employee in the controller unit was appointed responsible for producing the actual 'scorecards' before each management group meeting. The scorecards are implemented in an Excel sheet, so it only takes the controller one day per month to produce the binder for the management meeting (consisting of each unit's scorecard). Each scorecard is then sent to the respective responsible unit manager, who may

give some verbal comments on the development in the scorecard. These comments are then included in each scorecard, after which all scorecards are compiled in the binder and circulated to all members in the management team in due time before the meeting.

Hence, there are few formalized roles associated with the scorecard. The manager expects to receive the scorecard in advance of the meeting. One controller spends a day producing the binder, and the six unit managers add their comments to the performance report in the binder.

Oriflame
Centrally, Oriflame has set up a framework and guidelines for the usage and reporting of the scorecards. The local management team has full discretion to decide how to allocate responsibilities in the operation and reporting of the scorecards. Each country manager thus decides how to ensure that he is using the scorecard in accordance with its intentions. The corporate office will demand that performance information in the scorecard is compiled and reported on time.

Even then, however, it certainly helps if someone takes the concept to her heart. We saw in Chapter 3 how Skandia, which gave a lot of discretion to individual organizational units as to how they used the BSC and where it was also handled in rather different ways in different units, at an early stage appointed 'ambassadors' to the various units. Similar approaches were tried in other organizations:

Lund HLC
Out in the different wards there were also more and more people getting involved in the work. Karin Ottosson was one of the 'voluntary' enthusiasts at the centre who drove the process within her ward. To have someone leading the process from their own department or ward was important for the legitimacy of the process. External people, or even people at higher levels in the organization, coming into the ward to introduce a new concept had historically almost always directly caused resistance among the employees. New concepts and new ways of working were always frightening. But by, instead, having an enthusiastic member of the team, the whole process was made a lot easier.

In Ottosson's ward, almost all employees became engaged in the work. All took part in an off-site meeting where Bryder and Gyllenberg acted as coaches. 'We created the structure that we had in fact long wanted, and wrote down how we wanted it. This in itself had a big impact on our activities.' To continue what they had started, the ward appointed a steering group whose responsibility was to finish the scorecard that the whole ward had started working on, to communicate this out to the rest of the employees and to update it on a regular basis. The group also appointed a person who was going to be responsible for the updates in Dolphin – their IT system. This motivated more frequent use of the system because if the employees saw the changes it would be easier to take action. And because the system now became updated frequently, action was also taken more quickly.

Karin Ottosson regards her role as a 'co-driver' of her ward's scorecard effort. The head of the ward is responsible overall, but Karin volunteered for making sure that it works. She sees a clear link with the philosophy of 'constant improvements' that HLC subscribes to. 'That is the technique for driving this on, and it fits well with our scorecard and Dolphin.' Different wards have found 'fiery spirits' such as Karin but their backgrounds vary. It is important to prove that scorecard work can be done within existing resources, and have the support from Bryder and Gyllenberg.

Jönköping

To make the BSC into a tool to enable benchmarking and to develop the organization, and not a control tool, it must be communicated out in the organization through voluntary ambassadors. The initiators wanted to train tutors that could be available to the other employees and support them in their scorecard work. One tutor from each unit was to be trained. The administrative group sent out letters to the heads of all departments to get them to appoint tutors. They were, however, somewhat sceptic towards the work because they had not yet seen whether or not the BSC was a good way of working, and did not trust the administrative unit's capability to train the tutors. In the end, however, each unit had their own tutor. These tutors, consisting mainly of people in accounting and control, were trained during a two-day BSC course. They were also given a special manual on how scorecards could be developed.

The tutors were, in turn, supported by a couple of the organization's controllers who had been involved in the BSC work more or less from the start. These people developed the work with the scorecards, and had developed models and templates to make the work with the tool easier. These templates have become so widely accepted that they are even referred to as the organization's brand for the BSC work.

Despite these roles, the role-definitions in the organization have not been very explicit. Some enthusiasts have become more engaged in developing the scorecards, whereas others have put less time into the work. Management and the initiators have continued to play a central role. They require regular reports even though they want the scorecard to be a natural part of the employees' work.

Some organizations have given much thought to the role distribution in local units:

Nordea

For the business areas, Nordea has used the following list of BSC responsibilities:

- Responsible for BSC performance – business area head
- Focus area owner – one executive (i.e. the executive members share the focus areas – what is otherwise called strategic goals – between them)
- KPI owner – some person responsible for measuring and reporting outcomes
- Responsible for initiatives – obviously, each strategic initiative needs someone in charge.

The BSC coordinator in each business area is responsible for the completion of scorecards, for assembling metrics and for reporting. Scorecards are primarily discussed at quarterly intervals. There are clear instructions for all of the above as to what they should do two weeks, one and a half weeks, one week and half a week before these meetings.

'Scorecard ambassadors' also need to come together and learn from each other.

Helsingborg

To get on with the work the project was expanded to embrace also the executive part of the organization – the employees who were responsible for putting the plans into action. This group of people got to create and own their own scorecard, which was important for the continuous work. In all departments there is now someone – in some the controller, in others someone from the methods development – who is the local expert on scorecards.

In addition to these different roles, workgroups were created out in the organization. In schools, for example, a group of interested employees became responsible for their scorecard, for collecting relevant information and for updating the card.

Also, lower-level employees should take an interest in the numbers. The chief executive compared it with his jogging round: 'Although I'm not competing, I tend to check how many minutes it takes. In the same way, the scorecard measures must be something everyone is curious about and wants to follow.'

In public services, there may even be an ambition to involve ordinary citizens in the BSC project.

Helsingborg

An important ambition with scorecards in Helsingborg is to create a shared view of the city's service performance, through the presentation of measures on the Internet. As far as possible, these should be the same values that are used for internal control purposes. As a consequence, 'customers' (a term used in Helsingborg for citizens who receive city services) are asked to rate the performance, and the numbers are to be published on the city's website. This involvement is also meant to give the citizens a more balanced view of the service performance. 'If a department has 5000 customers during one day and one such contact is handled unsuccessfully, then people will understand that this is human. But if we cannot put it into perspective, it may end up in the papers as proof of our bad performance!'

It will be seen that no organization has identified a full cast of roles such as in Figure 8.1. There are scattered instances of new parts such as the 'KPI drivers' at Ericsson Enterprise. We also find it interesting how local units often have someone who more or less volunteers to become the local score-card champion or ambassador, such as Karin Ottosson in Lund HLC. To encourage these people and provide them with opportunities to develop their understanding and skills is vitally important. This is often a matter of training and networking.

TRAINING A SCORECARD 'COMMUNITY'

In Chapter 3 we learnt about the Navigator 'ambassadors' in Skandia and how these met repeatedly to learn about, for example, new ways of using the Dolphin software. Some organizations regard such meetings as build-ing a 'community' of scorecard people, but communities can also function in other ways:

Nordea

An internal BSC community has been established including one represent-ative from each business area, and from other units such as Group Treasury, IT, and HR. This group meets one day each quarter. They are also inves-tigating the possibility of an external community, but find it difficult to identify corporations that would allow relevant comparisons.

Among other organizations we studied, those in public administration made the greatest effort to train scorecard users and create networks for them. This may be because there is a long tradition of empowerment and 'codetermination' in the Swedish public sector, including a strong role for unions.

Helsingborg

More than 40 employees took part in a training programme about scorecards held in 2000–2001. The focus during the training was on the intangible values of working with the scorecard – the process rather than the numbers. This led to the ideas behind the tool being well communicated and understood.

Through taking an active part in the BSC seminars of the Swedish Association of Local Authorities, Helsingborg also made sure that they got access to experiences undergone at the same time in other Swedish cities. Helsingborg also teamed up with cities in Denmark, Finland and Poland to create additional commitment to its BSC project, and at the same time provide learning opportunities and boost the awareness about what Helsingborg was doing in this area. This involved leading people from Helsingborg presenting their experiences in seminars in the other cities, and a joint application for EU funding for continued work.

Lund HLC

The work with the BSC at the Lund HLC started more or less out of a coincidence. Arén, the head of the centre, had heard about the tool and thought that it could be a good way of supporting the new decentralized organization. He felt that they needed a tool that helped them identify a shared vision and goals, and to follow these up. He thought that the BSC could support this process. At a two-day workshop for the new organization, Arén introduced the scorecard to the other managers at the centre. He quickly got support for his belief that the scorecard could be a good supporting tool for the new organization.

The overarching centre scorecard was designed by a group of managers and staff representatives from different parts of the organization. After this work it was concluded that in order to get the BSC working they needed to introduce the concept in the entire organization. Courses available to everyone at the centre were therefore arranged. The thought was that enthusiastic participants from these courses would trigger others' curiosity and desire to start working with the tool. That way, the use of the concept would spread naturally throughout the centre.

To support the implementation process, discussions about what scorecards are, what they are for, and how they should look were held. Everyone at the centre was involved. People soon started to ask about 'when they would get to work with the scorecards'. This natural spreading of the concept was exactly what Arén had wanted, and what he also argued was the key to a successful implementation at the centre. The concept cannot be forced upon people.

When there is no formal BSC community, it may still be useful to try to learn systematically about how the BSC is succeeding:

Ericsson Enterprise

Enterprise has developed a model for performance assessment where each unit manager grades success in the following areas:

- Are there representative performance indicators and measures?
- Is performance level and improvement planning in place?
- Does reporting and follow up exist?
- Have improvement results been achieved?
- Does benchmarking take place?

This is done using a seven-grade scale, with verbal explanations of each grade to guide managers when they decide which level they believe they have reached. Through this process, Enterprise managers have identified an agenda for further improvements. These include improved cause-and-effect descriptions (cf. Chapter 6 for current procedures), and scorecards for processes and not only for hierarchical units. The final point seems especially important since Enterprise now concentrates on three processes: building partner relations; managing supply chains; and product provisioning. This is closely linked to its move from direct to indirect selling, since Enterprise has sold most of its sales units.

We also noted that some of the companies considered contacting other companies in order to set up BSC practice communities together.

RELATION TO OTHER PLANNING AND REPORTING

As we said earlier, several of the responsibilities that we identified may be assigned to an organization's controller department. This happens predominantly in corporations where scorecard control is viewed as the successor to traditional budgets and planning cycles. There is a natural tendency for controllers to be more comfortable with financial measures, and they may therefore give too little attention to other types of metrics. On the other hand, they may be well suited to tasks such as defining reports or analysing the impact over time from the strategies included in scorecards, i.e. learning.

In Chapter 3 we saw that in Skandia, the scorecard 'ambassadors' were mainly controllers and actuaries having close contact with organization management and control. Despite the fact that Skandia's aim had been that the Navigator was not going to become an 'auditing tool', it was now the controllers and the actuaries that became drivers of the implementation process. Perhaps the acceptance among the employees and the implementation would have been different if others had been chosen as ambassadors.

Here is how it is in some of the case companies:

Ericsson Enterprise

In Ericsson Enterprise, coordination of the scorecard process is located in the staff unit, Operations and HR, in close cooperation with the Business and Financial Control unit in charge of the financial rolling forecast and reporting, which is done in parallel with the scorecards. Asked about this, Sten Olsson, who coordinated the scorecard process, offered the opinion that

Control is more concerned about their 'products' – getting the financial reports out on time. As part of Operations and HR, we focus on achieving a shared view of where we should be heading. We offered to take part as facilitators. Some units 'lifted' our forms, to use as their own. This was an effective way to influence scorecard work in the units.

HP Services

There is a business control function in each HP company, which is the main unit responsible for its scorecards. The idea was that top managers should use the information available on the intranet for 'self-service'. So far, they need the assistance of the controllers, but in the future self-service is the goal.

SAS

As part of the new governance model for the SAS Group, its BSC project is managed from Corporate Business Control, which is a staff unit distinct from Finance and Accounting. One manager with previous scorecard experience from other airlines was hired to coordinate the introduction of the method.

Within each company, controllers are responsible for preparing the reports which focus the attention of company and group management, as well as, of course, company boards.

In one organization, controllers were at first openly sceptical. Management later took the opportunity to show that accounting and control now has to be compatible with the BSC, although, as we have seen, the BSC is not viewed as part of that department:

Helsingborg

At the beginning, Helsingborg's accountants were rather doubtful about the scorecard project. When the chief accountant (or financial manager) retired in 2000, this motivated an unusually prolonged search for a successor who would have the right qualifications and at the same time support the ideas behind the scorecard project. The city's chief executive commented that it is essential that the key people in the city all stand up for these ideas.

RECOMMENDATIONS AND IMPLICATIONS

Obviously the size and complexity of your organization will determine how much thought you need to give to the matter of roles and responsibilities. Then, in assigning people, we believe it is useful, as for any project, to think in terms of several variables:

- *Competence.* Specialized knowledge about BSC will rarely be needed (or available). But a good overview of the organization and its processes will be useful, as will some familiarity with previous control systems, information systems which may provide data, etc.

- *Availability.* As we have seen, some organizations regard scorecard work as a full-time effort, at least during the initial years. This needs to be understood – can your candidates for the assignments be allocated for BSC work?

- *Organizational status.* The nurses in our Lund HLC example show that legitimacy is not necessarily a matter of hierarchical position. But it certainly mattered that the head of the centre was the person who brought the BSC with him into it. So for different tasks and roles, formal position, authority, and legitimacy may all need to be considered.

- *'Fiery spirit'.* In several cases, we have met real enthusiasts. To appoint as BSC project leader an 'evangelist' with immense zeal in changing the entire organization also carries some dangers. Others in the organization may feel threatened, and sometimes correctly believe that this is a temporary phenomenon, since the enthusiast will soon attract attention from some other part of the corporation and move on. At least in our country, the most effective change agents tend to use more subtle means.

So where does this take us? In most of our case companies it was clear who was the owner of the BSC processes, and that units were responsible for their own scorecards. In some of them the assignment of such roles occurred naturally, and may not even have required any conscious decisions.

A few of them introduced more specific roles and even new positions in order to handle their projects. But we have not seen any who have explicitly considered the entire cast of characters we drew in Figure 8.1. We do not know if this would have improved their BSC processes – but we still would advise that the tasks are at least discussed at the initial stage of a project.

There may be some other general lessons to be drawn:

- Providing visibility for the scorecard process through appointing responsible persons is important in itself.
- Resource efficiency requires that you think through how skills and tasks are matched.
- Provide 'help-desk' services and document the process in its early stages.
- Safeguard competence by identifying key BSC tasks, and check how they are performed. Otherwise, it may well be that a few enthusiasts share all scorecard duties during the first months or years, and then depart or tire. A scorecard process has to grow roots among ordinary people in the organization.

Connecting Strategic Intent: **9**
Designing Interfaces
Between Scorecards

ONE FIRM, MANY SCORECARDS

Most writers on scorecards suggest that scorecards for subunits should be derived ('broken down' or 'cascaded') from the entire organization's scorecard. From the rationalistic perspective of normative management literature, this is obviously a good recommendation. In practice, the relationship is a good deal more problematic. Skandia in Chapter 3 provides an interesting example. Originally, scorecard use was meant to build from below. Later, top-down elements were introduced, but still not extensively:

Skandia
Some measures, mainly financial ones, are compulsory in Skandia and used for benchmarking. Apart from these, Navigators (i.e. scorecards) in different units are adapted to their own situation. Reporting performance to higher levels, managers summarize what has happened in the unit and how well this is aligned with its targets in its Navigator. The monthly reports are thus aggregations of the individual Navigators up through the units and companies to the corporate level. This process is currently becoming more structured, but as units use different metrics it is a logical rather than a mathematical exercise.

    Employees said they could not relate to a Navigator they had not themselves been involved in developing: 'It has been developed by our group manager and I don't even understand what's in it.' 'The current Navigator doesn't make sense. We haven't been involved in the process and therefore the variables in it don't have any practical implications for us. We must be involved in the process to be able to act accordingly.'

To adapt scorecards to the local situation is a good idea. Scorecards are useful primarily as communication tools. In Skandia Connection the communication we heard about in Chapter 3 was among employees, who then

used their new understanding of their task to communicate it to other parts
of Skandia.

This comes close to a view of the corporation as a federation, where each
unit proposes its own role. This may suit some organizations, but it is not
surprising that a company with a clear strategic focus such as Skandia
gradually has introduced more top-down elements into its BSC processes.
Still, they want to retain the sense of local ownership for scorecards.

In this chapter, we take a closer look at the relationship between the
multiple scorecards that may be used in any larger organization – and in
some not so large. We base the discussion on our case observations, but also
add some ideas for which we so far do not have any empirical evidence. The
relationship is, of course, primarily one between organizational units, not
scorecards. How scorecard measures in different units should relate is a
matter of intended synergies and how units co-produce results: how the
organization is structured, where power is located, methods of control, etc.
Subunits will impact on each other in different ways, and rarely agree on
how. As in budgeting and other forms of planning, there will be a tendency
to 'play games'. (This topic was investigated in Chapter 7.)

Sometimes discussing scorecards also helps to clarify some of these
issues. Here, we will limit our discussion to a number of questions about
scorecard use that we often meet, and which we now introduce.

SCORECARDS THROUGHOUT AN ORGANIZATION – HOW SHOULD THEY RELATE?

Figure 9.1 provides a graphical illustration of some of the issues we address,
using scorecards to symbolize organizational units.

- Is a top-level scorecard necessary? Some organizations do not have any
  corporate scorecards, although subunits do: British Airways, Lund's
  University Hospital, maybe Ericsson. Some started pilot cases preparing for later more widespread use. These had to do without the guidance from higher-level scorecards. But some just encouraged units to
  use scorecards without much attempt at cohesion. Or scorecards cropped
  up locally. How should we understand the relation between scorecards
  in such organizations – can they be used as a tool in building strategy
  from below, rather than deriving it from the top?

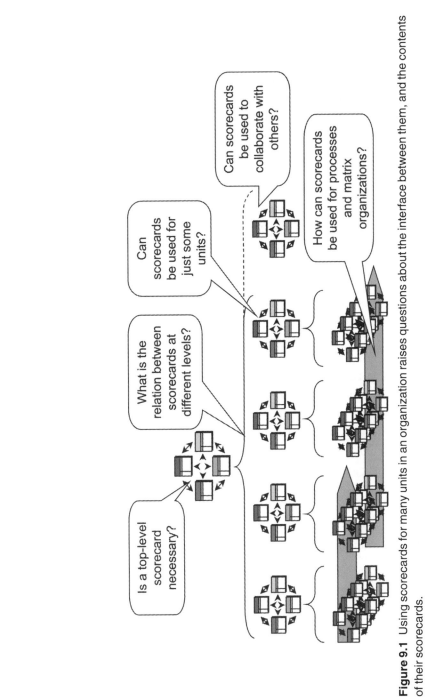

Figure 9.1 Using scorecards for many units in an organization raises questions about the interface between them, and the contents of their scorecards.

- *What is the relation between scorecards at different levels?* It is not obvious how to derive ('break down') goals and targets from higher-level score-cards. Some seem to regard this almost as a mathematical exercise, where tasks are subdivided into additive subtasks. Software for the BSC often assumes that metrics higher up in the hierarchy are sums or averages of measures for subunits. For most financial measures this holds true, but is it meaningful for other quantities? We regard the process as a logical, rather than purely quantitative, exercise. Still, it is, of course, practical to use similar metrics on all levels in an organ-ization. So how can this be handled? And should we break down score-cards all the way to scorecards for teams and individual employees?

- *Can scorecards be used for just some units?* Is it a good idea to use a scorecard if nobody else in a corporation is doing it? We see this happening especially for units that are different, often like a separate business. One case of this is an internal service unit: should its expected performance be presented in a scorecard (cf. Figures 2.7 and 2.8), even when no one else uses scorecards?

- *How can scorecards be used for processes and matrix organizations?* Some scorecards were meant to guide processes extending across several organizational units. Either they can be used as 'SLAs' between suc-cessive links in a value chain, or as common goals for an entire process. Such use of scorecards seems to have received little attention so far. Can scorecards be used to provide guidance in a matrix organization?

- *Can scorecards be used to collaborate with others?* Most managers today also manage outside their own organizations: partner relationships some-times called 'extended enterprises', 'virtual corporations', 'imaginary organizations' or just networks. Such relations rely on trust and require the exchange of information. Are scorecards useful for this – should there be additional scorecards to manage across organizational borders?

We address each of these issues in turn. We also comment on yet another relation between scorecards:

- *How do scorecards relate over time?* Each scorecard in Figure 9.1 will relate to some time period. It may show tasks or what has been achieved. How much should scorecards change over time? Strategic objectives may remain the same, but targets and performance values will be different during the next period. How should values relate over time?

The key to all these questions we believe is in the idea we stated initially: to use scorecards for communication. Scorecards are used to describe intentions and achievements, to help in realizing the intended strategy. In a top-down approach, corporate headquarters state their requirements. There may be little scope for discussion. In more bottom-up approaches, scorecards are used by subunits to propose possible courses of action. As in all planning processes there is an element of give and take, based on the knowledge of all involved. In preparing for the future, knowledge about possibilities and preferences is needed. Ideas about what is possible are scattered throughout the organization. So, too, are ideas about what would be desirable, but the organizational leadership has the ultimate authority to decide – at least in principle.

IS A TOP-LEVEL SCORECARD NECESSARY?

Scorecards help to introduce strategic thinking into planning and control. The task of each business unit has to be agreed on, and related to the overall purpose of a corporation. To provide strategic direction and to monitor progress, corporations with a strong common identity will usually want to introduce scorecards from the top. Strategic guidance is possible also in other ways, and other types of controls can be used. If the strategic role is sufficiently clear, then parts of a corporation may embark on scorecard projects for their internal benefit.

Ericsson
While the corporate leadership of Ericsson has endorsed the use of scorecards and many parts of Ericsson started scorecard projects in the 1990s, there are considerable differences between practices, metrics, etc. For some years, there was a corporate 'recommendation' to use scorecards, but in recent years it has been pushed more actively as part of the planning and review cycle for all units. So far, however, penetration does not seem to be complete, and Ericsson companies using scorecards do so more or less on their own.

This is even more apparent when the corporation is a conglomerate, managing a portfolio of businesses. If these are profit-seeking separate firms with no particular synergies across the corporation, then the decision to use scorecards could be left to each of them, regardless of practices elsewhere in the corporation. Corporate management may find that the mix of businesses makes a top-level corporate scorecard infeasible or unnecessary.[41] We believe that such a scorecard is useful even in such corporations. It would focus the strategic rationale of the corporation as such: corporate identity, investor relations, competences, common processes and practices, acquisitions and divestitures.

Sometimes scorecards are first developed for subunits, and then to some extent harmonized:

BA Heathrow

When BA Heathrow first started to develop scorecards for its separate units at the airport, no immediate effort was made to ensure that the airport's collective scorecard was synchronized with the units' separate scorecards. Instead, unit managers were asked to develop scorecards that would describe their units' performance according to how they thought the customers would evaluate them. This also meant that no actual synchronization was made on the horizontal level – between units within the airport. During the initial off-site workshop, however, all subunits participated, so some alignment naturally emerged as the participants spent time in the same hotel, informing their peers about their goals, strategies and ambitions. The actual scorecards have, however, not been explicitly synchronized in a comprehensive model.

Oriflame

Some selected units (mainly sales companies in different countries around the world, but also some units at the corporate head office) received instructions on how to develop the scorecards, and the results were presented at a joint conference where all countries took part. The scorecards especially focused on the logic behind the perspectives and metrics, i.e. the strategy maps describing each local company's business logic.

Following this, all country managers created scorecards for their operations, given local circumstances and established corporate guidelines. Every country manager operates a fairly isolated business and does not need to coordinate with many other units, only global production and marketing. The executive management team has developed a corporate scorecard which covers the whole organization.

We have also seen cases where *only* the corporate level uses scorecards. This may be because the firm is in an early stage of its scorecard project and will later extend its use to successive levels and units. But it may also reflect a view that the main benefit from using scorecards is to achieve strategic clarity in the leadership team, and that the control of subunits can be effected through other means.

WHAT IS THE RELATION BETWEEN SCORECARDS AT DIFFERENT LEVELS?

Most accounts of scorecard use do not discuss exactly what happens when scorecards are derived for successive levels of organization. Some CEOs prescribe a scorecard that is to be used by everyone, often accepting that a small number of 'local' metrics are added on a voluntary basis. Their emphasis is on metrics suitable for easy benchmarking and combination into values for larger organizational units. There is an obvious attraction in being able to calculate overall performance from that of lower-level units. Managers can pinpoint problem areas by comparing numbers and 'drill down' into the organization, just as they do with financial numbers. And measures can be aggregated into elegant 'dashboard' presentations of scorecards.

We started this chapter with Skandia's experiences. They expected scorecard use to spread spontaneously, but finally introduced more requirements from the corporate level. Even when there is strong central leadership, it may take a long time before scorecards exist at all levels:

Lund HLC

Thus far there are four scorecard levels where the top-level scorecard is the overall one for the centre. This top-level scorecard has existed since autumn 2000 and gives direction to the rest of the units.

The scorecards developed in the different wards have been given plenty of time to develop. The efforts must come from the employees themselves if the scorecard work is to be fruitful. In wards where there are BSC enthusiasts, or a need for new ways of looking at the work that is done, BSC work has been given a kick-start. In other wards, it has been slower. The head of the unit believes that you cannot force this kind of process upon the employees. That only creates resistance. Letting the initiatives come from the wards themselves instead creates curiosity and enthusiasm, making the whole process a lot easier.

A strong role for the corporate level does not mean that the contents of local scorecards needs to be mandated.

Nordea

Each unit will have a handful of 'themes'.[42] All of these should support long-term shareholder value. Links between scorecards for units at different organizational levels consist of these themes that guide the units towards the common goals in Nordea. Strategic objectives (in Nordea called focus areas), KPIs, targets, and actions (Initiatives) are derived from these – see Figure 2.4. Higher-level management does not prescribe which metrics to use. To be relevant, each scorecard has to reflect the local situation; increased commitment will result when local managers develop their own scorecards. Higher-level management may question the logic behind the metrics that are chosen, but if local management insist that their selection of metrics is the most relevant, then they will prevail. An exception to this may be that the same definitions shall be used for metrics that recur in several units.

By discussing the themes and their consequences for each unit, scorecards at Nordea also function as a way to build a common language and culture.

The Nordea project manager told us he would be sceptical if some unit proposed a scorecard identical to that of some other unit. He would see it as proof that they had not done a serious job.

The connection between scorecards is a matter of logic, not just mathematics. The same metric should be used for measuring phenomena which are essentially the same, and which appear in several scorecards, defining terms in a similar way. But this does not mean that this metric will be useful at all levels in the hierarchy. Adding numbers is not the only possible type of aggregation. Averages also cause difficulties, since they may hide large discrepancies. As an example, a group may want to achieve a more equal gender distribution, and set the target that no company should have more than 60% of either sex. The best measure of corporate performance towards this goal may be how large a proportion of the group's employees work in companies that fall inside the accepted range.

Another example: the competitive position of each business in a corporation might be measured as the market share relative to the largest competitor. If this metric is used, then it is certainly advisable to define it in the same way whenever it is used. But if the corporation is a diversified one, an average of all these measures may be meaningless. Its relative strength may vary between segments and markets. Maybe it should measure the proportion of target markets where it is one of the three largest players, or relate its performance to that of similar corporations. But it might also want to take into account that these may have emphasized other technologies, products, and countries. Comparing, for instance, Ericsson and Nokia requires an idea of what competitive position they try to achieve *as corporations*, not just summarizing their different businesses.

So any mathematical combination of lower-level measures has to be done carefully, taking into account strategies and the competitive situation. Conversely, deriving lower-level targets from overall goals will require strategic considerations and is certainly not just a mathematical exercise.

This has implications also for setting targets over time and providing incentives. Realistic goals and appropriate rewards are not a matter of mathematical formulas:

BA Heathrow

The scorecard for Heathrow is not an aggregate of the scorecards for its subunits. Instead, the scorecard at the airport level is designed to show the goals for BA at Heathrow and its strategies to reach these goals. Some metrics from subordinate scorecards are, however, also used at the superior level – but not as aggregates. They are there on their own merits.

Ericsson Enterprise

In addition to the scorecard for Ericsson Enterprise as a company, there are scorecards for its seven units. Scorecards for these were derived from Enterprise's company scorecard, following the hierarchical line organization. Within most of them, there are also scorecards for subunits.

In developing unit scorecards, there were a lot of discussions concerning how means and objectives should be considered to link into each other. How much of the company scorecard could be used unchanged at the next level? Several of the units just accepted the strategic objectives for the five perspectives as they are in the company scorecard. Maybe this was natural since they had just been part of the process to decide on them.

To explain the process, Ericsson Enterprise used the graphs reproduced as Figures 9.2 and 9.3. The logical sequence Strategic Objective → KSF→ KPI (i.e. metric) → Strategic Action is the same at each level. But the relation is 'staggered' so that higher-level KSFs become strategic objectives at the next level. And there has to be alignment back to the Enterprise level – common actions need to fit local needs. Yet there were several questions, and it is not certain that the same method will be used in coming years:

- The company scorecard had been prepared very carefully and resulted in strategic action plans (see Figure 2.4). These indicate on a high level what the subunits should achieve. Is it then really necessary to have complete scorecards for these? Maybe it would be possible to derive detailed action plans directly from Enterprise's scorecard?
- When the lower-level scorecards are developed, this involves an interpretation of Enterprise's goals. How large a freedom should the seven units

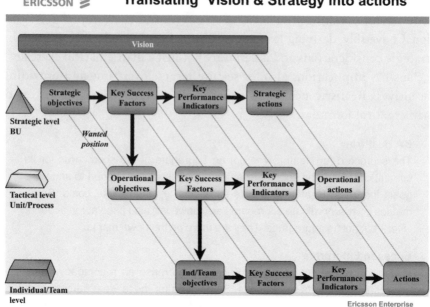

Figure 9.2 Deriving unit scorecards from top-level scorecards at Ericsson Enterprise. Reproduced by permission of Ericsson Enterprise AB.

have in this – or, to put it differently, what directives in addition to the company scorecard should they have?

HP Services

With a prescribed scorecard content for similar businesses across the globe, comparisons are easy. However, many numbers do not lend themselves to aggregating, and comparisons need to take into account differences in business conditions.

SAS

While the reporting format at the SAS Group is standardized, selection of KPIs (metrics) is up to each company. There are group definitions for cash flow, load factors, etc. – many of them reflecting industry practice – but no group requirements on which metrics to include. Companies with similar conditions are 'encouraged, but not ordered' to use similar measures. They should reflect the 'story' for each company – 'If they can explain that these are the most relevant ones for them, OK.'

In scorecard reports, KPIs are colour-coded red or green, and managers decide manually when preparing their reports. They also summarize their verdicts in an overall colour 'grade' for each of five perspectives. Originally,

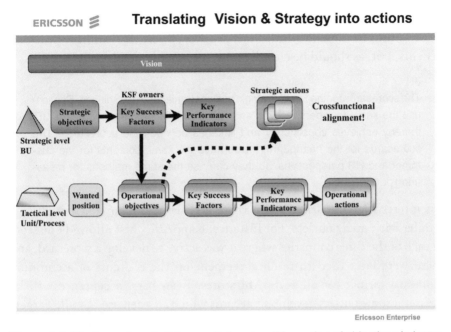

Figure 9.3 Aligning actions in Ericsson Enterprise. Discussion of objectives in lower-level units may result in requirements on common actions at higher levels. Reproduced by permission of Ericsson Enterprise AB.

there was the possibility to choose yellow, but this was abandoned since 'everything became yellow'.

There is no ambition in SAS to consolidate company KPI numbers into group metrics. 'We would never be able to, and don't want to.'

Xerox

During the past few years, there has been a realization that the scorecards used previously were too generic. Business needs to be conducted in different ways in different countries, and when the current difficulties have been conquered, it is likely that top management will focus sources of differentiation, unique competencies, partnerships, etc – making KSFs more varied across the organization. In the longer run, just having KPIs relating to cash flow will not be enough.

Xerox was successful in using metrics over a very long period through benchmarking between countries and units, and creating challenges for managers. When top management needed to take a more differentiated approach and create changes that require corporate management to act forcefully, this turned out to be of limited use.

For smaller companies with more uniform activities, it may make more sense to use the same or similar metrics everywhere. It does have practical benefits, but, as should be clear by now, we would not advise it.

> **JIT**
> The scorecards for the three strategic business units (Airline, Solution, Service) use the same four perspectives and CSFs as the corporate scorecard. JIT thereby achieves consistency and linkages between the scorecards. The scorecards for the headquarters also have the same contents for the customer and HR perspectives, so they can use the same methods for measuring performance.

An interesting case arises when there are many similar units, such as a retailer with many outlets. For instance, KappAhl[43] first allowed one store in each of the three countries where it was active to develop a scorecard, and these were later used to reach agreement on the contents of a common scorecard format for all KappAhl stores. Even here, acceptance will be greater if some outlets develop scorecards which are then used by all. Targets and strategic actions will then, of course, be different between stores, and change between years.

Even if managers and employees were engaged in developing their unit's scorecard when the BSC was introduced, it is important to find ways to refresh this experience in coming years. There is an obvious danger that the measures used last year are accepted almost automatically as still valid. We will come back to the relation between successive years later in this chapter. It may be necessary to revisit the logic, and certainly the target levels, in order to get a renewed understanding of the strategy and commitment to the goals.

Oriflame is a company with parallel operations in many countries, yet its country managers have been encouraged to use somewhat different scorecards.

> **Oriflame**
> The strategy map for each local company is translated into metrics in a scorecard. The local manager has full discretion to choose how many metrics he wants to use, but he must include approximately 10 common metrics that are used by all units for comparison as well as aggregation.
> As noted above, these scorecards have been developed by the local managers independently, even though the initial instructions on how to develop scorecards have probably influenced them to draw their maps in a

similar format and hence to include similar issues. Executive management has also intervened to some extent since they have made some metrics mandatory for use in all local companies. The purpose of this intervention is not however, primarily to ensure that information is compiled for a set of aggregated measures, but rather to ensure that the most important dimensions in the operation are not forgotten.

The local sales organizations operate quite independently from each other, so there is no immediate need for the scorecards to handle interdependencies between units in the organization. The most important dependency is the supply chain, which requires information about future demand in the market to be communicated to production quickly and efficiently. One metric that has been defined as mandatory for all local sales organizations is therefore the degree to which their product forecasts are accurate. Hence, this metric serves as a liaison between the local units' ability to predict future sales and the effects it has on the company's production schedules and product mix decisions.

When there are more scorecard levels, and the organization has a longer experience of using scorecards, it may seem practical and even necessary to use similar or identical scorecards for several units. We found some such cases in our public sector organizations. At least in Helsingborg, there may also be another reason. Helsingborg intends to publish data on its services for all citizens to see, and this, of course, makes it necessary to use identical metrics. But here, choice was from a predetermined list:

Helsingborg
There are several levels of scorecards in Helsingborg. There is one overall scorecard for the city. Then there are separate scorecards for its departments. How these work with their scorecards is somewhat different. Some units have one overall scorecard which they break down into operative scorecards at team level. Each team then has the same metrics and the same targets. The scorecards are made available for everyone in the unit, making it possible to follow what is going on in the organization. The purpose of having the same scorecards for all teams is that the members should be able to recognize and compare all scorecards.

The development of these scorecards has been done collectively, where members of each team have been involved. The goals and CSFs have been developed on the basis of a number of predetermined alternatives. The choice of metrics, on the other hand, has not been regulated. The regulations in the scorecard work have been set because the implementation should not take up too much time. The engaged actors should be able to reflect upon their work and their role in the organization but not feel that it takes too much time.

Despite the linkages between the department scorecards and those of the teams, there is no formalized connection between the scorecards. The focus throughout has been on the local processes, and defining how information should be openly provided to employees and citizens alike. By doing this, city management expects managers and employees to take appropriate action. So even if there is a hierarchy of scorecards, their relations are needed more to explain the logic of local activities than to create a chain of command. A result of developing and discussing their scorecards is, however, that several units have started to communicate in new ways as they begin to see opportunities for improving their cooperation.

Jönköping

In Jönköping there are several levels of scorecards. There is one overall scorecard for the organization that is being developed by the management board. This scorecard is then supported by scorecards at the administrative level, at clinic level and at department level. All levels of scorecards are compulsory and are developed on a regular basis.

These scorecards are thus aligned with each other even though they are individually developed and adjusted to represent each group's situation. The overall scorecard functions as an overall plan for the organization – it gives direction to the other organizational units. It is published in an official document where vision, goals, measures, and action plans are clearly stated.

On the basis of this plan, the administrative units develop their own specific scorecards, so-called 'planning scorecards'. These are more detailed and are often seen as more short-term than the overall scorecard. In these scorecards, focus is more on action plans than on strategic goals as in the overall scorecard. Goals, success factors and targets are clearly specified in the 'planning scorecards' but the focus is on how these goals are to be fulfilled. This makes the connection between the long-term planning and the short-term work visible for the organization. It also exposes the lead times that exist in the organization, enabling the employees to think about these and take them into account in their work.

On the basis of these 'planning scorecards', each unit then constructs activity plans. These are communicated through what they refer to as 'development guides'. These guides support the goals for each unit and describe how the employees are to reach them. Using the guides, reports are made three times a year communicating how well the unit has met its goals. These reports are made in special cobweb charts where measures are visualized within each focus area (Figure 2.6 is an example). These cobwebs have become a brand for the county's work with the BSC. They symbolize the qualitative and multi-dimensional work that the council does.

Even though the scorecards are connected to each other, there is a lot of freedom in how they are used. There are some measures that are compulsory to report back to management, but mostly the use of measures varies between the units. The employees have to feel that the measures that they use capture what is important to them, not only what is important to management. In some cases, this has led to the compulsory measures not being reported, but instead measures that the unit feels are more representative of their work.

An anonymous company which we quoted previously also had views on this. They strongly advised against considering the corporate scorecard as an aggregation of the units' scorecards:

If the corporate scorecard is considered an aggregate of the units' scorecards, then it is apparent that the organization misses out on many of the available synergies. As Goold and Campbell[44] have pointed out, the sum total of a corporation must be bigger than the sum of its parts. Hence, a scorecard that is constituted of the parts' scorecards does not indicate how the synergies will be realized. Instead, the corporate scorecard should tell the story of how the pieces fit together in a way that makes them – together – stronger than they are separately.

Each scorecard should be tailored to its specific context. Given this focus, it is unlikely that the superior unit will need to measure dimensions that are identical to its subunits. On the contrary, whereas the subunits might measure such things as customer satisfaction or retention rate, the corporate metrics would be the degree of integration between business units, cross-selling, or utilization of shared resources.

Our anonymous interviewees told us of their fight against the aggregation of scorecards. But the yearly business planning process in the company, which was logically based on the idea of aggregation, was so important that the scorecard process had to align with it. For two years they tried to prevent the corporate scorecard connecting with the business units' scorecards, but then they had to accept this notion.

One additional issue which needs to be addressed is how far down in an organization scorecards are meaningful. Since scorecards are about communication, a simple answer is: where there are some people who need to discuss business logic, ambition levels, and achieved performance. Extending scorecard work down to individual employees may prove useful when they have more independent tasks. Otherwise teams would be the normal level to stop. How useful this will be depends on a number of factors: the improvements aimed for in the project; links to development talks; effects on remuneration, etc.

Employees with individual tasks such as a consultant, sales representative, or a teacher may benefit from a personal scorecard. Three of its perspectives can be used to describe their work:

- The *customer* perspective: contacts with clients, prospects, or students. Measures may include the time spent on such activities, number of visits or classes, etc.
- The *internal processes* perspective: administrative duties, for instance, creating documents that are useful for colleagues, entering data into CRM[45] systems, or adding teaching notes to a school's database.
- The *development* perspective: identifying new prospects for the firm, or new materials for teaching.

Both processes and development can be measured in different ways: hours spent, the volume of documents created, or – better still – how much these have been used by colleagues. If a team of employees share their work and work closely together, then scorecards like this would be more relevant for the team.

It will sometimes be more difficult to find a meaningful role for the *financial* perspective in this kind of individual or team scorecard. Consultants or sales representatives may be able to measure their revenues, but probably not the teacher. There will be direct and indirect costs to measure connected with all employees. Sometimes the financial perspective can be interpreted in a broader sense of a principal's perspective. It then becomes an evaluation of the contribution the person or team has made to the organization. We will come back to this issue in Chapter 11.

CAN SCORECARDS BE USED FOR SOME UNITS?

We saw earlier that there sometimes can be scorecards only on some levels of an organization. Can it be meaningful to introduce scorecards just for one or a few units? One such case is BA:

BA Heathrow
Scorecards are not mandated within BA, so no alignment is needed between BA at Heathrow and the rest of the customer service organization in the corporation. However, the head of Heathrow, together with some colleagues, has initiated a discussion in the customer service unit (some 25 000 employees), to articulate the goals for customer service within BA. Since the manager at Heathrow has experience of working with the concept, some of the emerging goals might be structured and described according to the dimensions in a scorecard, but it has not been defined as the official control instrument.

Many organizations start their scorecard projects from the top, some with a pilot project farther down in the organization. Some never reach below the higher levels of the organization, others develop scorecards even for individual employees. Where to start is sometimes determined by the corporate leadership, sometimes it is the result of where the organization's 'fiery spirits' are located. Organizations that want to take a more premeditated attitude clearly first need to think about which of their activities should be covered by scorecards.

A local scorecard could be used entirely for internal purposes (motivating employees, etc.). It would normally also be used to agree on targets with higher levels of management, and report on performance to them. It might also be published on a corporate intranet as part of a description of the unit. Which of these dialogues scorecards shall be used for also needs to be determined.

If a BSC project is too broad in coverage and/or involves too many people, then there is a danger that the work will balloon and overtax the company's resources. It may then take too much time to gain the necessary support for the concept. Employees will not perceive scorecards as relevant (as at first in the Skandia case in Chapter 3), and the desired effects will not be obtained. Also, the project may consume so much of the time of key personnel that seeing it through to the finish is perceived as burdensome. Some companies seek to avoid this danger by starting with a pilot project at a subsidiary or department. The organization can then learn from its mistakes and have an easier time with further implementation of the concept. Oriflame even used a 'pre-pilot' project, followed by tests of the BSC in selected units:

Oriflame
A pilot project evaluated alternative modes of business planning and evaluation. Early on in the project the group zoomed in on the BSC and financial

forecasts as an alternative to the traditional budgeting process. The group's task was then to analyse whether these two control mechanisms would be a feasible alternative to the traditional budget. The sponsor of the project was the CEO of Oriflame. The project group's conclusion was that scorecards and financial forecasts would be a feasible alternative to budgets, and seven units were appointed to test these two methods to see how they would work in practice.

Another advantage of a pilot project is that it can help win the confidence of employees. What employees like and dislike about the concept may carry more weight than the pronouncements of top management or outsiders.

However, some companies believe in company-wide implementation of the concept from the very outset, reasoning that the concept raises issues with broader ramifications. This approach forces the entire company to change its philosophy of management control, and to look ahead to its goals for the future. The drawback is that the process – gaining support, spreading the message, and instilling appropriate attitudes – may take a very long time.

Among our cases, several have taken several years of rather modest trials. Even where a corporate function initiates the work, it may be advisable to have one or even a few years of pilot work before the BSC is introduced everywhere.

Jönköping

To get everyone involved in the work, the initiators decided to start from the top in the organization and move down. They thought this was the best way of getting engagement and motivation to work with the tool. The implementation therefore started in one unit, spreading from year to year until everyone worked with the BSC in one way or another. It is now compulsory for all departments to work with the BSC.

Where coverage is broad from the beginning, as in Nordea, there may still be acceptance that scorecards will reach only gradually into the lower echelons of the organization.

If one unit is chosen for the initial scorecard, then it needs to be fairly complete and self-contained, or have a clear task and vision assigned by its owners. Otherwise, the attempt to develop a scorecard will only result in a lot of questions about its vision and logic. Even that may be useful – some scorecard projects result in a 'proposal' from a subsidiary to corporate management about the role it wants. There are also practical matters involved: how large a part of the total organization will it be feasible and cost-efficient to include?

Sometimes the pilot is a volunteer who manages to convince the larger organization that it is time to try the BSC:

Lund HLC

At Lund's University Hospital, the policy was that all organizational units should work with QUL* – a TQM-like tool to ensure quality in healthcare. However, being a completely new organization, QUL was not regarded as a suitable tool for the HLC. They did not have an organization to measure. They therefore needed another tool that could support this quality-assurance process. The BSC was thought to fill the desired function, and management of HLC therefore convinced the hospital management that this tool would be a good alternative to the QUL reports. The BSC work was thereby given high priority and full attention in the organization.

If a pilot is needed, probably it should resemble other units in the group. But sometimes the criterion will be which units are most likely to benefit from scorecards. As their use is as communication tools, we should look for those where the need to discuss and reach agreement on priorities is greatest. This may be the case with:

1 *New businesses* or businesses with a great need to invest. These will invest in markets, new processes and development with a long-term focus, and scorecards will assist in reaching agreement on such investments.
2 *Crisis situations*, where it is necessary to reach agreement on problems and needed changes.
3 *Internal service and staff units*, where the scope of activities is not decided in contacts with an external market.

In the first of these situations, scorecards will be useful because financial targets may need to be set to show low or even negative results. The scorecard is used not only to justify this by proving the strategic importance of the venture, but also to safeguard that non-financial benefits – such as a growing business or improved capabilities that promise future profitability – are scrutinized and checked as closely as a traditional budget performance. As we learnt in Chapter 3, the huge investments needed in

---

* An acronym derived from the Swedish.

Skandia AFS started its quest for new ways to present its task and its performance:

Skandia

The investments that were made in the employees' development and learning only turned up as red numbers in the profit and loss account. This created a number of problems for AFS's managing director. During the first few years he found it difficult to get financial support from the rest of the organization because he did not show any profits. In addition, the company's financial value did not at all correspond with the company's potential future value. It was these thoughts that triggered the search for new tools to visualize and manage the organization's intangible assets.

In situations such as these it must be kept in mind that scorecards describe 'strategic bets', and to use them constantly to question these hypotheses – not to carry on with investments regardless of the signals from the marketplace.

The second situation is closely related, but here it is not so much the need for investing for the future, with a temporarily 'unbalanced' performance as a consequence, that is in focus. Here, rather, it is a major cultural change that is desired, and so many people inside and maybe also outside the organization have to start communicating about their tasks.

AMF Pension

AMF Pension's monopoly situation was to change with the new Swedish pension laws, and its management decided to compete aggressively in the upcoming 'pension elections'. This led to a strong awareness of change, and scorecards became one of the new CEO's tools for clarifying and communicating directions. Management in AMF Pension are agreed that they were valuable in changing a cost-conscious monopoly with tall walls between departments into a customer-oriented, cross-functionally operating modern company.

The third of these situations includes using scorecards for 'SLA's' with internal customers. An IT department, for instance, would often benefit from 'selling' not just current services but also a 'readiness' component – providing support and security – and monitoring new developments in technology of importance to the businesses in a corporation. Its activities to provide such benefits should be agreed with internal customers and the corporate leadership, and costs and performance levels should be included in its scorecard.

Nordea

As we saw in Chapter 4, Nordea's new PPMM consists of scorecards, rolling forecasts, and SLAs.

All SLAs are not yet in place. Their importance is to clarify roles, since group services now largely supersede the services formerly provided in each of the banks that merged to form Nordea. SLAs shall be used between four group service departments (IT, HR, Finance, and Legal) and their main customers (essentially the three business areas). For staff units, which are smaller, SLAs will not be used. In some cases, units may decide locally to use SLAs, but their number should be kept low.

There is no clear intention so far to use a scorecard structure for Nordea's SLAs. We believe this might be valuable, but there are other views. The project managers in the anonymous company referred to previously believe that

Scorecards should only be used in real business units. Functional scorecards in subunits, such as HR scorecards, IT scorecards, etc. do not generate any substantial benefits. A scorecard for a support function will not contribute to the unit in the same way as the scorecard is intended to when it is used in a real business. This requires three components: it must have shareholders, it must have real and external customers, and it must have an offering that the customer is prepared to pay for (and internal processes to produce this offering). Only real business units are free to design their vision and strategies. Internal units must always coordinate with the units they support, and they are dependent on these units' revenues that finally support them. Instead of scorecards, management control in and of internal units should be executed through, for example, process management and SLAs.

HOW CAN SCORECARDS BE USED FOR PROCESSES AND MATRIX ORGANIZATIONS?

Some firms see scorecards as an extension of their work to improve processes and relate the BSC to their quality programmes and introduction of process or workflow organization. That was the case already in the mid-1990s when ABB introduced scorecards in some of their units,[46] but we still have not found any fully developed example. Most, as in the cases we report in this book, remain ambitions for the future:

Ericsson Enterprise

Enterprise increasingly stresses processes that extend over several units among the seven. Would it be better to develop scorecards for the processes, rather than for the line units? To some extent this has been taken care of through the appointment of persons responsible for each KSF, the so-called 'KSF drivers'. In these roles, unit heads are encouraged to keep in mind that it is process performance and not their own units which determines Enterprise's success.

Lund HLC

The division of scorecard levels has become somewhat blurred due to the complexity of the organization. It is a matrix organization with process-based departments in the horizontal dimension and the medical specialities to which the doctors belong in the vertical dimension. To each department are coupled functional units such as wards, out-patient clinics, secretaries, etc. The scorecards for the departments have been rather difficult to develop because they embrace new and still somewhat abstract processes. There are, however, some attempts at such scorecards. The major part of the scorecard work has been done in the functional units so far.

To encourage the work with the scorecards, Arén's philosophy has been: 'Let it grow where there is a demand. People embrace it and find it is a good way of working.' By saying this he believes that an increased pressure will build up within the entire organization to start working with scorecards.

A company now using scorecards as an important tool in product development projects is VCC. Although the term 'scorecard' seems to have a somewhat different sense in Volvo, we find their model interesting:

Volvo Cars

For each new project started at the VCC, there are targets for investment and RoI. Especially in developing new product generations, RoI is a very long-term concept, and has to be translated into short-term, tangible targets. This is the purpose of the scorecards for product development now being developed. In developing these, the VCC builds on its methods for running such a project. The product development process is, in fact, two parallel processes: technological and commercial development, linked by a third, business development, which shall serve as the 'glue' between the other two. These three processes run throughout the three main phases of a project: the concept phase, pre-study, and industrialization. Scorecards are needed for each process and each phase.

These shall contain targets within each of four perspectives: Quality, Leadtime, Economy (i.e. efficient use of financial and other resources), and HR. The VCC shows this as the cube in Figure 9.4, where measurement should cover all 36 cells. Obviously, it is desirable if the same metrics can be used

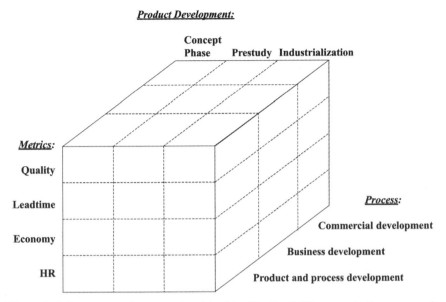

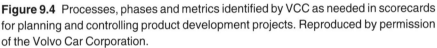

Figure 9.4 Processes, phases and metrics identified by VCC as needed in scorecards for planning and controlling product development projects. Reproduced by permission of the Volvo Car Corporation.

for, say, quality throughout, but it may mean different things during each phase and process.

When people from the line organization take part in projects, there is an interesting meeting between line and project responsibilities (Figure 9.5). Scorecards in the line organization will essentially cover the four main object-ives used throughout the VCC: profitable growth; customer satisfaction; next-generation cars; and next-generation employees and leaders. It will be seen that these are broadly similar to the Finance, Customer, and Development perspectives in a 'normal' scorecard. But they highlight the importance of renewing products and people at the VCC. In their matrix relationship with development projects, line units will emphasize competence development and staffing (How and Who). The projects will emphasize the deployment of people, and the efficient use of their talents (What and When). People may be assigned to projects part-time or full-time. They will agree with their line managers about personal goals, which should derive both from the line score-card and project scorecards. This relation has not, however, been formalized.

Whether or not an organization admits it, collaboration across the hier-archy often introduces an element of matrix into the organization. This involves responsibilities in two directions: vertically, to reflect, for instance,

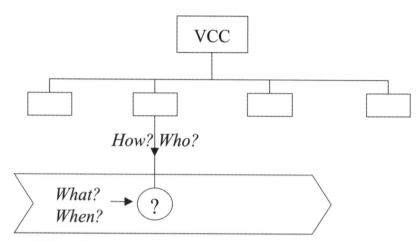

Figure 9.5 People working in a development project at VCC must relate to scorecard targets both vertically and horizontally. Reproduced by permission of the Volvo Car Corporation.

a functional or product dimension, and horizontally, to show the joint impact of several vertical units on the company's success with a particular 'key account' customer, or a specific industry. Scorecards could be used to depict this kind of double responsibility. Operational performance would then be largely a matter of a unit's responsibilities as part of one or more process chains, while maintenance and development of its capabilities could be agreed in a traditional hierarchical dialogue.

In matrix situations such as this, scorecards might work in different ways:

- Scorecards can be used to clarify interfaces in a process or 'value chain'. Just as they can serve as SLAs between internal support units and their customers, two functional units may use scorecards to agree on their tasks.
- Some metrics may be used throughout the value chain to focus attention on the performance of the whole process, e.g. customer satisfaction, to tell each link in the chain that this is not just of interest to the unit that deals directly with the customer.
- In relationships such as Figure 9.5, competences are normally a line responsibility. But it is important to learn from processes and projects. Targets and actions for this could be included in scorecards for processes, and in the scorecards for units taking part in the process.

As before, the key issue here is for what dialogues scorecards should be used. We suggest using the scorecard as a tool in whatever such discussions a corporation may have, for instance, when it introduces process coordinators or shifts responsibilities away from the traditional hierarchy.

Figure 9.6 is an attempt to illustrate this. It was originally drawn in a project where we assisted an airport – not Heathrow – in developing its performance measurement system. An example of the horizontal dimension is the arrival of passengers, where several different functional units are involved. For such horizontal processes there should be targets relating to customer satisfaction and the efficient use of facilities. There are even units not belonging to the airport (such as flight operators and customs officials) who have an impact on these metrics, as our case from BA at Heathrow illustrates.

The vertical dimension is provided by the different functions, and follows the traditional hierarchy of the airport. One of these, baggage handling, could be as illustrated in the figure. This unit also takes part in other horizontal processes, such as taking care of departing passengers'

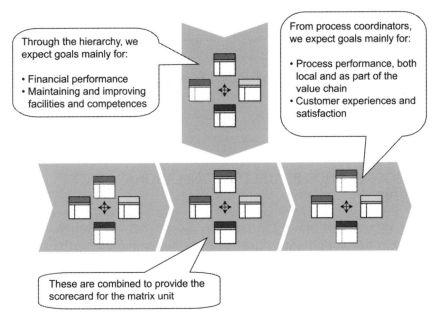

Figure 9.6 In a matrix organization, scorecards may be used to reflect expectations from both "vertical" and "horizontal" leaders.

luggage, and unclaimed luggage. There is a need to discuss baggage hand-ling's investments in new technologies, and the cost of this function. Since these decisions will have an impact on other processes also, such as departure, such discussions must take place in the vertical dimension. These discussions should provide targets for baggage handling relating to its HR, information systems support, etc.

Figure 9.6 illustrates how the meeting between the vertical and hori-zontal dimensions in a matrix may be thought of as a meeting between scorecard elements coming from these two dimensions. For instance, if a scorecard is used to discuss baggage handling for arriving customers, then targets relating to both their total service experience *and* to the functional unit's utilization of its information system are relevant.

This is even more apparent for functions requiring more extensive long-term investments. Following the recent downturn in the number of travel-lers, some airports find themselves with excess capacity in runways or terminals. Scorecards for such units within an airport will have to reflect *both* current utilization – a horizontal process dimension – *and* long-term development plans – a vertical, hierarchical dimension we may call owner-ship. They will be used to discuss responsibilities in both dimensions.

We would like to see a family of related scorecards, where, for instance, baggage handling's scorecard would include measures relating both to its functional (vertical) role and its ongoing utilization in (horizontal) oper-ative processes. As we show in Figure 9.6, operative measures such as these will dominate the customer and process perspectives, while the develop-ment and financial perspectives will contain measures that reflect their functional objectives.

CAN SCORECARDS BE USED TO COLLABORATE WITH OTHERS?

In our airport example in the previous section, service quality depends on close collaboration with actors who are not employed by the airport: flight operators, customs, and others. If we define the customer experience to include ground transportation, still more firms and people should be included. It is, of course, tempting to use scorecards within this larger group for discussing and agreeing on levels of ambition, and monitor performance jointly.

Increasingly, service that used to be in-house is outsourced, and cooperation in value chains or value constellations extends to outside partners. Such 'extended enterprises' or 'virtual' and 'imaginary' organizations[47] require formal or informal contracts which are more long-term than those in a normal market. In an outsourcing relationship, the lowest price for some pre-specified good will not always be a relevant goal. The aim is to achieve a mutually rewarding collaboration, and common problem solving may identify solutions which are better for both partners. Scorecards may be a very useful tool for arriving at and monitoring such collaboration.

Helsingborg
Contractors performing work for the city measure quality and customer reactions. Since they have the contacts with customers (e.g. unemployed attending the city's training courses, which are outsourced to professional training firms), it is also natural to have them take the measurements through customer surveys. These are part both of the evaluation of the trainers, and the functional department within the city responsible for this type of service.

In manufacturing and retailing, computers are increasingly used to link processes across several firms. There is also a growing interest in sharing financial information between companies ('open-book accounting'). It may also extend to data about customer experiences. Scorecards can be used to communicate across organizational boundaries, agree on current performance and on long-term investments needed to develop the collaboration further.[48]

HOW DO SCORECARDS RELATE OVER TIME?

Measures in a scorecard will reflect the current situation in an organization, or targets for the next period. In Chapter 6, we discussed how it should include both leading and lagging measures. For instance, progress towards a 'wanted position' (cf. Figure 2.4 from Ericsson Enterprise) concerning the Finance or Customer perspectives will depend on how we fulfil ambitions concerning Development and Processes. Maybe we should prepare scorecards for several time periods, linked through our assumptions about causality. But fine-tuning actions and targets for a sequence of future years can easily turn into a complex planning exercise involving simulation, mental or computer-assisted.

This is not the way it is done in any of the corporations we have visited. They derive their long-term targets, their wanted position some years from now, from an interpretation of what future competition will require. These targets will then guide the design of more short-term actions and targets:

Nordea

Planning takes place mainly in the third and fourth quarter each year, when 'stretch targets' are set three years ahead. In addition, targets are set for the next five quarters, i.e. the final quarter of the current year plus the four quarters of the next fiscal year. Obviously, not every KPI will be practical to measure every quarter, but essentially Nordea's scorecards include the expected trajectory over the next three years.

Thus, during Q3 of 2001, targets were set for Q4 and all four quarters of 2002, and also for 2004. During 2002, the quarterly targets are regarded as fixed. Only under exceptional circumstances will they be revised. This is partly because they are used together with RFFs. These provide a simpler and more regularly updated view of expected performance during the next five quarters. By 'rolling' these every quarter and stating clearly that they should be best estimates rather than targets, management always has an up-to-date basis for coordinating. Obviously, at the start of the year scorecards and forecasts are harmonized, but during the year they may drift apart.

When new scorecard targets are prepared in the autumn of 2002, this is expected to require less work since the strategic logic and the 'stretch' target for 2004 should normally still be relevant. Targets are now prepared for the three quarters of 2003, and for 2005.

Oriflame

From 2002, the scorecards have replaced the traditional budgeting exercise. Each subsidiary submits a financial forecast every third month (for the coming twelve months) to the corporate office. In the last forecast of the year, the scorecard is included (and the forecast is also extended to 15 months). Hence, it resembles the former budget but the production of it should not require as much resources. The forecast and the targets in the scorecard are then negotiated with the regional manager, and are used as an ambition statement for the coming year.

ARE WE BEING TOO RATIONAL?

Our discussion above, and also that in several of the firms we describe, may be criticized for presenting too harmonious a picture of relations within major corporations. Planning and budget processes have been described as 'games' played in order to promote subunit or personal interests (cf. Chapter 7). Surely the multi-dimensional targets in a scorecard will not change this?

Some will also question whether our view of an organization's preparation for the future as rational problem solving is relevant. Are not targets set primarily to provide motivation, often involving some 'stretch' factors rather than the global logic we advise?

Of course, arriving at targets and actions for the next year or quarter will involve a matter of negotiation. This should be based on facts and explicit assumptions. We agree that the budget game may invite featherbedding and delays in admitting that targets will not be met. But we believe that a good scorecard invites serious discussions and makes it much more difficult to cheat. There will obviously be an element of optimism and 'stretch' that cannot be verified from facts. But it will be clearer for everyone how, for instance, markets have to react, or what level of yield is required, in order for the scorecard logic to be realistic.

Shared views on strategy and business logic are necessary for many actors in today's corporations, not just managers but most employees. 'Trust' has been one of the most frequent concepts in management books in recent years. Scorecards can be used to identify win-win designs and prove that planning dialogues in large organizations need not be a zero-sum power game.

A THEORETICAL PERSPECTIVE

This chapter has discussed how subunits within a larger organization are coordinated. The main reason why management may sometimes be more effective than the market-place in coordinating human activities is the existence of transaction costs.[49] Put differently, if business units are combined to form a corporation, then they can only outperform similar units in a free market if the corporation uses some element of control. To create a corporation and limit control to using an internal, simulated market mechanism will not be enough. This additional control may involve financial cross-subsidization between units, operational synergies through shared activities, knowledge transfer, etc.

Traditionally, this additional control was achieved through hierarchical means: plans and orders. This was a top-down process with senior management subdividing the task for the entire organization into subtasks for each unit. Over the years, planning (e.g. budgeting) became less top-down and more of a coordination process. The input from subunits now is essential for arriving at agreement on suitable tasks for each unit. Only in this way will managers of these units be committed to do their best.

Goals for subunits also became fewer and less detailed. Elements of market mechanisms were introduced and often influenced day-to-day actions of units as much as plans and agreed goals.

Top-down or bottom-up planning processes, internal markets, or some combination of these may be useful in different circumstances.[50] Use of scorecards has to be considered also in relation to other means of control. Tasks which can be easily decomposed into individual subtasks, each to be separately optimized, should be left to the market and not included in the kind of coordinated human enterprise we label 'firms' or 'corporations'. Conversely, decomposing ('breaking down') tasks in a firm will require us to articulate dependencies between subunits: synergies that will often be non-linear. Using scorecards is a good way of showing such dependencies, since subunits, instead of a too-simplistic optimization of some single goal such as unit profit, are directed to pursue a balance between several different goals, reflecting how they contribute to corporate success in different ways.

By themselves, scorecards do not constitute management control. They are introduced, however, as an important tool for strategic management. In this context, they need to be related to other current concepts such as 'value-based management', 'shareholder value' and 'intellectual capital'. In many corporations, the challenge now is to arrive at a suitable mix of financial controls and scorecards.

In our experience, financial controls (sometimes called *performance management*, and usually focusing return on capital) are sufficient only when management is remote and does not have a viewpoint of its own concerning the business logic and success factors. This may be true in conglomerates or holding companies, where the different businesses are viewed just as financial investments.

As soon as control is based on some strategic vision, corporate leaders will need to communicate with management about this vision and its business logic. They need to agree on it *ex ante* and monitor progress *ex post*. So-called *value-based management* uses revised monetary measures such as

Economic Value Added (EVA) to stimulate activities leading to shareholder wealth. While still predominantly financial, this type of control is not limited to measures found in standard financial reports (profit and loss, and balance sheet). Here, business units may be regarded as long-term investments, where projected cash flows over time are the main focus.

Using BSCs for control can be labelled *strategic management*. Here, control metrics should capture the strategic aims and logic of business activities, making it natural to include also non-financial measures, and to indicate as clearly as possible linkages between actions and metrics.

Figure 9.7 shows this in a highly simplified manner. To the right, where corporations are pursuing synergies, scorecards will be used at fairly high corporate levels – even at group headquarters. To the left, where corporations are managed like portfolios, more traditional controls will continue to be the most important ones. At division or business unit level, however, scorecards will be valuable for communication about visions and business logics.

Financial measures used for control to the left in Figure 9.7 will normally be included also in the scorecards used to the right. To decide how to use the BSC, an organization needs to identify its mix of different

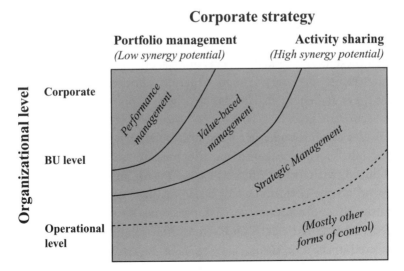

Figure 9.7 Dominant modes of control at different organizational levels in large, multibusiness corporations pursuing different basic strategies.

kinds of control for each level of the organization. Scorecard projects easily lead into a reconsideration of strategy and management control.

All the issues discussed in this chapter reflect different problems arising from this. How can we use scorecards to direct a unit's efforts, and provide managers and employees with the semi-separate task they need in order to feel motivated? And at the same time take into account that *corporate* success is a complex function of the achievements of several units?

RECOMMENDATIONS AND IMPLICATIONS

'Orchestrating' activities, and creating a joint focus in an organization, should be one of the great payoffs of good scorecard use. To do this, we should:

- Decide early in the process whether a corporate scorecard is desired, and – if it is – use this as the departure point for lower-level scorecards. Scorecards can be introduced for parts of corporations. This may be useful if these units have clear tasks and roles within the larger group, and their role is not to optimize profits. Local enthusiasm for trying the BSC will also help.

- Regard the relation between scorecards at different levels as logical rather than mathematical, but use identical metrics if the same KSFs are relevant for different scorecards.

- Have strong local involvement in the development of scorecards, even when there is an overarching corporate scorecard to guide the process. And arrange meetings to share experiences between similar units, so that they can benefit also from each others' insights in developing their own scorecards.

- Consider carefully whether scorecard metrics should describe just the situation for the local unit, or also measure conditions that are co-produced with other units (such as customer loyalty, which may depend on the performance of different units meeting customers). A healthy effect of scorecards is that it becomes clear that responsibilities need to be sorted out – and sometimes remain shared – with this reflected in the scorecards.

Through careful handling of the issues we have discussed in this chapter, several benefits may occur, such as being able to

- Take advantage of the knowledge existing in different parts of the organization as people are encouraged to contribute their views about what should be done, but do this with an improved understanding for intended strategies.
- Cut out unnecessary spending on development efforts in local units that will be worthless because other parts of the firm are not preparing for the same future.
- Improve horizontal communication so that managers collaborate for the benefit of the whole, rather than the glory of the parts.
- Assist in finally making matrix organizations viable, where the business logic makes them attractive.

How to Balance the Incentive System

10

ARE FINANCIAL REWARDS REQUIRED TO OPERATE A BSC?

When we talk to clients and participants at conferences, the question of how to connect scorecards to incentive systems always comes up. Some practitioners argue that they have not succeeded in their BSC efforts because their incentive systems have not promoted the intended behaviour. Others argue that it is impossible to change any behaviour unless it is associated with a substantial reward. In general, it is interesting to note that so many practitioners say that they plan to connect their scorecards with their incentive system in the future. Both Nordea and Oriflame, for example, anticipate that they will embed the scorecard in the incentive models, but first they say that the scorecards have to sink into the organization.

Even if incentives may play an important role when implementing scorecards – or in any other change programme for that matter – we do not believe that incentives or reward mechanisms are generic success factors. On the contrary, we have seen numerous situations where the incentive systems have been aligned with the organization's strategy and goals, but where the employees have still behaved in ways other than those that the incentives encouraged. When asking the employees why they disregard such behaviour that would yield rewards, they often say that the incentive models are based on perceptions of the workforce that are too simplistic and instrumental. The reason why they do what they do is not because it results in one Euro more or less, but because they want to contribute to what they believe should be the organization's goals; belong to the group; or be true to their profession.

At this point, it may be important to stress that our practical experience from working with strategy and management control projects mostly comes from the Scandinavian countries, as do the majority of the cases in this book. Our attitude to financial rewards may differ from other writers. The attitude to remuneration and compensation differs greatly between countries, and our presentation is naturally grounded in a Scandinavian approach to incentives and rewards that at least until recently has de-emphasized financial gains as motivators. However, even a seasoned American writer such as Peter Drucker recently challenged some common assumptions on incentives and bonuses:[51]

> *We already know what does not work: bribery. In the past 10 or 15 years, many businesses in America have used bonuses or stock options to attract and keep knowledge workers. It always fails. ... The management of knowledge workers should be based on the assumption that the corporation needs them more than they need the corporation. They know they can leave. They have both mobility and self-confidence. This means that they have to be treated and managed as volunteers, in the same way as volunteers who work for a not-for-profit organization.* The first thing such people want to know is what the company is trying to do and where it is going. *Next, they are interested in personal achievement and personal responsibility... Above all they want respect, not so much for themselves as for their area of knowledge* (emphasis added).

We believe it is necessary to implement incentives and reward mechanisms with great care. This is partly because these instruments may have a strong impact on the organization (hence, it is important that they focus on the 'right' things, to avoid an unbalanced execution), partly because we think that there are other levers that may be used to promote the utilization of scorecards (cf. Chapter 7).

Ericsson Enterprise

In Ericsson, bonuses are a significant part of compensation. They are currently linked to three things: cash flow, operating margin, and the BSC. Cash flow and operating margin are measured for Ericsson as a corporation, while scorecard metrics are selected from among those in the scorecard for the unit of the person involved. (It should be kept in mind that there is no scorecard for the corporate level in Ericsson.) Compensation is normally linked to the fulfilment grade of the whole scorecard but occasionally to only one or two selected metrics on the scorecard. Some people argue that it is better to include the whole scorecard, since the danger otherwise is that those few metrics achieve a greater importance than the rest of the scorecard. Using the whole scorecard is also considered to be simpler from an administrative point of view.

In Ericsson Enterprise there are incentive models for management and for all employees. These are linked to corporate and Enterprise finances and to all or selected KPIs on the BSC for Enterprise and their own unit. The compensation range, in the form of bonuses, varies for the different management levels and for the broad incentive for employees.

The feasibility of a reward system is contingent on many factors in the organization. Hence, it is impossible to say whether or not incentives will support a BSC project. In this chapter we therefore discuss how incentive systems can be aligned with scorecards in order to promote realization of the intended strategy. Drucker seems to be critical of monetary remuneration that is based on an idea we will call *behavioural control*, i.e. that there is an immediate connection between behaviour and a financial reward. Experts on 'compensation management' would probably point out that there are numerous ways to package rewards, also including other kinds of incentives. We will here limit ourselves to a distinction between behavioural controls and *profit sharing*.

When planning to implement an incentive system, the first question to answer must be whether the system's main purpose is behavioural control or profit-sharing. If it is profit sharing, then the incentive schemes will primarily serve as a method to define how the profit should be divided between the members in the organization. A scorecard structure could thus be used to summarize an individual's or a group's performance. This performance evaluation then defines how the profit will be distributed between the employees (an alternative distribution mechanism would, for example, be to split the profit equally between all employees).

In addition to this, a decision must be made on which profit to share. Most organizations calculate profits at various levels in the organization: an internal profit centre may show one profit, the company may show another profit and (if applicable) the corporation may show yet another profit. The profit-sharing system must strike a balance between cooperation and suboptimization. Sharing in one's own unit's profit may result in suboptimization (but also create a sense of focus and drive), while sharing the next level's profit may promote cooperation (or be perceived as irrelevant because such results are too remote). In literature, it is often argued that profits shall be shared on the next higher level in the organization, to promote cooperation between units.

If the incentive scheme will be used mainly to influence behaviour, then it is important to think about the reward package in another way. The money used to fuel the incentive model should be seen as an operating cost, and should not be conditioned to whether or not the company is making a profit. This cost is incurred on the basis of operational performance – not on financial performance. Hence, it might be the case that the 'rewards' (if the company is true to its BSC beliefs) are paid even though the company is making a loss.[52]

Regardless of the discussion above, there is one general reason why incentives should be linked to the scorecard. This reason does not, primarily, focus on the stimuli–response logic inherent in most reward structures, but rather on management's responsibility to demonstrate their belief in the scorecard. If the company is prepared to reward its employees for their efforts in the Customer, Process, and Learning and development perspectives, then it conveys that it believes in the hypotheses in the scorecard. For no other reason, this might be enough of a trigger to institute some kind of reward system linked to the BSC.

MULTI-DIMENSIONAL REWARDING

Above, we have argued that any organization thinking of linking their incentive scheme to their scorecards should be careful and evaluate the benefits and drawbacks of an incentive system in their particular context. Hereafter, we will therefore discuss some of our experiences as to how scorecards can be embedded in the reward system.

A balanced incentive system should be based on drivers as well as outcome metrics. In our view, the balanced incentive system should not only include a range of goals (regarding finances, customers, processes and learning and growth), but also strike a balance between drivers and outcome.[53] If the incentive system contains only singular goals, or if it solely focuses on behaviour or results, then we do not regard it as balanced.

Even when multiple goals are used in the scorecard, there are different ways they can be used. One practice we have come across is to aggregate all measurements into one combined index. In Figure 10.1, this means moving to the left in the figure. Even though this single index is an aggregate of different indicators, rewards are then grounded in one dimension only. It may be argued that in calculating a monetary reward, the multi-dimensional scorecard will ultimately be reduced to a single dimension. However, it is more in line with the intentions of the scorecard to keep the different metrics also in the incentive scheme. The more transparent the system, the better. Hence, all or some measures should be selected from the different perspectives and be used as explicit denominators in the reward structure, preferably combining both leading and lagging indicators, i.e. moving towards the right of Figure 10.1.

We use the concepts incentives and rewards synonymously, even though we have noticed that the two words sometimes are interpreted differently. The word incentive indicates a notion of financial remuneration, whereas reward may include various kinds of compensation. Also, incentive indicates an inducement that is known *ex ante*, whereas rewards may be decided *ex post*. Beyond the nuances of the words, the differences in interpretation also reveal different attitudes towards what the employees are believed to value. Some managers seem to view financial incentives as the only available alternative, while others experiment with various kinds of rewards.

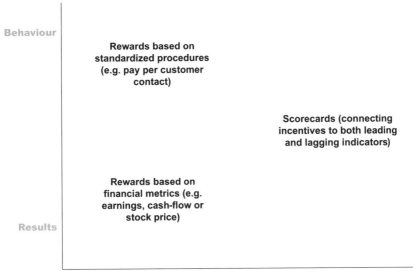

Figure 10.1 Alternative ways to link rewards to metrics.

In the literature, for example, we have found instances of companies that have not been allowed to implement financial incentive systems (due to existing agreements with the unions) and hence have tried to emulate a financial reward system. In doing so, they have implemented a system where points are awarded instead of money. These could be exchanged for valuables, such as merchandise, tickets, hotel nights. Although they were not defined as financial rewards, they carried an obvious monetary value (since the recipients could use the points to purchase items that they would otherwise have to use cash to buy). These compensation schemes are, thus, almost as financially oriented as cash bonuses.

When designing a reward package, the company should think beyond financial or pseudo-financial bonuses, and instead consider a range of different types of rewards that target the individual receiver's needs or wishes. Such rewards can range from tangible and apparent items with an obvious market value (pseudo-financial rewards) to intangibles that may be appreciated by the receiver but are difficult to set a price on (such as meeting an interesting thought-leader, attending a closed seminar, or getting time off for a personal project).

Marketing literature has elaborated on the need for personalized offerings and customization. Companies should stop treating every customer in the same way, and instead recognize that they are all individuals with different needs and different expectations. Every client should be served as an individual and unique person. In a similar way, reward mechanisms should be tailored to reflect the desires and requirements of different employees.

Skandia

The connection between indicators and bonus was not easy. The employees were different and aware that a specific connection could lead to sub-optimizations in the group. The only satisfying solution was therefore that the bonus be given on an individual level rather than on the group level, i.e. depending on each individual's behaviour, s/he got a customized bonus connection. This was thought to lead to the group's goals being fulfilled while the employees had their own way of getting there.

Instead of trying to create one reward system that is equal to all, the company could try to create a set of reward mechanisms that are as specific to the individuals as possible. Instead of relying on money, which has a high generic value but no specific value (the employee has to turn the money into something that she considers valuable), management should try to understand their employees' interests and aspirations, and offer them rewards that are aligned with these.

Such rewards, which also embed a meaning and a thought, are often most appreciated. These rewards may sometimes carry a low generic value (they cannot be changed into something else), but a high specific value. An alternative to a financial bonus could, for example, be an experience, such as if an employee gets to attend an interesting seminar or meet his favourite football team. In between these extremes (pure financial rewards versus individual experiences) are, of course, a host of different alternatives. Ranging from points exchangeable for goods and merchandise, via fringe benefits such as domestic services, to time off for studies, experiences, or a sabbatical. According to the literature, 3M, which is famous for its innovative capacity, rewards its successful employees with time, not money. This is time that the employees' must spend on non-core activities. Over the years, this incentive mechanism has also proved to be valuable to the company, since many new and profitable innovations have come out of these periods of absence.

The structure in the BSC promotes multi-dimensionality. Hence, the compensation packages linked to the scorecard should also allow for rewards in different dimensions. Instead of applying the same reward formula to everyone, the organization should tailor the rewards to suit the individual employees' aspirations and dreams.

EMBEDDING SCORECARDS IN THE INCENTIVE SCHEME

Regardless of whether the incentives are financial or non-financial, they may be related to the scorecards. Besides 'putting the money where its mouth is', i.e. showing that management actually believes in the scorecard to the extent it is willing to reward performance according to it, incentives may also focus employees' attention on certain behaviour – but only as long as the dimensions in the reward scheme possess some general characteristics. To have any impact on an individual's behaviour, the measures in the reward system must be:

- *accepted as true*. The first line of resistance is to think, 'This must be wrong!'

- *considered valid.* The second line of resistance is to say, 'Well, but that isn't really relevant!'
- possible to *link to* some *known action*. The third line of resistance is to say, "Yes, it's a pity isn't it, but we can't do anything about that.'
- possible to *link to* some *action of which the individual is capable*. The fourth line of resistance is to claim, 'That's nothing I can do anything about!'
- *linked to* some such *action for which* the *individual has incentives*. The last line of resistance is to say, 'I could do something about that, but why should I?'

Only if measures are perceived as true, valid, and linked to some action of which the person is capable will they influence the behaviour in the organization.

Rewarding performance according to leading indicators in the scorecard calls for some specific design choices to avoid suboptimization. In discussing performance drivers (leading indicators) and outcome measures (lagging indicators) in Chapter 6, we noted that these usually form part of a means–ends chain where an outcome such as a new customer contact is also as a driver of future sales. Even though rewards should be connected to leading indicators, these indicators could be measured as 'leading outcomes' rather than 'leading activities'. We prefer to avoid incentives on activity-based metrics such as 'number of customer visits' or 'number of cold calls'. These metrics may be interesting indicators of what is to come, predicting future demand, but if they are rewarded as stand-alone metrics, then there is a risk that they will be perceived as ends in themselves.

Such metrics may be interesting to monitor in order to get a feeling of the heat in the organization. But they may be dangerous to include in the incentive system. Instead their output counterpart could be used, such as 'number of new customers'. Consequently, the metrics in the scorecard play different roles. Some of them may be included in the incentive scheme, whereas others will serve only as indicators of future demands and capacities.

The links in the scorecard are, as mentioned earlier, only hypotheses about the logic of the business model, where some relationships (i.e. strategic bets) probably are stronger than others. Hence, only the metrics that are strongly correlated with the end result should be included in the incentive scheme. Different metrics have different uses.[54] In Figure 10.2 we show that some metrics may only be used as indicators FYI, whereas others may serve as a basis for rewards and remuneration. In the same way, some metrics are only used internally – and may hence be tailored to the specific situation – whereas others are used to inform the public and thus need to be understandable by outsiders.

It is interesting to note also that simpler metrics, which are primarily used as pure indicators may contain some 'rewarding' characteristics.

Lund HLC
Some employees find it rewarding in itself to be able to spot the development over time. Even when no targets are set for the metric, and definitely no rewards are linked to it, the information in itself may serve as a catalyst for action. Being able to see the development, recognizing past achievements, makes it worth the effort to put in some extra energy.

We have also received similar comments from other respondents in the public sector, where incentive schemes are not as usual as in the private sector. When embedding metrics from the scorecard into the incentive system, it becomes important to set realistic goals. This makes it more

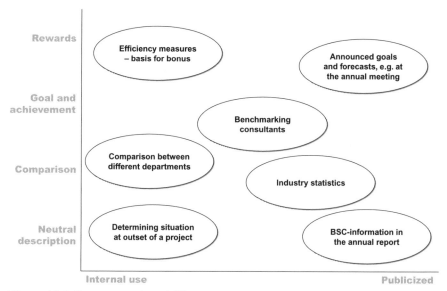

Figure 10.2 Some examples of different purposes and uses for measurements. (From *Performance Drivers*, p.126.).

difficult to work with stretch targets (as we discussed in Chapter 7), which deliberately serve as long-term aspirations. If the targets are too ambitious, then they will be very difficult – if not impossible – to reach within the coming year. Hence, the rewards will be out of reach for the employees. The pragmatic tactic to solve this dilemma is to strike a balance between stretch targets and reachable targets. Stretch targets could be set for metrics that are used to indicate long-term aspirations, and more modest (and reachable) goals can be set for the metrics that are embedded in the incentive system.[55]

Cosmetics retailer

One former client has implemented an incentive model for their store managers, which is linked to the company's BSC. The compensation package consists of three components:

1. Base salary, dependent on the job specification.
2. Salary increase, if the manager reaches the targets for four agreed metrics in the scorecard:

   • *Customer-satisfaction index* (the outcome is compiled by a research company, which receives questionnaires from customers who have been randomly selected by the cash register)
   • *Employee-satisfaction index*
   • *Paying customers/visitors* (measured as the share of persons entering the store who actually buy something)
   • *Inventory turn-around time*

3. Bonus based on financial results

   The targets that are used to define the salary increase are set in a dialogue between the store manager and headquarters. The four metrics account for 25% each in the formula. Hence, if the manager reaches the target for two of the metrics, she receives 50% of the proposed monthly salary increase. The targets are, however, set so that they are achievable. In this way, the metrics become relevant to the store manager.

We find it interesting that the incentives here are permanent salary increases. However, these obviously carry an expectation that performance should also have improved permanently. If these had been temporary bonuses, managers might hesitate to raise the level of performance expected from them in the future for just a short-term reward. The company had made calculations showing that the average store would profit from improving the four metrics more than enough to pay the increased salary. In communicating this to the store managers, it actually used a profit-sharing logic. The link from inventory turnover to profit seems fact-based: it should be possible to calculate the savings from improved turnover quite exactly. We would regard the link from employee satisfaction to profits as a hypothesis (strategic bet), although there are probably studies proving their connection. In basing rewards on this hypothesis, top management is proving its faith in the assumption it makes in encouraging store managers to take good care of their employees.

Connecting scorecards and an incentive model, as in the cosmetics company, switches some of the risk-taking from the principal (the organization) to the agent (the employee). Instead of promising the employee a gross salary, some part of it is conditioned relative to certain indicators. Employees who feel that they can influence these indicators will consider this fair. For instance, in the cosmetics company, store managers will readily accept the benefits from increasing turnover, but they may be hesitant as to whether improved employee satisfaction will increase profitability. Still, by rewarding managers for it, top management sends the message that *it* will risk 'betting' on this hypothesis. The risk that remains for the store manager who accepts this salary model is that she will be able to improve her employees' satisfaction.

Hence, it is important that the employee will be able to influence the domain that is captured in the indicator. If, for example, the board decides to invest in a national marketing campaign, then they should be held responsible for the business outcome of it, not the employees in the marketing department. Running a campaign does not only include marketing activities, but also ensuring that customer-service units, logistics departments, sales representatives, etc. can handle the new customers that are attracted to the company. Aligning these different processes, making sure that they operate in harmony, is management's responsibility. The employees in the marketing department are responsible for producing the best campaign possible, and should hence be rewarded for this. The model used in the cosmetics company comes rather close to what we termed behaviour control. Store managers are rewarded for 'leading outcomes' and not activities, and they can find their own methods for improving employee satisfaction, etc. But they are not encouraged to try alternatives to the business logic focusing on the four metrics that top management has mandated. An alternative would be to use a profit-sharing model instead. If compensation were related to store profit, then similar behaviour could result if store managers share top management's view of what creates success. If cooperation between stores is desired, then a profit-sharing model might link their compensation to the profits of a group of stores, maybe those in the same city. They might then start trying common advertising, training, or share personnel if one store has a temporary vacancy.

Our view is that behaviour control and profit sharing may both be useful. But the different logics of the two models need to be considered. If profit sharing is used, then the profit that is to be shared must be defined in a way that will encourage the desired behaviour. If behaviour control is used, then it should be realized that the choice of metrics for linking compensation has important implications in terms of risk bearing and freedom to act. Probably this is the reason why some large corporations use a combination of both:

Industrial company

(The company considers this information sensitive, and has asked us to with-hold its identity.)

Incentives are based on employees' level in the organization:

- Top management has 40% of their expected compensation in the form of bonuses. Half of this is linked to corporate cash flow, half to its operating margin.
- For the next level, 30% are bonuses, split equally among cash flow, operating margin, and scorecard metrics for this person's own unit.
- Below this, there is a level of managers who receive 25% split 8–8–9 between the three parts.
- For all employees, there is the so-called broad-based incentive scheme, where 8% are split between cash flow (2%) and scorecard metrics (6%).

We can see that as we go further down the company, incentives make up a smaller part of total compensation, and are based more and more on score-card metrics rather than financial results.[56] This certainly reflects the perceived discretion of these managers and employees. It will be seen that top management even get the signal that it should be concerned primarily about the whole corporation.

A risk when embedding scorecard metrics in the incentive scheme is that it may turn the strategic bets into perceived truths. But, the strategy map, and the metrics in the scorecard, do not provide a *guaranteed* road to success! On the contrary, it is the organization's best bet (or guess) on what the customers will value and be prepared to pay for, as well as why this particular organization will be able to deliver this offering. Even if the long-term goals (the outcome) may remain over time, strategic bets may prove to be incorrect and call for re-examination. If some of the metrics have been implemented in the incentive model, then it is an apparent risk that it will impede the organization's flexibility. The employees will probably be reluctant to change the 'contract' they have agreed upon, which has guided their efforts and focused their attention on some particular areas in the business. The scorecard may thus prevent change, even though its purpose is the opposite.

SAFEGUARDING AGAINST OPPORTUNISTIC BEHAVIOUR

Before implementing or redesigning the incentive system, it is important to analyse its integrity, so that it does not generate suboptimization. Measurement routines must ensure that the rewards are given to the employees who deserve them. Employees must not be enticed to tamper with the system in order to gain rewards and advantages that they are not entitled to.

Let us say that an organization decides to include the metric 'number of customer visits' in the incentive model, even though this is a leading activity rather than a leading outcome. Management's experience is, however, that there is a high correlation between an experienced salesman's number of visits and the revenue he generates. Hence, management is prepared to reward number of visits, because it is something that the salesperson can control. Number of new customers, on the other hand, would be a better leading outcome metric, but it does not reflect the salesperson's efforts only. Other factors also influence this outcome, and therefore management has decided to reward customer visits.

Management's intention obviously is to promote customer interaction. There are, however, also other implicit expectations embedded in this. Even though the metric does not address it, management expects that the salesperson – who visits the customer's site – will present the company's offerings in a professional and selling way. This expectation is not explicitly addressed, since most salespersons understand this tacit expectation (they have probably been trained in this) and the metric thus serves as a beacon along the road to revenue and profit. Some salespersons, however, may still not understand what (or how) they shall do when they meet with the prospect. This calls for the need to communicate the full picture: communicating that the salesperson should leverage the personal meeting with the customer to make him interested in the company's products – an interaction that will generate sales, which will lead to revenues and finally profits.

Fortunately, it is not very common that the employees are as ignorant as this, even though many scorecard opponents claim that this is a problem when 'managing by the numbers': that the employees will not understand the big picture, but only optimize on what counts. Of course, such persons may exist, but to our knowledge they are not very common. We refer to this as *ignorant* behaviour, when an employee does not grasp the full picture. This is the case when the incentive model communicates that the salesperson, shall, for example, visit as many customers as possible and devote his full time to this – but in carrying this out neglects to leverage the customer encounters. The 'measure' will drive him from one visit to the next, not giving him time to sell anything. If this is the case, it indicates that the strategy map and the scorecard have not been communicated thoroughly so that the employees understand the grand scheme. Or that other methods to influence activities, such as sales training, have failed.

Deceitful behaviour, on the other hand, takes more effort to manage. Whereas ignorant behaviour results in poor performance due to incompetence, the latter is a consequence of conscious opportunism. In this case, the salesperson is fully aware of the hypothesis underpinning the metric in the incentive model, but decides to focus his efforts on the issues that will yield the greatest possible returns. Instead of behaving in the intended way, the salesperson focuses only on activities that 'count' in the scorecard, to generate the highest possible personal returns.

How employees relate to scorecards is usually a bigger issue than the metrics themselves. Hence, if the salesperson tries to fool the system by carrying out as many customer visits as possible without trying to leverage the contact with each customer, then there is probably a deeper cause than the new management control system as such. Or, as the saying goes, 'If there is a will, there is a way.' The problem is not the measurement system *per se*, but rather the context in the organization that influences the employee's priorities. Rather than redesigning the control system, maybe the atmosphere in the organization should be addressed. This problem may be dealt with using strategy maps and scorecards to invite the employees to participate in the development of the organization's future.

It is also important that the measurement procedures are reliable, which both makes it more difficult to tamper with the results (i.e. reducing the risk of opportunistic behaviour), and adds to the performance information's credibility. If there is a suspicion among the employees that the outcome is not measured in a systematic and reliable way, then they will probably not rely on the information as a solid base for incentives. In addition to that, the management team will not accept the metrics as a valid representation of performance, and hence refuse to take necessary corrective action based upon them.

BA Heathrow

The manager confronted this dilemma when he used the check-in system to monitor availability at the check-in desks. His belief was that not all desks were open during peak-load. For some time, however, the responsible subordinate refused to accept the data the manager retrieved from the transaction system. Finally, to validate the information in the system, the manager himself went down to the check-in area and counted the number of open stands. Afterwards, he compared his own observations with the data in the system, and found that the information in the check-in system was valid. From that date, the subordinate could not question the validity of the performance information, and had to take action to increase the capacity during peak time.

As mentioned before, the scorecard contains a set of hypotheses – not a blueprint for success. As long as the scorecard is not linked to any compensation scheme, these strategic bets may be regarded as shared 'best guesses' on what will yield the best results. Ideally, the strategy map and the scorecard should contain the whole organization's collective knowledge and hence best bets on the future, and constitute a shared perception of the best design of the business model.

When incentives are linked to the scorecard, however, the scorecard may change character. Instead of serving as a set of shared hypotheses, it may turn into a contract with two distinct parties involved – a principal and an agent. The principal (i.e. management), ultimately has to decide what dimensions will be included in the contract, and the agents (the subordinates) are responsible for executing the (principal's) intentions. Preferably, the contract should be designed to satisfy both parties' wishes, but the underlying framework still awards the principal the right to judge whether or not the agent has performed satisfactorily. If incentives are not linked to the scorecard, then this asymmetry will not emerge.

Turning the scorecard into a contract, however, carries a lot of practical implications. First, it is likely that the target-setting exercise will change character from being a shared process where stretch targets are set, to a process where the agents will probably negotiate targets as low as possible to be able to meet them and receive the awards. At worst, the agents may try to manipulate the measurement system (or perform activities with the sole purpose of influencing the numbers in the scorecard) to look more efficient and hence gain the incentives. When turning the scorecard into a contract, a distinction is made between different stakeholders in the organization – between principals and agents. Before connecting the scorecard to the incentive system, these risks must be evaluated, and the potential benefits must be considered more valuable than the costs of the risks.

OPERATIONAL CONSIDERATIONS WHEN IMPLEMENTING A BALANCED INCENTIVE SYSTEM

Be explicit about the incentive system before implementing it, and when relying on it in the operation

Any incentive model, regardless of whether or not it is connected to a BSC, requires an explicit introduction. Few things create as much hassle in an organization as compensation schemes. Even though the incentive pools may not contain much money (compared with other accounts in the organization), the rewards also embed an implicit message – who is considered valuable and who is not.

Thus, the reward structures must be communicated with care. It must be clear to everybody why the schemes are to be introduced, how they will be managed, how performance will be measured, how goals and targets are set, etc. To make the expectations on the reward system realistic, it is also wise to define clearly to what extent the new model is a profit-sharing instrument or a behaviour-control tool. If the former is chosen, no employee will expect to get any rewards from the company unless it shows a profit. Whereas the opposite may create a lot of tension: if rewards have been anticipated for achievements in the different perspectives, but are not given because of poor financial results, then the scorecard will lose credibility.

When incentives are linked to the scorecard, it ceases to be a shared set of hypotheses, and becomes a contract between employee and employer. In this case, it is not unlikely that the employees will pay more attention to the dimensions (and metrics) in the incentive model than those that are left out. When 'contracting' performance in this way, the organization must accept an increasing degree of suboptimization, following from the fact that management is actually asking the employees to pay extra attention to a handful of issues.

Communicate performance regularly

To make the incentive models actionable, management must pay attention to them. To begin with, when incentives have been linked to the scorecard, the target-setting exercise becomes more important. Naturally, it becomes more difficult to propose stretch targets that are unrealistic to meet within the coming period. For the metrics in the incentive model to make any difference, the employees must be able to reach the goals. Otherwise, they will only create frustration in the organization. Most likely, the agents (the employees or subordinate unit managers) will try to depress the targets as much as possible to make them reachable.

In the literature, some examples are given of a dual negotiation process. In this, rewards are given on a combination of the outcome relative to the target as well as the difficulty of the target. This is an elegant approach to encourage the agents to suggest targets that are as bold as possible. The challenge is, however, to define 'boldness', since it necessitates subjective judgement.

Unless performance is communicated to the employees, the scorecards are not likely to generate any effects. One challenge in many organizations has been to encourage the employees to pay attention to the scores. Regardless of whether they are communicated in monthly company meetings, or whether the employees are expected to look up the scorecard on the intranet, performance information generally does not seem to be very interesting to most employees. However, when incentives are connected to certain performance indicators, this may generate an interest in the metrics. Hence, it is important that the organization can satisfy this interest with continuously updated information. When BA Heathrow offered incentives on a set of indicators, the performance was continuously published on internal TV screens. And it was obvious that the employees' interest in the specific metrics was much higher when incentives were connected to them than it was before.

It is also important that management respects the targets that have been set for the metrics. It is not uncommon that managers sometimes want to compensate a unit that has just missed the target, for their good effort. Even though this might be a positive thought, management should stick to the targets that have been set. If a unit fails to meet its goals, then the employees should not receive the bonus. Rather, management should refocus its attention from *ex post* kindness, to *ex ante* support, i.e. management should strive to help the units to exceed their targets. This becomes extra important as a period is coming to its end, and there is still time for the unit to reach the goal. Under such circumstances, management should do anything they can to help the unit increase its performance. Hence, it is important that management continuously monitors performance against targets, and takes action if it sees that a metric is deviating from plan. If rewards are paid, even though the targets are not reached, then it will erode the respect for the incentive model. But, if management participates and supports the units in taking proactive action – to make sure that they reach their targets – the incentive system as well as the BSC will gain credibility.

Avoid winner-takes-all schemes

Some incentive systems deliberately try to instil a sense of competition between units in the organization. This is not wrong. On the contrary, some kind of collegial rivalry between units may better the performance, both because many employees find it satisfying to perform better than their peers (winning is rewarding in itself), and because comparison between units may indicate what levels of performance are reachable. One organization we worked with, for example, deliberately encouraged the unit managers to log on to the intranet to find the best-practice outcome for each specific metric, values that could be used when setting targets in their own unit.

It is, however, sometimes dangerous to embed a competition component in the incentive system such that the unit that beats its peers gets the rewards. There is often a risk of internal suboptimization, especially when units interact on an internal market, or in some other way are supposed to perform together. This connects well to the line of reasoning used by opponents of transfer pricing. They usually argue that internal negotiations will focus the employees' attention on internal matters rather than external. Instead of regarding external competitors as the biggest threat and external customers as the foundation for the business, all efforts are instead focused on beating peer groups and pleasing other internal departments. The scorecard's purpose is to promote cooperation within the organization to realize the intended strategy, which typically requires all participants' contribution. One way to analyse this is to consider whether the relation between departments or units is 'sequential' or 'parallel'. A retailer's stores would normally operate in parallel, and competing for rewards will usually not be harmful. Competition between marketing and production in an industrial company, on the other hand, should be avoided and certainly not encouraged by scorecard-based incentives.

Somewhat similar to this is the relation between the different metrics in the same scorecard. A scorecard promotes multi-dimensionality. Sometimes, the rewards should be unbundled such that the employees can be rewarded for their achievements in each perspective separately. This was the case with the cosmetics store managers earlier in this chapter. Each of the four metrics seemed of value for the organization, and each was rewarded separately. But at other times it makes more sense to communicate that all the perspectives are indeed important. The company could have used another model, for instance, requiring the goals to be met in some particular order for rewards to be paid.

Even though the perspectives should be treated as distinct dimensions in the incentive system, the incentives should not be designed so that the employee may focus solely on one of them. This could, for example, be the case if the reward connected to one of the perspectives is so high that the employee will be satisfied with the compensation, maximizing just that one dimension. (The fictional case about a Polish subsidiary in Chapter 5 was an example of this. Its CEO received a bonus on just one measure: profit.) Instead, the rewards should be balanced, i.e. high enough per perspective such that the employee deliberately tries to balance her achievements in all four perspectives. Balance can also be mandated through thresholds that must be reached for every perspective before any bonus is paid. These thresholds must, however, not be too high, because that might neutralize the efforts in the other perspectives if bad performance in one perspective cancels anticipated rewards for other achievements.

The relation between different measures can be analysed in a way similar to our discussion about sequential and parallel organizational units. Here, the corresponding concepts are whether measures indicate effects on future success which are largely additive (separate) or multiplicative (co-producing the desired outcome). The four metrics in the cosmetics store seem to have been four different, separate ways of improving profits. But in other situations, a good performance on one indicator may be meaningless without an equally good performance on another.

Merkantildata A/S57

Merkantildata is a Scandinavian IT corporation offering consulting, out-sourcing, implementation, and operation services, which has embedded the scorecard in the incentive system. The Danish operation employs some 900 persons. Merkantildata A/S' BSC has been embedded in the bonus system for all management levels throughout the organization (including some 70% of the employees). The bonus system includes three perspectives: employee satisfaction, customer satisfaction, and financial performance. The maximum bonus equals one month's salary if all the targets are reached in all per-spectives. Even if the employee does not reach all his targets, he may receive some part of the bonus.

Promote team-based incentives

A closely related question is what behaviour to promote: individual achievements or group achievements. All together, we find the scorecard an effective instrument to show how individuals, and groups, fit together and how they may create more value together than they do separately. Hence, it is natural to use group achievements as the denominator in the incentive model.

Some authors argue that there is a risk associated with group-based metrics, namely, that some employees might receive rewards that they do not deserve. In some situations, this might be the case, but still such opinions are very difficult to validate in practice. Arguing that someone in a group has received a reward that he or she does not deserve opens up complex discussion on who is 'actually' doing what with regard to the joint achievements. If this were to be the case – that someone in the unit was gaining advantages that he did not deserve – then our experience is that that person would eventually (probably sooner, rather than later) be confronted and have to increase his efforts or leave the unit. The risk of a free-rider problem is hence not severe enough to stay away from group-based incentives. The opposite is, however, true: implementing an incentive system where considerable rewards are given on the basis of an individual performance will foster a solitaire culture where the sum of the whole eventually becomes less than the sum of its parts.

Ensure the validity and reliability of the metrics used in the incentive system

Regardless of whether or not the scorecard is embedded in the incentive system, it is important that the performance information is compiled and calculated in a systematic and reliable manner. Especially when the indicators determine whether or not a bonus is paid, the measurement procedures become even more important.

As mentioned above, the measurement procedures must be designed so that employees may not manipulate the information. If an employee behaves deceitfully, it is not a result of the scorecard, but probably of some other, bigger, contextual issue in the organization. In addition to protecting the measurement systems against manipulation, it is also important that the performance information is reliable, so that employees can rely on it in their decision-making. The most effective way to signal the validity and reliability of the metrics and the performance information is to be explicit about the metrics' definitions, how the data is compiled and from where, as well as how it is processed. Describing the measurement procedures explicitly allows employees to scrutinize the quality of the information as well as suggest how the measurement procedures could be further improved.

Most of the information in the scorecard will probably have to be gathered internally. For some of the metrics, data can be compiled from existing transaction systems. It then becomes important to assess their validity, i.e. to ensure that they really measure what they are supposed to represent. The discussion in BA's management team focused on this question. The subordinate manager argued that the data, which the manager retrieved from the transaction system, did not represent the area of interest. The manager then had to validate the information in the system by personally inspecting the real world (the entrance hall) and comparing his own observations with the data in the system. The data in the transaction system turned out to be a valid description of the capacity in the check-in stands and could thereafter be used as a shared indicator of performance.

When embedding the scorecard in the incentive system, it is important that the data is valid and reliable. To ensure the information's credibility, some organizations therefore purchase performance information from external providers. This is most frequent, of course, when it comes to customer and employee satisfaction indexes, but also information about delivery precision, store appearance, the employees' product knowledge and many other issues can be bought from external research companies. The perceived quality of the information acquired from an external and independent provider may very well compensate for the additional and visible costs that this mode of data gathering will incur.

RECOMMENDATIONS AND IMPLICATIONS

Incentive systems are not required to make scorecards actionable. Most organizations implement scorecards without any connection to the incentive schemes. There are, however, some aspects to think about when analysing the connection between scorecards and incentives.

- Make sure that existing incentive systems do not contradict the intentions of the scorecard (for example, focusing solely on financial returns or cash flow).
- Use measures in the incentive model that reflect the strategic aims of the activities they portray (relevant and logical scorecards).
- Ensure that the metrics can be measured by valid and credible methods (accepted and practical).
- Offer the employees rewards that are multi-dimensional, i.e. tailored to the individual's expectations and desires.

If the incentive systems are connected to the scorecards, then it is likely that the employees in the organization will pay more attention to the scorecards:

- The scorecards will gain credibility if rewards are connected to the leading indicators (i.e. management is putting the money where the mouth is).

- A more balanced view will evolve in the organization as long-term initiatives are also promoted and rewarded.
- The employees will show an interest in the performance statistics when incentives are connected to the individual metrics.
- However, connecting incentives to the scorecards may turn the scorecards into contracts where the parties may engage in a negotiation process (creating we and them). There is also a risk that some employees will try to manipulate the performance statistics to gain personal rewards.

Using IT to Leverage the Scorecard   11

Whether or not a BSC is to make a difference in the company's strategic discussion and learning processes depends on whether or not it is continually updated with current and operationally relevant information. Thus, a critical question for the company is how to establish procedures and implement systems that collect information and communicate it to management and employees.

Regardless of whether simple and straightforward procedures (based on manual input) or a more sophisticated software solution is chosen, success depends on actually using the tools and communicating the right level of information to the right people.

Software companies from different segments in the IT industry have discovered the potential for new management-control IT solutions, and introduced specialized applications designed to suit BSC projects.

Initially, the market was not ready for these packaged applications. Instead, most organizations started to implement BSC support applications in existing software environments such as Excel or Visual Basic, focusing mainly on high-level management – providing them with information in the four perspectives. But as the BSC concept began to gain more widespread acceptance, demand grew for more advanced solutions, and there are today numerous specialized BSC applications on the market (in an examination recently, Gartner Group evaluated 28 different systems).

When evaluating alternative software options, the company must first determine why it needs an IT solution and then compare the alternatives with these requirements. In this chapter, we discuss how IT can be used and suggest how the alternative solutions can be compared.

WHEN SHOULD IT BE USED IN A BSC PROJECT?

Typically, BSC software is thought of as an application that retrieves numerical information from the organization's wide range of transaction systems, and presents this as speedometers and performance reports in four perspectives. These features are, of course, important in any BSC software, but we believe that IT can also play an important role in other stages of a scorecard project: from the initial development of the organization's vision and the creation of the strategy map, to the day-to-day administration of action plans and to-do lists. This would include, in addition to the number-crunching functionality, tools to draw and validate strategy maps, features that connect vision, strategic goals, CSFs, measures, and action plans, as well as forums that allow members in the organization to share knowledge and insights in order to improve the business. IT can thus be used at different stages throughout the scorecard effort:[58]

- IT support in the initial stages of the scorecard project
- IT support when breaking-down and linking the scorecard
- IT support when setting targets and monitoring performance
- IT support when managing strategic activities.

IT support in the initial stages of the scorecard project

As mentioned above, BSC software is most often thought of as number-crunching applications that retrieve, process, and present available numerical information in four boxes. Some kind of administrative support is, however, often also needed in the early stages of the project. Typically, such a system should feature some basic project management tools for document sharing, managing e-mail lists, setting up shared calendars to record project milestones and deadlines, etc. These services may already exist in other administrative tools in the organization, which may be used if the employees are familiar with them. Regardless of whether a specialized project management solution is used, or whether these features are offered in the BSC application, it is important that the documents produced during the initial stages of the project will be accessible later on, directly from the BSC environment. This is important because many of these documents and databases contain valuable knowledge about markets, competitors, trends, reviews of internal strengths and weaknesses, etc.

A retail company

A couple of years ago we worked with a big retail corporation in Sweden, helping several of its business units to design and implement scorecards simultaneously. The project was structured such that the business units worked separately but occasionally met and reviewed each other's score-cards and learned from the collective scorecard experience in the corporation. To support the local administration of each project, as well as stimulate cross-unit learning, a project web site was developed. The site offered some basic features such as file sharing (open as well as password protected), access to shared resources (corporate guidelines and strategy documents), discussion boards, 'yellow pages', summaries and excerpts of relevant litera-ture, Internet resources, and a metric proposition database (see Figure 11.1).

Although, the project management software does not have to be embedded in the BSC solution *per se*. It should be connected with the future BSC environment to promote reuse of already produced knowledge. All too often, customer analysis reports and competitor reviews are produced once and then forgotten.

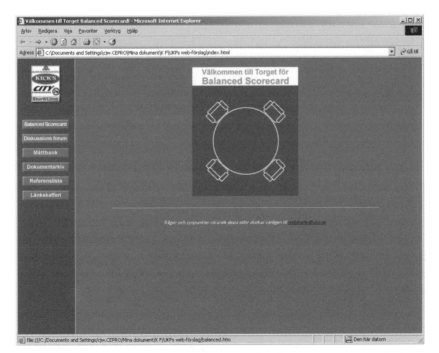

Figure 11.1 Screen shot from balanced scorecard project management web site.

More specific to the scorecard effort are the tools that can be used to create strategy maps. Most companies seem to use Microsoft PowerPoint, which offers a straightforward way to produce graphs. Its use is probably widespread because most people know how to use it, and most computers are delivered with Microsoft PowerPoint today.

There are, however, some disadvantages using PowerPoint to produce strategy maps. One problem is that it is difficult to link the content of the strategy map to the other parts of the scorecard: to the CSFs and the metrics. This means that it is difficult to backtrack from the metric, through the success factors to the strategy map, and find out why a certain metric is used and what it represents with regard to the bigger picture.

Another functionality that is missing in a simple presentation slide is the ability to embed dynamics in the map. The links that are drawn in the PowerPoint map are 'dumb' in the sense that they do not embed the logic they represent. The dynamics (the *if this increases... that decreases*, etc.) in the strategy map must hence be imagined by the perceiver. If, on the other hand, the map is drawn in a software with simulation capabilities, then the links can be logically tested. In addition to visualizing the relationships between the entities – suggesting a positive or negative flow – the effects of the links in the map can be validated. The simulation engine allows the user to test what happens in the model if some of the key assumptions are changed. The business model can thus be logically validated while it is still on the drawing board.

Oriflame

Testing the strategy map in this very rational manner is, however, rare in practice. In Oriflame, where strategy maps have been developed for every sales company, no units have evaluated their strategy maps in this very detailed way. The strategy maps were instead created in PowerPoint or Word, which was considered convenient enough since the maps were not thought of as real representations of reality that needed to be statistically checked and tested. Rather, they were seen as instruments to communicate the intentions of the business model and the corporate beliefs. The maps did not have to be mathematically consistent to serve this purpose, hence Oriflame did not consider it worth the effort to draw and test the maps in a simulation application.

Skandia

Dolphin, the web-based solution, can be used to link the vision, success factors, activities and indicators, creating a chain of cause-and-effect linkages. A built-in function, named Process Model Relations, allows the users to connect the vision to the success factors, and then to activities and indicators.

Working with the Process Model and thereby linking the vision to a success factor, to an activity and then finally to an indicator has thus been an effort to create a language that tells the story of the strategy. This is central to the work with the Navigator. By looking at a unit's Navigator, one should be able to tell what is done in the organization to reach the vision. In this story, the indicators play an important role. They tell whether or not the unit or organization is on track towards the vision. In Dolphin, indicators are identified through work with the Process Model and are visualized in the Navigator.

Industrial Company

Another client we have worked with quickly saw the potential in linking its strategy map (which they refer to as a 'Driver Model', linking all cause-and-effect relationships between the four perspectives) to the individuals working on initiatives within each item in the model. This placed interesting requirements on the presentation capability of the software since the company demanded the ability to click on the Driver diagram, in say the 'increase customer satisfaction' box, and immediately see a list of all initiatives and the owners. Conversely, any one owner of a strategic initiative would be presented with the driver model colour coded for the areas in which he was personally involved, but the software would shadow all areas where he was not involved. This made it easy for individuals to see how their activities related to the overall strategy map and how the activities in which they were involved were achieving strategic targets.

IT support when breaking down and linking the scorecard

Following on the articulation of the vision and the strategy map, the corporate scorecard is often broken down into scorecards for the separate business units or even smaller entities. Some organizations, for example Skandia, have even chosen to break down the scorecard all the way to the individual employee. (See Chapter 9, Interfaces.)

Similar to the way in which the links in the scorecard show relationships between perspectives, and between leading and lagging indicators, the breakdown of the higher-level scorecard into lower-level scorecards shows the subunits' contribution to the whole organization's goals. The scorecard software should enable the user at a lower level to contextualize her scorecard, and see how it relates to the success of the whole company. This linking exercise is generic in the sense that every scorecard on a lower level must relate to the scorecard on the next level above, not only in a logical fashion (as discussed above, when talking about simulation capabilities) but also from a pedagogical point of view. The scorecard must tell the company's story: the sum of the whole must be greater than the sum of the parts.

Lund HLC

An IT solution was considered important to support the BSC work. A web-based, stand-alone solution was installed at the centre fairly early in the project, which has come to serve as a communication and information system, providing information from the different parts of the centre. In the system, documents are collected and stored, which can be reached by the 'right' employees in the organization.

The overall scorecard is accessible to everybody in the hospital and to the employees in other hospitals in the region as well (since they all belong to the public health organization and HLC uses the common intranet to publish the information). The results of the measures can, however, only be reached after logging on to the web-based system. In the future, HLC's ambition is to publish information about their scorecard and some of the measures on the intranet, so it will be accessible without logging in on the scorecard system (see Figure 11.2).

The software should also allow backtracking or drilling down in the scorecards. As the user browses through her unit's scorecard, she may backtrack by clicking on a particular perspective, or metric, and reach the immediate level above, hence understanding how the local efforts contribute to the collective achievements. Likewise, the user should be able to drill down by clicking on a metric and see what constitutes that metric and what initiatives have been taken to improve its performance (more about this under IT support when managing strategic activities).

IT support when setting targets and monitoring performance

Target setting and continuous monitoring have attracted most attention among BSC systems developers during the last years. As we discuss in the next section (Choosing software) the functionality of a specific software often reflects its origin. Most applications come from a management control (often financial) discipline, where non-financial indicators have been added on top of the general framework and the system itself. It is therefore natural that most scorecard applications are rather elaborate regarding how

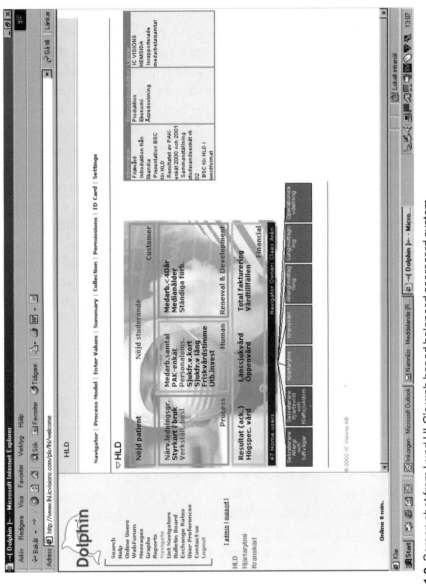

Figure 11.2 Screen shot from Lund HLC's web based balanced scorecard system.

they access, retrieve and present information from different financial transaction systems in the organization.

Still, the BSC software should satisfy more requirements than just data compilation and processing. Target setting is a more creative, non-linear and intuitive process than is often thought (contrary to the perception of a bureaucratic budgeting procedure). Supporting this process, the software must naturally satisfy all necessary security requirements (that only those who are authorized are allowed to enter data etc.), but in addition, the system should also encourage a dialogue in the organization and between organizational levels. The system should, for example, allow the individual manager (or anyone else setting targets), browse through the system and learn from other units.

The system should also support the actual entering of targets. If targets are set for each month, then it should be possible to enter the yearly expectations for every metric and then allow the system to distribute the target values over the year. This distribution could be made in different ways: dividing the target evenly over the months (12 company meetings per year equals one per month); allocating the same target value to every month (market share shall always be above 13.6%, every month during the year); automatically distributing the target for the year according to last period's business cycle (the goal is to sell 23 500 products during the year. Based on last year's result, we expect to sell 13% of the volume in January, 11% in February, 5% in March, and so on). When the targets have been set for each metric, it must be possible to adjust the values for each period. Preferably, the system should generate a matrix with the metrics in the rows and the months in the columns. Each cell will then contain a value, which the user can adjust individually.

It is not uncommon that organizations want to present outcomes in an intuitive format, such as a speedometer, a red light or a thermometer, in addition to figures and charts in the performance report (see Figure 11.3). The benefit of presenting performance as a red light is that it is very communicative: if the light is red, then all employees understand that performance has been below that expected. The intellectual challenge, however, is to decide and set the thresholds for categorizing the outcome. How much should the outcome deviate from the target to be labelled as red? Minus 20%? And when shall it be yellow? On target, or below target?

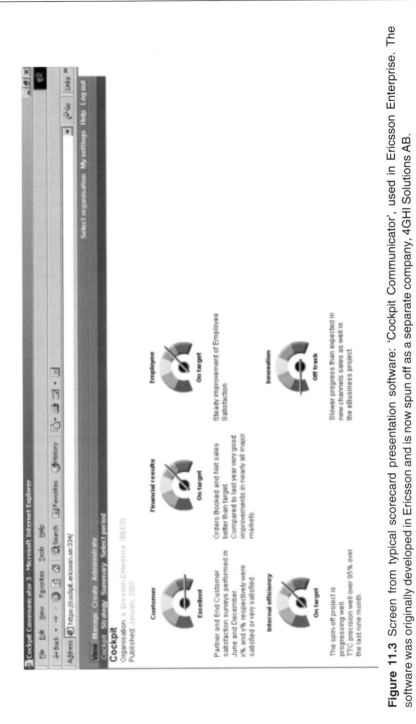

Figure 11.3 Screen from typical scorecard presentation software: 'Cockpit Communicator', used in Ericsson Enterprise. The software was originally developed in Ericsson and is now spun off as a separate company, 4GHI Solutions AB.

The system must also be able to handle goals where the outcome is preferred to be lower than the target (for example, lead time) and vice versa (profit). Some targets may also be set as an interval, where 'good' is defined between certain limits.

Performance data for the system can be compiled in two different ways, even though most BSC applications seem to imply that most data can be automatically compiled from other computer systems. This is, however, rarely the case. Ken Gøran Bjørk, at the Norwegian Air force, claims that only 20%–40% of the metrics in their top-management scorecard can be updated automatically.[59] The rest must be compiled by hand and entered manually into the system. At Oriflame, the corporate business controller, Robin Chiabba, expects that they will be able to provide some 60% of the metrics with information automatically. The rest will need to be compiled manually. Hence, the solution must be designed to enable easy recording of manually compiled performance information.

Oriflame

When all units within Oriflame had developed their individual strategy maps and scorecards at the end of 2000, the BSC team started to look for a software package that could support the operation of these 70 different cards. Oriflame evaluated several alternatives and finally decided to select a package that was designed as an Enterprise Resource Planning (ERP) add-on module (even though they were not running that particular vendor's ERP system at the time). The choice of supplier was made, partly, to test that vendor. Hence, implementing the BSC module was a pilot project by which they could test the vendor's abilities.

The BSC module that Oriflame implemented is a web-based solution, mainly offering reporting facilities and a presentation interface. When the user logs on to the system, she can view her unit's scorecard and drill down to see the results and development regarding the specific metrics. Through the system, it is also possible to access the unit's strategy map and strategy document. At present, these documents are not connected to the metrics in the scorecard, but are stored as pure PowerPoint or Word files.

During the initial period, data for the metrics will be entered by each local organization. The figures will be recorded manually, or compiled from other administrative IT systems, and then entered manually on a special page in the system. In a similar way, targets are entered for each metric in the system. The system also allows the user to define thresholds of acceptance, so the system can produce 'speedometers' to indicate whether the metric is on target, over performing or under performing. These intervals are set manually for each metric. Charts and trend indicators also aid the analysis of the scorecard.

In the future, a data warehouse will be implemented so that data can be automatically derived from other systems and be presented online in the scorecard. Oriflame expects that data for some 60% of the metrics can be provided automatically from various computerized systems, whereas the rest of the metrics will have to be measured and recorded manually and locally.

Also the information that can be compiled from other computer systems may need some attention. The databases are sometimes not as consistent as expected, which may require some cleaning of the data. Middleware may, for example, be implemented to translate data from one format into another. The ambition must be to design interfaces between the BSC solution and available databases, such that the data can be retrieved and quality assured automatically. Many of the BSC software packages that are available in the market today have emerged out of the analytical data-processing domain. These applications hence are well tailored to process vast amounts of information, allowing extended drill-down capacity to deepen the analyses on any specific question. This capacity can also be used to summarize data across various organizational units so that they can compare their performance.

Besides the analytical effort to evaluate performance based on data in existing transaction systems, the software package must present the results in an appealing style. An up-to-date scorecard should always be available on the corporate intranet, so that it can be reached by anyone in the organization, at anytime and wherever they might be. Ideally, these presentations should cover all the functionality mentioned above: drill down to understand what data has been used, backtracking to contextualize the individual scorecard, as well as checking what specific actions have been taken to improve the particular measure. The BSC software should not only be perceived as an analytical tool, but also as a knowledge-management solution, offering the employees in the organization the opportunity to share information about the business. Hence, it should be possible for any person in the organization to make a comment on anything in the system, asking questions or replying to them. In Skandia, for example, anyone can submit a question or comment regarding a specific measure, and the 'owner' of that metric must respond to the question within a certain time limit.

Helsingborg

In the city of Helsingborg, which utilizes scorecards throughout the organization, the need for a well-functioning IT solution has increased over time. Most importantly, they want to collect and communicate data easily through the scorecard – within the organization as well as to the citizens in the community. This will require a scorecard solution that can handle multiple scorecards and at the same time be easy to use.

Until May 2002, the city of Helsingborg did not have any shared solution. Internally, one of the departments uses an IT tool called *Gyrot* (see Figure 11.4), which was built on a data warehouse solution. The indicators in the system are collected automatically from other IT systems in the organization. This solution, however, has been found insufficient for the whole organization, since all employees should be able to add numbers, make comments, etc.

Helsingborg regarded it as paramount that all employees must see immediately the connection between the scorecard and their reality, for the system to fulfil its purpose. The solution must create a feedback loop that clearly displays the changes that are made in the organization. It is also important

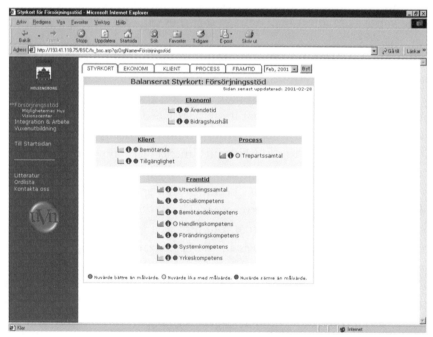

Figure 11.4 An example of the development department's scorecard visualized in Gyrot.

that access to certain information in the system can be restricted, so that scorecard owners can decide who shall and who shall not have access to what data.

It is not likely that all employees access the intranet at all times, or look up the BSC section in it, so management must continuously refer to the scorecard and use it as a means of discussing whether or not the strategy is realized. Except from publishing the scorecard on the intranet automatically, the system must also be able to produce physical performance reports directly.

Lund HLC

A web-based BSC solution was implemented early in the scorecard effort. In some units at the centre the system has become the primary information system. So far, however, in some other units, only a few employees log into the system to see how the scorecards develop. Therefore, the scorecards in the system are often printed and put on the notice-board in the wards. In this way, the centre still communicates what is going on, but it reduces some of the benefits of having a web-based system.

Some solutions therefore offer 'presentation generators', which automatically produce a set of overhead slides (with the company's logo and so on), with the last period's outcome according to the scorecard. This material can then be used during the monthly meetings or be included in the monthly company newsletter. Another feature that some systems offer is to alert different employees (configured to suit the individual company) via short message service (SMS) or e-mail when the figures in the scorecard have been updated, if the outcome deviates from the pre-set target or if a to-do item is delayed.

IT support when managing strategic activities

Much literature on BSC implementations has thus far focused on the connection between strategy development and how performance can be monitored to check whether or not the organization is realizing its strategy. The final step in the scorecard process has sometimes seemed to be the measuring and evaluation of performance. But in Kaplan and Norton's original articles, the final component in the model was the action list, not the metrics. This is an important distinction, and it should be recognized in the BSC solution as well. It is not enough to monitor performance. It is not even enough to monitor and compare performance with the pre-set targets. The purpose of the scorecard is to trigger a new behaviour in the organization, such that the intended strategy is realized.

Some of the BSC software packages in the market therefore include a, often rudimentary, activity management module. Managing strategic initiatives and activities does not require an IT support system *per se*, but it might contribute to the organization's ability to ensure that its initiatives are executed as intended. An activity management system is a type of workflow management package that helps the employees in the organization to ensure that activities are carried out as expected.

BA Heathrow

Deliberately, no dedicated BSC system has been introduced. Instead, they have implemented a template in Excel that retrieves data for the metrics from existing transaction systems. This Excel sheet enables the controller to produce the scorecards (for all the units at Heathrow) in less than one day. It is also considered a benefit that the scorecards are produced by hand, since it is believed to add to their credibility. Figures that are automatically produced from a computer system may be questioned in a different way from a performance report that has been produced by hand. It is also possible for BA Heathrow to rely on a simple Excel solution, since only six to eight scorecards are produced in each batch (once a month).

In addition to the separate scorecards that are produced in the Excel system, the resulting performance report binder also includes the to-do items that were decided on at prior meetings. These activities are manually compiled on the first pages in the package so that the group can browse through them at the beginning of each meeting and inform each other about what has happened since the last meeting. When an item is completed, it is removed from the list, so that it will contain only items in progress.

The simplest kind of activity management feature in a BSC solution is to link 'to do' items to individual metrics. If the organization decides to take some action to correct for a negative trend regarding a certain metric, then information about this initiative can be entered in the system – and be linked to the individual metric. The activity is then allocated to someone who is responsible for executing it. When she has finished, the activity is marked as completed.

The workflow functionality can also be extended to allow different paths of escalation, and allocation of different responsibilities to different employees. The system may also keep track of the action list and alert the person responsible for a certain activity when the deadline approaches. The system may also keep track of the initiatives that have been taken regarding a specific issue, so that it is possible to see who has done what in relation to it.

Finally, the system can create a feedback loop. The system should allow the user to see whether or not an action has created the anticipated effects. Some time after an activity has been completed, the system can summarize whether or not the metric has changed in the desired direction. If, for example, the company has faced decreasing customer satisfaction and has decided to take a short-term initiative to increase customer communication, then an alert could be set in the system, e.g. three months after the activity was executed, to inform the user about the effects of the initiative on the customer satisfaction index.

CHOOSING BSC SOFTWARE

The first step to take when choosing a BSC software is to decide whether it shall be purchased off the shelf or if it shall be developed in-house. It has been common, in many organizations to play around with simple Excel or Access solutions before any standard package has been implemented. As the BSC concept has matured, however, numerous alternative standard solutions have been released in the market. Even if they all claim to support the operation of a BSC, they vary a lot, based on their origin of development. Some solutions have been developed on top of traditional financial consolidation packages, whereas others have been developed from scratch as web-based solutions (which can even be rented from independent service providers over the Internet).

If the organization decides to purchase a standard BSC application, then it is paramount to examine where the product comes from, and consider whether the embedded logic in the system (inherited from its origin) will fit the organization's context and the purpose of the BSC implementation.

Gartner Group, a consultancy, and Cranfield School of Management (Marr and Neely, 2001), have developed a decision framework which they propose as an instrument to evaluate and choose a BSC application. The framework consists of 10 evaluation criteria (Table 11.1), which can be applied to the applications under evaluation.

To get a better understanding of the different systems and solutions in the market, we prefer to divide them into five categories. Any solution,

Table 11.1 Evaluation criteria

1. Company and product	When evaluating the supplier issues such as the company's background, its expertise and credibility, as well as the price structure of the application are of interest
2. Scalability	Focus on the ability to grow with the system and add additional scorecards as well as users
3. Flexibility and customization	Flexibility focuses on the possibilities to tailor the system to the organization's specific scorecard dialect and whether it supports personal scorecards and personal views of performance
4. Features and functions	Addresses whether the system can assign owners to measures and objectives, if and how access rights can be enforced, how scorecards can be linked to reward schemes, if it offers features to manage action lists, alarm features and can generate hard copy performance reports, etc.
5. Communication	Is the software web-enabled? Does it allow the users to make comments about goals, targets, and results? Will the system alert the user as to whether new information is available in the system or whether some action is expected from her?
6. Technical specification	Does the system run on the existing infrastructure? What hardware and software are required to operate the application?
7. Data presentation and views	Presentation focuses on the application's capacity to visualize information in, e.g. strategy maps, links between metrics and goals, descriptions and definitions of measures, etc.
8. Functionality analysis	Functionality refers to services in the system, such as drill-down capabilities, possibilities to compare and benchmark outcomes, online analytical processing (OLAP) as well as statistical, simulation, and trend analysis features
9. Service	What kind of additional services does the vendor offer, such as consulting, education and support?
10. Future	What are the future plans for the application? Will new versions be released and how often? But also the company's aspirations: what is its vision and how financially robust is it?

from any one of the categories, may hence serve its purpose, given the above evaluation criteria. Therefore, we do not think that any type of system is inherently better than any other. Rather, we would like to emphasize the need for a fit between the intentions of the scorecard and the characteristics of the IT solution.

In-house productions (productivity-suite solutions)

The simplest solutions are typically developed in a productivity suite such as Microsoft's Office package. Today, these Excel-based solutions are probably the most frequently used, where the internal IT department or the business controller has developed a set of sheets in a spreadsheet program, which is used to produce graphs and performance reports. Data are either registered manually or retrieved from other systems. Some data may also be exported automatically from other applications and formatted into the spreadsheet. If the scorecard is getting more complex, the solution may be migrated into a personal database format, such as Microsoft Access.

The benefit of starting with a solution in this environment is, of course, that it is fast and cheap (considering up-front costs). These systems are also very flexible, since the organization has direct access to the logic of the scorecard and hence may change the system if the scorecard changes. The productivity-suite environment is also advantageous since it is often widely spread: most computers are equipped with it, so it is easy to share the solution without any need to install additional software or to pay additional licence fees.

JIT

JIT uses Excel and paper-based measurement routines to monitor performance. The information is compiled monthly and stored in the Excel environment. In addition to using Excel for numerical processing, the strategic objectives also are stored and managed in an Excel interface.

KappAhl

KappAhl, the Swedish fashion company, which has been working with scorecards since 1995, has not implemented any dedicated BSC solution. According to the CEO at the time, Thommy Nilsson, most such tools are too complex and inflexible. Hence, they restrict the development and utilization of the scorecards. Instead, KappAhl relies on Excel sheets and PowerPoint documents to present the performance information.

One disadvantage is, of course, that of scalability. If the complexity of the scorecard increases just modestly, it is difficult to maintain the solution. Similarly, the solution can neither handle volumes of data that are too large, nor interact seamlessly with other transaction systems in the organization. A productivity-suite solution is also usually limited to the 'number-presenting' domain outlined above. Such systems rarely serve as a knowledge management tool where individuals in the organization can communicate with each other, neither does it serve as a workflow system where actions and initiatives can be managed.

The other major disadvantage with these applications is the maintenance of accuracy. Errors in the application tend to be discovered when new data values or types are entered and are often fixed on the run in the updating period. This invariably generates secondary errors, which are difficult to identify. The net result is that metrics can be calculated incorrectly and when users discover this, it causes the organization to lose faith in the application.

BSC stand-alone solutions

The natural next step for many organizations seems to be to migrate the logic of the spreadsheet solution to a web-based internal BSC portal. Both Ericsson and Skandia have developed advanced web applications that support their scorecard implementations. Both also offer their solutions to external customers.

The benefit of these systems is that they have been deliberately developed to support a scorecard implementation – from start to finish. Most often, they are also convenient to implement, since they can be leased on a subscription basis. No applications need to be purchased and installed in the local IT environment. The only equipment the users need is a computer with a web interface. As with all standard packages, it might also be an advantage to rely on an external company that specializes in BSC-software development, instead of allocating internal resources to such projects. Recently, some dedicated companies have also been established that offer BSC systems as web-based ASP solutions.

Lund HLC

Some wards communicate everything through the web-based solution. They have appointed a person who is responsible for updating the scorecards and ensuring that everyone in the ward gets the updated information either by logging into the system or through printed material.

By presenting performance information in the scorecard system, the scorecards become more interesting. One employee argues that seeing the changes on the screen has triggered action in itself. She continues, 'as long as you do not see what happens in black and white, little will be done to change the situation. The system has been crucial to trigger this action'. Or, as the head of the centre summarizes it, 'putting the information into the system has become an incentive to measure things. And things that are being measured will also change.'

One disadvantage, compared with the productivity-suite solution, is that the BSC stand-alone application is designed according to a generic scorecard structure and process, whereas a solution in Excel is easy to adjust to the local and specific circumstances. In Skandia's solution, for example, the 'scorecard dialect' is heavily influenced by their own work with their equivalent to the scorecard – the Navigator. Compared with the number-crunching solutions, however, most stand-alone applications include more of the communicative services as well as the possibility to present strategy maps visually.

Data warehouse solutions

The third category of solutions is based on data warehouse products. These solutions' advantage is their ability to retrieve and analyse vast volumes of data, searching for patterns as well as consolidating and presenting information in a comprehensive way. One important capacity of any data warehouse solution (be it BSC focused or not) is its ability to interact with other transaction systems and retrieve data for calculation, analyses, and presentation. It is therefore natural to think of a data warehouse solution when most of the performance data in the scorecard can be assumed to reside within existing transaction systems. Hence, these solutions offer a convenient interface that can be used to retrieve information from existing digital sources within the organization.

Of course, it is possible to record information manually in a data warehouse solution as well, but it seems to be an expensive and complicated path to presentation. If most of the data must be measured and registered manually, then the Excel or BSC stand-alone solutions mentioned above, may do. If, on the other hand, numerical processing is at the core, the data warehouse solution will offer interesting opportunities for analysis and maybe even simulation of the scorecard.

Similarly, if manually input data adds value to data in the data warehouse, then it is important that the BSC application has 'write' as well as 'read' capabilities to the data warehouse.

Add-ons to ERP systems

Many suppliers of ERP solutions have also started to develop software for scorecard purposes – modules that can be integrated with the company's existing ERP system. Implementing these kinds of systems was a big trend in the late 1990s. Most ERP systems have a much broader scope than just focusing on the company's financial transactions. They are typically equipped with modules to handle most of the administrative functions in any organization, such as HR management, production planning, inventory management, purchase, sales.

A fully implemented ERP system hence stores information about most transactions in the organization. This information can then serve as a source for the BSC. The benefit of using an ERP add-on is that it will be tightly integrated with all the other components in the ERP solution and it will enable easy retrieval of information 'that is already there'.

Nordea
Nordea has implemented an add-on solution to their existing ERP package. The new IT solution, yet with a limited number of scorecards and users, will support the entire PPMM process. The platform for the solution is a new data warehouse that will include all planning and performance data. In due course it will be accessible for all 40 000 employees over the intranet, but the roll-out will be fairly long – in 2003 the goal is to have 2000 people linked up.

Relying on an ERP solution is often secure since most ERP vendors are financially stable, and because the integration between the modules is assured. The risk is, however (beyond the price tag), that the ERP add-on is only a competitive alternative when the performance information can be found in the modules within the ERP solution. If, on the other hand, the information resides in other applications, or even on paper, then the ERP solution is probably not the most cost-effective alternative.

Add-ons to process management systems

The final category of solutions has emerged from the domain of software dedicated to model and analyse process efficiencies. These systems are used to describe and model processes and their activities. Each activity is defined thoroughly and its cost elements are listed with references to the corresponding accounts in the accounting system. When the system has been implemented, it is possible for the controller to analyse the organization's costs according to the ABC approach. Systems such as QPR and ProDacapo hence allow the organization to find out its processes' and the products' 'real' costs.

Many process management systems have, lately, been extended to include also some kind of BSC engine. The strength of these applications is often that they have the capacity to model processes and link activities in the processes to information sources in other systems (typically the accounting system).

An illustration

AMF Pension

When the new business year 2000 started, management wanted to provide high visibility to scorecard measures, providing access for everyone to targets and performance reports, including comments and action plans. It was therefore decided that this information should be made available on the corporate intranet.

AMF Pension did not feel ready to undertake a large and expensive software project for this. They wanted to have a solution available during the first months of the year in order to make the scorecards visible and used. Faced with a price for software products ranging from less than US$2000 to up to a hundred times that sum, they purchased one of the cheapest products they could find. It provided little more than a customized web page with links to spreadsheets that required manual input. After toying around with this for a few weeks, an employee in the IT department built a similar but more suitable tool, and it was decided to use this instead.

This software is seen as a temporary tool. It requires managers to input measurements manually for their departments, but as yet many of these come from various informal systems or are personal estimates, so they would have to do this anyway. There may even be an advantage in doing this, since the managers have to take personal responsibility not only for inputting values, but also for providing comments and suggested actions. As they do this monthly, it is, in fact, like publishing a report on their department's performance for everyone in the company to see. It is also widely known that management uses these intranet pages during its regular meetings to judge progress and discuss future plans.

After using this simple tool for less than a year, a discussion ensued about buying some 'real' software for scorecards. AMF Pension was now in a better position to do this, thanks to its makeshift solution. It also proved that as long as one tolerates – maybe even prefers – some manual tasks and can live without sophisticated links or access rules, using standardized tools can be both cheap and fast. However, the outcome of this new discussion again was to use a 'do-it-yourself' solution, now with an improved HTML functionality.

IMPLEMENTING BSC SOFTWARE

Implementing a BSC system is not very different from implementing any other administrative information system. Hence, we will not elaborate extensively on this issue, but just point to some general concerns to keep in mind.

Establishing the task-force

In the presentation of Skandia earlier in this book, we stressed how important it is that the scorecard effort does not turn into a computer project. In Skandia, some employees kept referring to the Navigator – their equivalent to a scorecard – as a computer system for reporting business statistics, not as a management tool.

When electing members to participate in the selection and implementation of a BSC system, it is therefore important that they represent the coming users of the system, not the implementers or operators. Of course, the group must also be staffed with persons who know the technology, but these must not be in the majority.

Apart from staffing the task-force with coming users, it is also important that the task-force receives its mandate from the business side of the organization – from the units who are implementing scorecards as their new management control instrument – not from the IT department. In case of uncertainties or diverging ambitions, the business people will have the right to decide what to focus on and what to neglect.

Defining the requirements of the solution

The first step, before evaluating different alternative solutions, in any implementation project must be to take one step back and consider the purpose of the scorecard implementation. Why has the organization decided to implement this form of management control? And who are the intended 'users' of the new management control system? Is the purpose of the scorecard project to monitor and present performance along the dimensions in the scorecard, or is it to create strategy maps? Will the scorecards mainly be used on a strategic level in the organization, ensuring that the business units are on track, or will it play an important role in the daily operation: informing the employees about performance and managing ideas for improvements? Are the metrics complex, requiring advanced retrieval and computational capacity, or are they easily compiled from manual measurement routines and other administrative systems? Who will use the information in the system? Will it only be presented in the management team (in a physical binder) or will it be published on the organization's intranet?

It is not likely that all available BSC solutions are equally well tailored to cater for all these different purposes. On the contrary, it is more likely that some alternative solutions match some requirements perfectly, but are impossible to use in any other approach.

To structure the requirements, we suggest that the task-force uses the simple framework we presented at the beginning of this chapter. A simple and straightforward way to compile the requirements is to list all possible functions, which could be of interest, in four boxes on a whiteboard (IT in the initial phase, IT when breaking down the scorecard, IT when setting targets and monitoring performance, and IT when managing strategic activities). This requirements list can be produced in a brainstorming session, where the members are asked to suggest what they might expect from the system during the different stages. To boost the discussion, the moderator in the meeting should have compiled a list of possible functions that she can throw in to stimulate the group's creativity. As is always the case in brainstorming sessions, the more creative the ideas, the better.

When the group has filled the whiteboard with functions they wish present in the future solution, the functions must be compared with each other. Rarely can all the wishes be satisfied, hence there is a need to agree on which functions are required and which are considered 'nice to have'. The easiest way to carry out this activity is to give each member in the group 10 small dots, which they may place next to the items they find most important. At a first glance, the whiteboard will indicate when in the scorecard effort the IT solution is most needed. The next step may be to extract the functionality that has emerged as important and run it through another round of prioritization – to find the relationship between the qualified functions.

Selecting or developing the solution

Now that the scorecard concept has matured, and there are numerous different standard solutions available in the market, the preferred first step would be to look for a standard application in the market, rather than developing it in-house. There are, however, some situations when an in-house product could be a suitable alternative, e.g. when there are only a handful of scorecards in the organization and they are primarily used by the top management team, or if the scorecard effort mainly focuses on strategy mapping rather than on the continuous monitoring of performance. In these cases, existing productivity suites, including programs such as Excel and PowerPoint, may suffice.

If, on the other hand, scorecards will be implemented as *the* management control instrument in the organization, then it will probably require a robust IT environment. Even so, attitudes towards the scorecard concept may vary, hence there is a need for a requirements document, as described above. Most solutions today have emerged from the management control domain, so they are typically oriented towards retrieval, compilation, and presentation of numerical data. If this particular functionality has attracted most interest in the selection process, then it will probably not be difficult to find a suitable solution. If on the other hand, strategy mapping and simulation is considered more interesting, then the task-force will probably have to look for vendors in other domains of the IT industry.

Designing roles and responsibilities

In Chapter 8 we discussed roles and responsibilities, in general. When putting the scorecard software into operation, there are a handful of responsibilities that must be carried out with care.

Some of the information in the scorecard will probably be retrieved automatically from other information systems, but some indicators still need to be monitored and recorded manually. If these data-gathering responsibilities are not assured, then the scorecard system will not contain the outcome information anticipated. According to some respondents, the manual compilation and processing of data may even add value to the information. Apart from getting to know the sources, the personal processing will also create a sense of ownership of the information.

As we said before, some of the information in the scorecard can probably be found in other computer systems, and hence just needs to be transferred from one system to the other. However, information might not even exist in any database, and someone must make sure that it is manually recorded throughout the organization and is entered into the system.

Producing the scorecards may also require some effort. If the organization relies on an Excel-based solution, then it is likely that someone will have to create the spreadsheets, print and staple them (or publish them on the intranet) – as in BA Heathrow. This person may also need to distribute the packages and make sure that the receivers pay attention to them. If, on the other hand, a fully integrated scorecard solution has been implemented, then this manual effort should not be required. Instead, the solution will automatically retrieve data from different systems and produce the individual scorecards. Human attention to the scorecards can, however, not be automatically ensured even if the system produce the performance reports. Typically, someone has to promote the information in the scorecard and build an interest in it. Of course, this is the manager's responsibility, but it is often advisable to have someone supporting him in this effort.

Educating the users

Depending on which solution has been implemented the need for education varies. If, for example, an integrated scorecard solution has been installed, which publishes the monthly performance reports on the intranet automatically, then there is no immediate need to educate the employees as to how to use the system. Since the information is available on the intranet, most of them know how to retrieve it (still, there might be a need to encourage them to look up the scorecard information on the intranet).

Instead, this solution may require that a handful of super-users be taught how to set up the system, and how to re-design the scorecards if their structure is changed. If, on the other hand, a simpler Excel-based solution is used, then it might be important to teach the employees how to find the performance reports and how to interact with them.

Education is probably also necessary if the organization wants to develop strategy maps in a simulation environment. These tools are often much more complicated to use than, e.g. PowerPoint. The pay off, may, however, be that the strategy maps can include elaborated and 'tested' relationships before they are accepted. Yet, it is not realistic to expect someone without experience of using this type of software to be able to design a strategy map in it.

Both the simulation package and the back-end of an integrated score-card solution are intended for specialized users. These will probably belong to the core group of the BSC project team, and hence have time allocated to scorecard development.

Relying on the scorecard software to manage strategic activities, how-ever, targets the ordinary employee in the organization as an important information provider. If the scorecard solution includes an activity management module, then it is important that the employees are intro-duced to the system so that they know how to interact with it and what is expected of them. The same is true if the organization has broken down its scorecards all the way to the individual employee, such as Skandia did. Under these circumstances, the employees are expected to interact with the system on an operational basis – which will require some basic under-standing of how the solution is designed and how it should be used.

Skandia

Workshops were arranged where technical information about the system was given, as well as information about the Navigator and its purposes. In some units, three-day computerized business games, built on the Navigator con-cept, were arranged so that the ideas behind the tools really would sink in. Management and the group responsible for the implementation of the tool emphasized the importance of both understanding the system and the con-cept to make the work successful. The workshops and the business games were seen as important parts in creating this understanding. And it seems as though the communication of the ideas had some success. The business game workshops seemed to have given some real 'aha'-experiences.

Still, learning from Skandia's experiences, it is important that the introduction of the computer system is not confused with the implementation of the new management control process, so that the scorecard risks being interpreted as a new computer program.

In some cases, users will be responsible for generating their own scorecards as part of the yearly planning and review process. This places special requirements on software which make it easy to input data in a web environment and allow on-line collaboration between managers and employees in agreeing goals and metrics. If this type of solution is successful it greatly simplifies the performance and development review process for managers and employees.

ENSURING THAT THE IT INVESTMENT PAYS OFF

Does IT pay off? During the last decade this question has attracted considerable attention, and most authors agree that it is difficult to observe explicitly the positive effects of investments in IT. Over the years, however, more and more voices have argued that IT investments, on an aggregate level, generate more value than they cost. Still, this does not imply that every IT investment is likely to yield the expected pay off. One reason for this is that most IT investments serve as an infrastructure, giving the organization the opportunity to operate differently than before. But this does not mean that they will start to act in the new way, just because the technology allows it.

The gap between the intended and actual use of the technology (in operation) is interesting. All too often, managers make investment decisions based on the assumption that the organization will start to use the new technology as it is intended, and as it has been described in the investment appraisal or outlined in the business case. But there are numerous reasons why it is unlikely that the new behaviour (enabled by the new information system) will emerge. The employees may, for example, not have the necessary skills to take advantage of the features in the new system; the system as such may be too complicated to use; or the employees may decide not to use the technology because they do not see why it would benefit them or the organization. All these reasons, and variations of them, may explain why the actual use of IT deviates from the expected. And, if the systems are not used as intended, then it is unlikely that they will create the anticipated effects – and in the end pay off.

In discussing the challenges a knowledge-based firm (in this case, a management-consulting company) faces when it wants to ensure that its investments in IT pay off, a distinction has been proposed between input and output challenges.[60] The former refers to the efforts needed in the organization to encourage the employees to spend time on recording information in the systems. This is not as effortless as is sometimes suggested. On the contrary, many companies have realized that their knowledge or customer relationship management systems have failed to meet the expectations because no one has entered the necessary information into the databases. The latter – output challenges – focuses on the utilization of the information in the system. Just because information about customers, lessons learned from previous projects, etc. is available, it does not mean that the employees will search for it and retrieve it from the system. To realize the expected value from the specific information system, both input and output activities must be systematically performed.

These same two challenges are also relevant when operating any BSC application. Unless information about the organization's goals, strategies, and performance is stored in the system, it cannot be retrieved, analysed, and used to trigger corrective and enhancing efforts.

The need for input activities can be found in all stages of a BSC effort. Initially, the working material from the strategy sessions must be compiled and codified in the system. Ideally, the strategy map will explicitly link the overarching goals with the more concrete success factors and metrics in each perspective. Breaking down the scorecard also demands a set of input activities, since the relationships between different scorecards must be made explicit and every metric must be explicitly defined in a compact and comprehensible way. Operating the system also requires continuous input activities: once-a-year targets must be set for each and every metric, and periodically (monthly) the metrics should be updated with the last period's results. This effort may be labour-intensive, unless the scorecard solution is designed to fetch performance automatically statistics from other transaction systems in the organization. Even so, many metrics must still be measured and entered into the system manually, which is an important, but often neglected, activity. Finally, if the BSC is supposed to trigger new behaviour, then an activity management package may be included in the software. Similarly, if information about the suggested activities is not entered into the system, it will not help the organization to execute them.

Still, even if all the information mentioned above has been registered in the scorecard system and its databases – but is never retrieved and viewed, it will not make any difference and hence not contribute to creating the anticipated effects. Thus, there are key output challenges in operating a BSC solution as well. Most often, the vision statement and the goals are rather dense and may need some elaboration to be understood. In a hyper-link environment, these kinds of clarifying linkages can easily be made. It may, for example, be possible for any employee (e.g. a newly hired person) to browse through the system and grasp the essence of the company, finding out the organization's purpose, as well as how it is to reach its goals.

More important, probably, is the systematic proliferation and utilization of the performance information in the scorecard. Regularly, management must turn to the figures and analyse the outcome, as well as present the results in the scorecard to the organization. Management should both present the outcome orally at monthly company meetings, and encourage the employees to check it out on the corporate intranet. Our experience thus far tells us that if the organization does not manage these output challenges – ensuring that the outcome is presented and used – it will destroy the employees' interest in supplying information to the system (i.e. making the input responsibility even more difficult). If the solution is equipped with an activity management module, then it is also important that the list of suggestions and activities in progress is regularly monitored and managed, such that decisions are made regarding proposed activities. This module may support activities to be carried out according to their deadlines. If no one pays attention to the activity management system, then it is quite probable that the members of the organization will stop paying attention to the activity list that the scorecard has triggered.

Unless the scorecard application is used, it will not create the intended effects in the organization. Even though it is rarely addressed in the literature, there is – more often than not – a gap between the intended and the actual use of the systems. According to our experience, many BSC systems suffer from this gap as well. To ensure that the investment in an IT solution pays off, it is thus important that it is used as intended – in practice. There are two challenges on which the organization needs to focus:

1. ensuring that the relevant information is recorded in the system (from vision statements, via performance statistics, to suggestions for improvements) and

2. ensuring that the information is used by the members of the organization.

Managing these two generic challenges (input and output), will diminish the gap between intended and actual use of the scorecard application.

What we have proposed here is to focus (i.e. invest) resources in the utilization of the technology as well as in the technology itself. In practice, this would imply that any investment appraisal regarding BSC software (developed internally, implemented as an add-on to the general ERP solution, or bought as a stand-alone package) should also address how the input and output challenges will be handled. Normally, this 'utilization tactic' may require some additional investments, for example, in designing processes that will encourage the employees to contribute to, as well as retrieve information from, the system (which we talked about in Chapter 7). Such a program would not only include education (how to use the system), but also communicate why the system should be used, to ensure that management actually uses the information in the system, etc. These initiatives rarely come for free, but they typically contribute far more to the realized utilization of the system than they cost. Using IT to leverage the scorecard hence requires investment in processes that encourage input and output activities. It is therefore important to strike a balance in the IT investment budget between development of the technology and development of the utilization.

RECOMMENDATIONS AND IMPLICATIONS

In this chapter we have demonstrated how IT can be used during the different stages in a scorecard project. It is, however, important to stress that we do not think IT solutions are required to operate a scorecard. But, if the organization decides to evaluate alternative IT solutions, we find it important to be explicit about the purpose of the IT system. Hence, we believe that:

- It is important to define why and when the IT solution will be used. Will it mainly support the early stages in the project or will it be used for numerical processing?

- Most projects benefit from modest investments in IT during the first year. It is usually enough to begin with simple solutions in Excel or Access, before more advanced solutions are implemented and rolled out in the organization.
- The future users of the scorecard solution lead the IT project and make the priorities.
- It is vital that both input and output activities are managed thoroughly.

If an appropriate IT solution is chosen and implemented, then it will contribute to the scorecard effort, and hence play a role in the realization of the intended business strategies.

- The IT solution will provide the scorecard with up-to-date information on the organization's aspirations and achievements.
- Existing digital resources may be re-used and create additional value at a low marginal cost.
- The IT investment will pay off.

Prospects: BSC as a tool for modern management   **12**

CREDO

In this final chapter we summarize our arguments and look forward. We started out with a question: 'fading fad or maturing management?' We confess to a bias, since we do believe in the BSC as a useful, maybe necessary, tool in achieving strategic control. However, in working with scorecards over the years, and also learning about the experiences of others, we have come to realize that using scorecards in itself is no guarantee of success. Quite a few implementations of the BSC have been based on ambitions quite different from those we advocate. To us it is not surprising if these organizations have not achieved the benefits we regard as possible with the BSC. These are to mobilize the organization's potential for strategic thinking, and to focus its activities on the realization of intended strategies.

These important benefits from scorecards are possible when they are used as:

- Tools for communication and dialogue, especially about the intangible resources that are increasingly important in all organizations known to us.
- Visualization of hypotheses and strategic bets.
- Documentation of shared views about strategic intentions.
- An aid in realizing strategy, since progress is monitored and discussed from multiple perspectives.

It is obvious that scorecards can be used in other ways, for instance, checking performance against benchmarks that are imposed from the top of the organization. There may be situations where this is still a relevant way to run an organization. But we believe that they are increasingly rare, and our enthusiasm for the BSC is closely linked to another perception of how managers should act.

In modern life in business and public administration, most of us need a good understanding of the fundamental logic of the organizations where we are employed. One reason for this is selfish: it is more fun to work at something you understand than just performing duties you get paid for. Many people also feel more comfortable about their employer that way. Ethical concerns, risks of unemployment, etc. are easier to tackle if you are invited to share some of the basic ideas of your company, hospital, or whatever.

That by itself will probably benefit the organization in terms of lower personnel turnover, lower absenteeism, etc. But for the employer, there are other reasons that may be more compelling. As employees, we all have to act in situations that are changing and unpredictable, and where we need to take initiatives of our own. To be able to do so in the best interests of our organization, we need guidance from an understanding of its strategy. From our daily work, all of us should bring back observations and ideas that may influence the strategic thinking in our organizations. We should also develop our knowledge and capabilities, and this will happen more easily (and in more interesting ways) if we can put our own actions into a larger perspective. We gradually develop this through taking part in discussions about the logic behind what our organization is doing.

We do not mean that all employees should have views on corporate strategy. Most people will prefer to limit their interest to much more local issues. Our discussion of Skandia in Chapter 3 provides good examples. When management shows its interest and provides time and opportunity, most people in organizations want to contribute their views on improvements, and appreciate getting a better understanding of what they do, and why.

The benefits from the BSC – to mobilize the organization's potential for strategic thinking, and focus its activities in the realization of intended strategies – come about through its usefulness in discussing ambitions and achievements. The BSC here refers to a family of tools and organizational processes, where proven, easy-to-understand formats are used to provide a multi-dimensional, richer description of what an organization is doing, and why.

The designs will vary. So will the processes where scorecards are used. To use scorecards in the way we want to see them used, an organization's culture needs to support the idea. Trust in people is needed. So is willingness and ability to discuss the reasons for actions, and to reconsider them in the light of experience. Managers at all levels, and those employees who want to, must feel they are invited to engage in a shared quest for success.

Just introducing something resembling scorecards will not automatically provide any benefits at all. It may even be negative, cost a lot of money, and give the BSC a bad reputation. Apart from reflecting our enthusiasm for the BSC, this book was written out of concern that a good idea was being misunderstood and misused. After 10 years of scorecards, it was time for stocktaking.

A SUMMARY

We have used a broad range of cases to illustrate and provide food for thought, rather than identify what has worked and what has not. As we have said, scorecard success is closely linked to other aspects of how an organization is managed. Therefore, it is not possible to judge in isolation whether or not one or other of the practices in our case companies is good. So the following summary is a list of the arguments we have put forward, rather than a condensation of all our cases:

- The hype surrounding scorecards has probably peaked. Those who introduced the BSC because it was the modern thing to do are hopefully leaving the arena. Those who remain should persevere, because the BSC is no quick fix. We find indications that, with patience, scorecards will enable organizations to work in new ways. We cannot prove that this will always be more profitable, or more effective. Maybe business success depends largely on short-term manoeuvring, or sheer luck. But if you believe that strategies, coordination, and focused, yet flexible, execution of agreed intentions is of any importance, and that more than a handful people need to be involved in constantly keeping strategies relevant, then scorecards are a good idea for you. It is time now for the pay off from the hype – if we manage to design the BSC use right!
- Failures are giving the BSC a bad name among those who have not bothered to find out what it really is about. That is why we wrote this

book: to explain in detail what it takes, and also warn that it is no quick fix.

- Organizations need control, because organizing is about coordination. Even short-term, adaptive control in a highly operative context usually needs a long-term basis consisting of ideas about the world in which you operate. People in an organization need to arrive at those ideas together, and gain a shared understanding of their consequences, because only then will they be able to act as quickly and wisely as they inherently are able to do. Some of those ideas will concern how this organization shall become successful in what it is doing. Strategic control essentially is making sure everyone knows about this, and acts on it. Control is about realizing intended strategies.

- The ideas and shared understanding we just mentioned are hypotheses: 'if–then'. If we develop our skills, then we will be able to provide improved services. If we do that, then customers will like it. If customers like that, then there will be one zillion more people who are willing to become our customers, etc. Some of these hypotheses will be 'almost-truths', fact-based, and proven by experience. Others will be conjectural, because no one has ever tried it before. Most will fall somewhere in between. We call them strategic bets. Strategy maps and scorecards document them for us to make it easier to agree on them; question them; find support for them, or refutation – to use them in our daily activities as a guide for what to do. And to give them adequate time to be tested. But never believe them to be eternal truths.[61]

- We need to involve many members in our organizations to discuss these hypotheses. They need to know about our strategic bets, and understand their role in trying to realize the intentions. They may also contribute their knowledge and improve on them.

- All of this provides the backdrop to the BSC and explains why we need to use strategy maps and scorecards to visualize strategy: not for multi-dimensional performance measurement as such, but to enable communication. Our 'challenges' in Chapter 5 were about providing adequate motivation and resources for the application of the BSC that we attempt in our organization. Application, motivation, and resources have to be matched.

- We advise you to do this through a systematic design of your BSC process. The six 'design issues' that we introduced must in themselves be balanced. There is no such thing as a best design for strategy maps, a best set of roles, or the best BSC software. How these and the other issues are tackled depends on the situation: what you want to achieve through the BSC; other types of controls; organizational culture, etc. By learning from our cases it is possible to identify the issues to be tackled, and get an idea of the range of possible designs.

Introducing scorecards into an organization is perhaps best viewed as creating a business language. The words and phrases that are needed in the language will depend on each organization's situation and intentions. But when people talk, there are certain constants even across different cultures. What we may have been able to describe here is partly about the grammar of the scorecard language. But we have also tried to give a flavour of the situations where it is spoken, since this, after all, is more important than the details of the language. These will anyway vary between different organizations. The main thing is to get the communication going.

THE FUTURE: COMBINING SCORECARDS AND OTHER LEVERS OF CONTROL

The concept of a BSC has proved influential to such an extent that today it is difficult to define any 'proper' use of scorecards. Instead, it may well be that the simple format of a scorecard will be integrated into a variety of uses and situations. Maybe even the term BSC will go away, and a 'balanced' set of metrics will be considered the natural way of describing any organization's work?

Scorecards will have to be reconciled with other planning processes (market and production plans, etc.). We have already mentioned management's need to communicate the primacy of scorecards – employees need a clear idea of what is more important, to stay within budget or to fulfil what has been agreed and documented in the scorecard.

In Figure 9.7 we linked the use of scorecards to strategy and organizational level. Management control based on financial numbers tends to be rather similar across industries. Scorecards, on the other, hand need to reflect the highly specific conditions for each company. Hopefully, what will emerge is a combination of budgets and other traditional controls with scorecards, adapted to each particular company's quest for uniqueness.

Linking the BSC to other aspects of management, as we have done in this chapter, broadens the perspective even further. Scorecards and strategy maps will be used as an organization's common language for discussing the rationale behind actions. This rationale is partly fact-based, partly based on strategic bets. Many members of the organization are invited to these discussions – indeed, are expected to contribute to them.

The successful use of scorecards thus becomes a matter of the organization's attitude to people: employees but also owners, partners and customers, and others with whom it needs to discuss its intents and achievements – an attitude that should balance strategy and control, and make the intended strategies actionable.

Notes

[1] That book was written by two of the present authors, Nils-Göran Olve and Jan Roy, together with Magnus Wetter. We refer to it as *Performance Drivers* in the present text.

[2] For 2000: `http://www.bain.com/bainweb/expertise/tools/mtt/balance_scorecard.asp`

[3] Total Quality Management; Business Process Reengineering; Activity-Based Costing.

[4] Mintzberg (1994, p. 24) makes the distinction between intended and realized strategies. It may be important to point out, however, that our use of 'intended' should not imply inflexibility – intentions should be adapted as new facts emerge.

[5] As reported in *The Economist*, 4 May, 2002, based on a study by Baruch Lev of New York University.

[6] *Asian Productivity Organization News*, May, 2002.

[7] We find it difficult to maintain absolutely clear distinctions between 'metrics', 'measures', and 'measurements'. In general, 'metrics' are used when we refer to the chosen scale for describing the attributes of something, such as dollars or customer visits. 'Measurements' are individual values observed through the act of measuring, leaving 'measures' as the most general term indicating scales, target values, and achieved performance.

[8] See Chapter 10 in *Performance Drivers*.

[9] 'The balanced scorecard – measures that drive performance' is the title of Kaplan and Norton's *Harvard Business Review* article in 1992.

[10] Skandia has been much discussed in connection with 'intellectual capital' – cf. Edvinsson and Malone (1997), Hedberg *et al.* (1997, 2000) and Olve *et al.* (1999).

[11] They are directed to Kaplan and Norton (1996, 2001); Olve *et al.* (1999); or Olve and Sjöstrand (2002).

[12] Scorecards and strategy maps may some day provide a road for developing the public disclosure of information, but organizations need to achieve maturity in conducting such discussions in-house before thinking about using scorecards for external reporting.

[13] Scorecards for, e.g. IT and HR have attracted considerable interest lately. As consultants we have worked jointly with clients to develop thoughts on this which have been reported in publications from The Concours Group (www.concoursgroup.com).

[14] For a much more extensive discussion, readers are referred to *Performance Drivers*.

[15] This chapter is mainly based on material from a forthcoming dissertation: Roy, S., 'Navigating in the Knowledge Era', PhD Dissertation, School of Business, Stockholm University.

[16] We are unsure whether or not these differences (or similarities) are conscious.

[17] IC in *FuturICing* is short for intellectual capital, symbolizing the expected future pay-off of the organization's intellectual capital.

[17] A few indicators are automatically reported into the system from the administrative systems.

[19] This help function is similar to the help functions in Office, except that there are some graphical illustrations added.

[20] What the employee means here is that one of the perspectives in the model lost value when there was an imbalance between the investments in the different perspectives.

[21] See Hedberg *et al.* (1997, 2000), *Virtual Organizations and Beyond*.

[22] Some examples of compulsory indicators are given in the last part of this chapter. These measures are mainly financial and used for benchmarking between the different companies within the Skandia Group.

[23] The sales managers also belonged to Skandia Connection, supporting the customers, i.e. the distributors and brokers, with information about new products, new regulations, and changes on the market. The support unit's role was to answer questions about products and issues related to these. It was more of a back office function than that of the sales managers, but they still worked closely together.

[24] Sales managers (försäljningschef), the employees at Skandia Connection who are responsible for the distributors' and brokers' training and sales. They are spread all over Sweden and travel around to brokers, entrepreneurs and others that sell Skandia's products to make sure that they are updated on product development, and try to make them focus on selling Skandia products instead of other companies' products.

[25] Skandia Connection has, however, always been a profitable company but they still need to take these new requirements into consideration.

[26] An example is given in Figure 11.3.

[27] 28 March, 2002.

[28] Material on Ricoh was collected for Olve and Sjöstrand (2002) and is reused here.

[29] VCC's use of scorecards in the late 1990s was described in Olve *et al.* (1999).

[30] Material on Xerox was collected for Olve and Sjöstrand (2002) and is reused here.

[31] In *Performance Drivers*, we described the XMM as a model with a strong resemblance to the BSC, and considered it as Xerox's response to the same pressures that motivate other companies to introduce scorecards.

[32] This corresponds to a typical situation where scorecards are particularly useful, which we will come back to in Chapter 9.

[33] Ericsson's COO Per-Arne Sandström in *Kontakten*, 28 March, 2002.

[34] 'The strategic themes reflect the executives' view of what must be done internally to achieve strategic outcomes. As such, the themes typically relate to internal business processes.' (Kaplan and Norton, 2001, p. 78).

[35] A new book by Kim Warren (2002), *Competitive Strategy Dynamics*, provides a good introduction. See also www.strategydynamics.com.

[36] A view of planning as a systematic meeting between the organization's knowledge of possibilities, and management's knowledge about preferences, is provided in Nilsson and Olve (2001).

[37] According to Kaplan and Norton, 85% of executive teams spend less than one hour per month discussing strategy (*Balanced Scorecard Report*, September–October 2001, vol. 3, no. 5).

[38] Porter (1996).

[39] Cf. *The Economist*'s Survey on Management (9–15 March, 2002) where Charles Knight's article in *Harvard Business Review* from 1992 is cited: 'In that article he wrote: "What makes us tick at Emerson is an effective management process." The essential elements of that process are still drilled into every manager. They include a strong commitment to planning; a well-functioning system of control and follow-up; an insistence on being the lowest-cost producer in each business area; a determination to "keep things simple"; and a desire (in true Missouri style) for action and results. Mr Knight believes that companies don't fail because their analysis is faulty. "Management usually knows what to do", he says, "but for some reason it doesn't do it."'

[40] From Olve *et al.* (1999, pp. 269–70).

[41] See Nilsson and Olve (2001) concerning the link between corporate strategy and use of scorecards and other control instruments.

[42] On the topic of strategic themes, see Chapters 2 and 6.

[43] See *Performance Drivers*, p. 77.

[44] See Goold *et al.* (1994).

[45] Customer Relations Management.

[46] See *Performance Drivers*, pp. 85–89, and p. 179.

[47] cf. Hedberg *et al.* (1997, 2000).

[48] This would realize the ambitions for control in the imaginary organizations in Hedberg *et al.* (1997, 2000) – cf. their Figure 12.2.

[49] Ronald Coase in a 1937 paper is commonly seen as the originator of this argument. Later contributors (with different views) are Williamson, Porter, Teece, and Goold and Campbell.

[50] The following section is based on Nilsson and Olve (2001). Also see Simons (1995) and Goold *et al.* (1994).

[51] Peter Drucker, in *The Economist*, 3 November, 2001, p. 18.

[52] Cf. the media attention when a manager gets a bonus even though his company is not making a profit. Given the assumption that the manager's only responsibility is to report a financial profit, this might be offensive, but if his reward is based on some driver of future profits, it is not as sensational as the media sometimes describe it.

[53] Ouchi (1979) elaborates on the differences between results and behavioural control, and argues that the latter should be applied when it is difficult to define the results explicitly or when a multitude of different results are acceptable.

[54] See *Performance Drivers*, p. 122ff.

[55] Other aspects also need to be considered: Do employees expect to remain part of the organization, so future rewards are of interest to them? Does the (national and corporate) culture encourage 'realistic' targets, or is it part of accepted behaviour to set highly ambitious goals that are maybe never met, etc.

[56] Linking compensation to cash flow and especially operating margin, we consider rather close to a profit-sharing model, although profit is measured before various costs, which probably this corporation feels are not possible for people to influence.

[57] This case is presented in Bukh *et al.* (2001, p. 205).

[58] Our sequential elaboration is similar to the Balanced Scorecard Collaborative's Functional Standards (2000) for BSC applications. Their requirements are: (1) *Balanced Scorecard Design* (drawing strategy maps and managing links between measures and objectives) (2) *Strategic Education and Communication* (capacity to document and communicate descriptions of objectives, measures, targets, etc.) (3) *Business Execution* (management and linking of issues that are taken to execute the strategy) and (4) *Feedback and Learning* (features that present feedback on past

performance compared with targets in figures and graphical indicators). See www.bscol.com.

[59] In Hoff and Holving (2002, p. 246).

[60] Dunford (2000).

[61] It is a pity that 'scientific management' has century-old, different connotations, because essentially what we are arguing here is a scientific approach to management: using all knowledge that is available to the organization for a constant, 'scientific' debate about how it should act.

References

Bukh, P.N. *et al*. (2001) *Balanced Scorecard på dansk*. Køpenhamn: Børsen

Dunford, R. (2000) 'Key challenges in the search for the effective management of knowledge management in management consulting firms'. *Journal of Knowledge Management* 4 (4), 295–302.

Edvinsson, L. and Malone, M. (1997) *Intellectual Capital*. New York: Harper.

Goold, M. *et al*. (1994) *Corporate-Level Strategy*. New York: Wiley.

Hedberg, B. *et al*. (1997, 2000) *Virtual Organizations and Beyond*. Chichester: Wiley.

Hoff, K.G. and Holving, P.A. (2002) *Balansert målstyring*. Universitetsforlaget

Kaplan, R.S. and Norton, D.P. (1992) 'The balanced scorecard – measures that drive performance', *Harvard Business Review*, January–February, 71–79.

Kaplan, R.S. and Norton, D.P. (1996) *The Balanced Scorecard – Measures that Drive Performance*. Boston: HBS Press.

Kaplan, R.S and Norton, D.P. (2001) *The Strategy-Focused Organization*. Boston: HBS Press.

Marr, B. and Neely, A. (2001) *Balanced Scorecard Software Report* 3 (5). (A Business Review Publication from Cranfield School of Management with contributions by Gartner, Inc. Infoedge.)

Mintzberg, H. (1994) *The Rise and Fall of Strategic Planning*. Hemel Hempstead: Prentice Hall.

Nilsson, F. and Olve, N.-G. (2001) 'On control systems in multibusiness companies: from performance management to strategic management'. *European Management Journal* 19 (4), 344–58.

Olve, N.-G., Roy, J. and Wetter, M. (1999) *Performance Drivers – a Practical Guide to Using the Balanced Scorecard*. Chichester: Wiley.

Olve, N.-G. and Sjöstrand, A. (2002) *The Balanced Scorecard*. Oxford: Capstone.

Ouchi, W. (1979) 'A conceptual framework for the design of organizational control mechanisms'. *Management Science* 25 (9), 833–47.

Porter, M. (1996) *Competitive Advantage*. New York: Free Press.

Roy, S. (2003), *Navigating in the Knowledge Era*. PhD Dissertation, School of Business, Stockholm University.

Senge, P.M. (1990) *The Fifth Discipline – The Arts and Practice of the Learning Organization*. New York: Currency Doubleday.

Simons, R. (1995) *Levers of Control*. Boston: HBS Press.

Wallman, S. and Blair, M. (2001) *Unseen Wealth*. Washington: The Brookings Institution.

Warren, K. (2002) *Competitive Strategy Dynamics*. Chichester: Wiley.

Index